The Inspiring Life of
Abdus Salam

Mujahid Kamran

University of the Punjab, Lahore

ALSO BY MUJAHID KAMRAN

The Grand Deception
Corporate America and Perpetual War (2011)

Einstein and Germany (2009)

Pas e Parda: Almi Siasat Kay Makhfi Haqaiq (2008)

Relativistic Quantum Mechanics
A Quick Introduction (2005)

Dr. A.Q. Khan on Science,
Education and Technology, Editor (2004)

Jadeed Tabiyat Kay Bani (1997)

Dr. A.Q. Khan on Science and Education
Editor with S. Shabbir Hussain (1997)

Jadeed Tabiyat Kay Mashaheer (1988)

The Inspiring Life of Abdus Salam

Published by the University of the Punjab
Lahore, Pakistan
www.pu.edu.pk

Printed and bound at the University of the Punjab Press
ISBN 978-969-9325-11-3
First Edition

To
the people of Italy and the UK
who valued and hosted Salam

Contents

Preface

This book is an offshoot of a book on twentieth century physicists that I began writing in October 2009. The title of the book, *Variety of Physicists*, was an adaptation of C.P. Snow's famous book *Variety of Men*. I had completed several chapters when I began the article on Salam. He was the only one of the personalities in the book whom I knew personally. The chapter on Salam, however, grew well beyond the 50 page or so limit that I had set for each personality. I, therefore, decided at the end of November 2009 to convert it into a small biography. However, on account of my commitments as Vice Chancellor the work was delayed. The recent discovery of the Higgs or "God" particle, however, forced me to sit down and complete this work.

Several biographies of Salam have appeared in English already. Most of these were written while he was still alive. Gordon Fraser's biography[1] is probably the only one in English language that appeared after Salam's

[1]Gordon Fraser: *Cosmic Anger: Abdus Salam The First Muslim Nobel Laureate*; Oxford University Press, 2008. I am grateful to my former student Dr. Mansoora Shamim for having sent me a copy of Fraser's book. She also sent me the chapters on Salam in Moffat's book. Sadly Gordon Fraser passed away in January 2013.

death. Another highly useful biography was penned down in Urdu by Salam's younger brother Abdul Hameed Chaudari.[2] This biography is not available in bookstores in Pakistan for reasons unclear to me. However fortunately, Aatika Aziz, a former student of Punjab University was kind enough to get it for me. I am thankful to her. These two books have been of great help.

A compendium of writings by, and on, Salam compiled by Dr. Anwar Dil has been highly useful.[3] This book contains more than 70 articles, or excerpts from articles, on Salam. I found these articles most helpful and it saved me a lot of time and labor. I am thankful to Dr. Anwar Dil for having gifted me a copy of his book. I have generally referred to this book while quoting various authors, instead of going to the original source, as, in many cases, I did not have access to the original source. I am thankful to Dr. Anwar Dil for allowing me to quote from his book.

In addition to the aforementioned books, Salam's own writings have helped me in forming a picture of his views on various issues that dominated his mind. Further, some

---

[2]Abdul Hameed Chaudhari: *Alami Shohrat Yafta Sciencedaan Abdus Salam* (World Renowned Scientist Abdus Salam); published by Ahmad Salam, 8 Campion Road, SW 15, 6 NW, London; 1998; this book is written in Urdu.

[3]*Science for Peace of Progress Life and Work of Abdus Salam* compiled by Anwar Dil, publishers Intercultural Forum, San Diego and Islamabad (iforum@aol.com), 2008.

of Salam's writings contain useful biographical material. I had collected almost all books, and numerous articles written by him, during my visits to Trieste during the period 1982-1992. Over the years I had maintained a file on material pertaining to Salam. With my interest in lives and works of great physicists it was inevitable that I would write something on Salam one day.

In fact, in the mid 1980s (sometime during the period 1985 -1987) Salam had himself said something that seemed to indicate that he wanted me to be his biographer. I was at Trieste and his wife Dr. Louise Johnson was there along with their two children. Salam introduced me to her very briefly during a lunch. Afterwards, in his office, he said that Loiuse believed that I could write a biography of his. Salam had apparently shown her an article that I had written on the Russian theoretician Lev Landau for the daily *The Pakistan Times.* Just over a quarter of a century later this wish has come to be true but sadly, just as the book was nearing completion, Professor Dame Louise Johnson, Salam's English wife, passed away.[4] As Salam's biographer I also feel that I missed an opportunity of asking her about their life, as I

[4]Professor Dame Louise Johnson was David Phillips Professor of Molecular Biophysics at Oxford from 1990-2007. She died on September 25, 2012, a day before her seventy second birthday. Please see: http://www.telegraph.co.uk/news/obituaries/9594182/Professor-Dame-Louise-Johnson.html

had originally planned. It was not meant to be that way.

During the course of years I had contributed several articles to newspapers and journals on Salam. In particular I had written a three part article for the magazine section of the daily *The Pakistan Times* in the year 1992.[5] This has been incorporated in the final chapter of the present biography as well as in the chapter on electroweak unification.

I am thankful to Professor K.L. Mir for having shown me the file on Salam that he had recovered from the office of the Punjab University Mathematics Department and allowing me to photocopy it. Just as I had almost completed this work, he also pointed out the existence of a very valuable article on Salam by the writer K.K. Aziz. I thank him for this also.

I thank Mr. Shahid Kamal for having pointed out the existence of a book by John W. Moffat that contained two useful chapters pertaining to Salam at Cambridge and at Imperial College. I also thank him for providing me with a copy of Salam's Faiz Memorial Lecture delivered in Lahore, as well as Salam's Edinburgh Lecture and his detailed biodata. Mr. Shahid Kamal also proof-read the book and made many useful suggestions. I am thankful

[5]It is sad that *The Pakistan Times*, which was, for almost half a century, one of the two foremost dailies of English in the country, has now been reduced to the level of a dummy daily by a large media group which bought it.

to him. I am also thankful to Prof. Dr. Mansoor Sarwar for his constant interest in the work. To Mr. Amjad Pervez, Director of the Punjab University Press and Publications Department, I am thankful for his constant help in the printing and layout of the book and for designing the cover pages. But the person who continually provided me with incisive comments all along was my wife Shazia Qureshi, herself a former Cambridge law graduate. I thank her for her objective feedback and constant interest in the work.

I have typed the book in LaTeX. I remain solely responsible for any errors and omissions that may have escaped scrutiny.

Mujahid Kamran
January 29, 2013
Lahore

Chapter 1

Introduction

Abdus Salam's emergence from the backyards of Jhang in the Province of Punjab, currently in Pakistan, to a dominant position on the stage of twentieth-century physics is a dramatic story. In some ways he reminds one of Lord Rutherford. Both were born in far-flung areas of colonial Britain with parents in the teaching profession (Rutherford came from New Zealand) and both were outstanding students who, by sheer strokes of luck, won scholarships that took them to Cambridge. While Rutherford became the most powerful scientific figure in the British Commonwealth, Salam assumed the mantle of "People's Emperor" of Third World scientists.

The kinship between Salam and Rutherford goes deeper. Rutherford won his Nobel Prize for his researches into radioactivity, a phenomenon accidentally discovered in 1895. It was in 1932 that Enrico Fermi, the Italian genius, found that a new fundamental force of nature was the cause of this phenomenon. It was named the weak nuclear force,[1] and Fermi propounded a theory for the weak force. Salam made a major contribution to elucidating fundamental aspects of this force in 1956-57 and then went on to unify the weak force with the force of electromagnetism in 1967-68. Albert Einstein had set himself the task of unifying the forces of nature but he was on the wrong track - he wanted to fuse gravitation and electro-magnetism into one underlying reality. He failed and while gravity still eludes incorporation into some unified frame, Glashow, Salam and Weinberg have succeeded in unifying electro-magnetism with the weak force - the electro-weak force as it is now called.

In 1979, following confirmation of some of the crucial predictions of the theory, Sheldon Glashow, Abdus Salam and Steven Weinberg were jointly awarded the Physics Nobel Prize for their work. While the $W^{\pm}$ and Z_0 particles predicted by this theory were discovered in 1983, the final missing link, the Higgs particle, was discovered only recently. Its discovery was announced by scientists on July 4, 2012 in Geneva at CERN (European Organization for Nuclear Research). This discovery was the result of a marathon search spread over almost three decades.

[1] For brevity the weak nuclear force is sometimes simply called the weak force.

Chapter 2

Early Life

Abdus Salam was born on January 29, 1926 in a village Santok Das in District Montgomery[1] of the Province of Punjab, in British India. In those days it was usual for expecting mothers to go to the homes of their parents for delivery - babies were not usually delivered in hospitals. Salam's maternal grandfather lived in Santok Das. However, having spent a traditional period of forty days with her parents, after Salam's birth, his mother rejoined Salam's father in Jhang. It was in Jhang that Salam grew up. Interestingly, he never told anyone that he was born in Santok Das. During his lifetime biographies and ar-

[1]The city of Montgomery has been subsequently renamed Sahiwal. During the 1947 division of the Indian sub-continent, Montgomery became part of Pakistan.

ticles written on his life always mentioned Jhang as his place of birth. Salam never corrected this error. In fact, in his Dirac Memorial Lecture he mentioned Jhang as his birthplace.[2]

In an article written after Salam's death, his sister, Hameeda Bashir Begum, revealed that an uncle of Salam's father was a Punjabi poet who composed a few verses on Salam's birth. Her Urdu article was translated into English and published in 1997.[3] The aforementioned verses mention Santok Das as Salam's place of birth. Their English translation, carried out by Dr. Rasheed Syed Azam, goes as follows:

> A letter has come from Santok Das
> Bearing the glad tiding
> Of Abdus Salam's birth
> Brother, Friday is a blessed day,
> The day of Abdus Salam's birth
>
> A thousand nay a million thanks
> Praise do we render to Allah
> On the birth of Abdus Salam.

[2]Abdus Salam: *Unification of Fundamental Forces*; Cambridge University Press, 1990; p 35. The lecture notes were compiled by Jonathan Evans and Gerard Watts.

[3]Hameeda Bashir Begum: *My Glorious and Beloved Brother: Professor Dr. Abdus Salam*; translated by Dr. Rasheed Syed Azam, Quaterly *Al-Nahl*, vol 8, Issue 4, Fall 1997, p 58.

> May Allah give him long life
> And best of luck.

Jagjit Singh's biography[4] of Salam describes Jhang in the following words:

> Although British rule brought peace to the region, it did little towards the town's development. It had no electricity, piped water supply, roads, radio or telephone. Uneven dirt tracks full of potholes were negotiated by bullock carts and one-horse contraptions which jolted along precariously.

In the first ever Dirac Memorial Lecture given at Cambridge in 1988, Salam, while speaking on the unification of fundamental forces, referred to the non-availability of electric power in Jhang in his school days. He narrates:[5]

> I still remember the school at Jhang in Pakistan (Jhang is my birthplace). Our teacher spoke of the gravitational force. Of course gravity was well-known and Newton's name had penetrated even to a place like Jhang.

[4] Jagjit Singh: *Abdus Salam: A Biography*, Penguin Books, 1992; p 1.

[5] Abdus Salam: *Unification of Fundamental Forces*; Cambridge University Press, 1990; p 35. The lecture notes were compiled by Jonathan Evans and Gerard Watts.

> Our teacher then went on to speak of magnetism; he showed us a magnet. Then he said, "Electricity! Ah, that is a force which does not live in Jhang, it lives only in the capital city of this province, Lahore 100 miles East." (And he was right. Electricity came to Jhang five years later.) And the nuclear force? "That was a force which lived only in Europe. It did not live in India (or Pakistan) and we were not to be worry about it."

Jhang however was the setting of the famous Heer-Ranjha romance, a Punjabi equivalent of Romeo and Juliet. The romance was immortalized by a Punjabi poet Waris Shah. This romantic poetry is sung in the most melodious tunes ever conceived by mankind. This rather remote town was to produce Abdus Salam, who was to become one of the foremost physicists of the twentieth century, as well as Majeed Amjad, one of the most original and outstanding poets of Urdu.

Salam's parents got married in 1925 and had eight children - seven sons and one daughter. Salam's mother, Hajirah Begum, was twelve years younger to her husband Muhammad Hussain who was born in 1891 in the town of Jhang. It has been pointed out that Salam's ancestors were Hindu princelings, Rajputs, as they are known. Under the influence of a Sufi (i.e. mystic) Saint, the well known Bahauddin Zakariya, they converted to Islam in the twelfth century.

In his book, *The Coffee House of Lahore*, the writer K.K. Aziz, who knew Salam well from their student days has, however, described Salam's ancestry in the following words:[6]

> Salam was the son of Chaudhri Muhammad Hussain, a schoolteacher of Jhang and Hajirah who belonged to Faizullah Chak near Batala. Muhammad Hussain was a jat and Hajirah a Kakkezai. Now I know that Faizullah Chak was an almost exclusively Kakkezai village because my mother's mother belonged to it and the family had lived there since time unknown. The Kakkezais were a close-knit community, mixed well among themselves, and formed a close network of relationships within the tribe. The problem of working out or tracing a relationship in Muslim (and non-Muslim) families is that the genealogical trees concern themselves with males only. Therefore I presume with some justification and optimism that Hajirah was a member, however distantly placed, of my grandmother's larger family. That makes Salam a cousin of mine, it doesn't matter at how many removes.

[6]K.K. Aziz: *The Coffee House of Lahore - A Memoir 1942-57*; Sang e Meel Publishers, 2008, p 200.

Salam was the eldest of their children. Hajirah Begum, it appears, was a wise mother. Salam's brother has written that their mother never punished her children physically. Corporal punishment is quite common in those parts of the world even today. The maximum threat in response to mischief would be "I 'll tell your father".

There is an interesting incident connected with Salam's birth. This has been narrated by Salam's brother in his biography of Salam and has been taken from the diary of Salam's father. On June 3, 1925, Salam's father prayed with great fervor and had a vision in which he was promised a son by the name of Abdus Salam. He apparently wrote to his wife about it as she was visiting her parents at the time.

In a memorial article written by his daughters Aziza Rahman and Bushra Salam Bajwa this story is narrated in the following words:[7]

> Our father's extraordinary story began when our grandfather was given the news of his birth in a vision ··· He had just recited the prayer "Our Lord, grant us of our spouses and children the delight of our eyes and make each of us a leader of the righteous." (Holy Quran 25:75)" when he saw a vision in which he was

[7]Aziza Rahman and Bushra Salam Bajwa: *My Father, Abdus Salam*; in Quarterly *Al-Nahl*, Special issue on Abdus Salam, Vol 8, Issue, Fall 1997, p 50.

> handed a baby boy. He asked "Who is this?" and was told "This is Abdus Salam."

Aziza Rahman and Bushra Salam Bajwa also note:

> From early years he showed signs of great intelligence. He actually won his first prize at the age of two for being the healthiest baby in Jhang.

Interestingly, Salam started speaking a bit late. A visitor, who was known to be spiritual and religious, was informed about Salam's silence by the worried mother. She requested the visitor to pray for him. He took the little boy in his lap, said a few words to him, and then pronounced: "When Salam speaks, he will speak so much that the world will hear him". The age at which this incident took place has not been mentioned by Salam's brother, who himself confirmed this incident from that particular visitor in 1960.

Salam was an unusually bright child. When he was still very small, his mother used to send him often to bring yoghurt from a shop near their residence. Enroute the shop was a Hindu school where Salam would overhear the boys learning mathematical tables by rote. His mind was so good that he learnt all the multiplication tables just by overhearing them. He, therefore, knew the mathematical tables at a very early age.[8]

Salam had a close brush with death at a very young age. His father had brought home rat poison which was left inadvertently in a bag strung by his father's bicycle. Salam mistook these for something meant to eat and took them. He vomited immediately afterwards and told his parents what he had taken. He was rushed to a nearby doctor who induced further vomiting to clear his body of the poison. Medication then alleviated his condition further. The doctor was of Hindu religion as the Hindu community had taken to British education much earlier than the Muslim community.

Salam's sister Hameeda Bashir Ahmad writes:[9]

> Our brother was well organized from his childhood and all his things were placed at the right place. His books could be easily located where he placed them when needed. He was a guiding light for all of us. He was taught by our father to do his work on time, sleep on time and offer his prayers on time.
>
> Our father always used to bring seasonal fruits

[8]This was narrated to me by Salam's younger brother, the late Abdul Hameed Chaudhri in 1997.

[9]Hameeda Bashir Begum: *My Glorious and Beloved Brother: Professor Dr. Abdus Salam*; translated by Dr. Rasheed Syed Azam, Quaterly Al-Nahl, vol 8, Issue 4, Fall 1997, p 58.

> on his way home from office. All of us were given the equal share but unobserved we used to put a portion of our share in his plate. He would smile but would also say "Everybody should eat their share."

Salam's parents took a very keen interest in their son's eduction which started at home. Both parents were involved. His mother taught him to read and write and his father oversaw this education. He maintained a diary from which the evolution of his son can be followed. He narrates in his diary that he used to give Salam easy to read story books and magazines of Urdu language. Sometimes stories were narrated to him by his parents. He noted that Salam was an avid reader. There came a stage when Salam already knew so many stories that he would tell his parents that he already knew the story being dished out to him. His father would also ask Salam to narrate the stories that he had already read or heard. In the words of his father, as quoted by one of Salam's brothers,[10] this was done to "to improve Salam's power of retention and expression."

When he was able to read and write to the satisfaction of his parents, Salam was taken to the M.B. Middle

[10] Abdul Hameed Chaudhari: *Alami Shohrat Yafta Sciencedaan Abdus Salam* (World Renowned Scientist Abdus Salam); published by Ahmad Salam, 8 Campion Road, SW 15, 6 NW, London; 1998; p 27; this book is written in Urdu.

School Jhang.[11] After evaluating him the school Head Master decided that Salam be admitted directly to class four. He was seven at that time. The Head Master knew Salam's father personally. On account of this acquaintance, and also on account of his unusual abilities, Salam received special attention at school. In fact Salam's father would complain to the head master if he felt that Salam was not receiving attention.

In a privately recorded video interview in the late 1980s Salam reminisced:[12]

> My father took me to school and asked the teachers to test me. I was about six or seven years of age then. I had been taught at home. Since I could read with ease and my math was good I was admitted directly to class four probably. That's my earliest recollection of school ··· I was in class five or six probably. We were taught Arabic by Maulvi Mohammad Latif. He once mentioned the word *kataf* for shoulder and said he could not recall

[11]In primary schools the highest class is fifth, whereas in middle schools the highest class is the eight class. In high schools the highest class is tenth class, also known as the matric class.

[12]I am thankful to Mr. Akhtar Said, former Minister of Education Punjab and a former Punjab Education Secretary, a career bureaucrat, for having provided me with a copy of this interview. The interview was conducted by Mr. Akhtar Said in Punjabi, Salam's mother tongue.

> whether it was an Arabic or a Persian word. At the end of the period I picked up the dictionary and went to him and pointed out that it was an arabic word. The teacher was drinking water and said "My son, at least let me drink water and let me live." That is one of my earliest recollections that my teacher wanted to slow me down ··· Our other teacher was Sher Afzal Jafri, the poet. He taught me prose. He was a great man. I once wrote an essay and showed it to him - he wrote *aafreen*[13] thrice on the essay and said to me that each *afreen* that he gave me was the equal of an *ashrafi*[14] ...

In the above interview he also mentioned his Hindu teachers Lala Bhagvan Dass and Lala Butni Nath. Since Salam passed his matric (class 10) in 1940 and since he was admitted directly to class four, and since his year of birth was 1926, one can easily infer that he was admitted to school between the age of seven and eight years. He was therefore, almost certainly admitted to school in the year 1933.

Right from early age, Salam's ability to concentrate intensely had been noticed by elders. Stories describing his unusual absorption in reading have become part of the

[13]It is a powerful expression of spontaneous praise.

[14]Gold coin.

family lore. His first cousin and his wife's brother Col.(R) Iqbal[15] told this author that one day Salam could not be traced. The entire family searched for him and there was a lot of commotion. Eventually he was found absorbed in reading something after hiding himself behind a stack of quilts. He was totally oblivious to the commotion. Col.(R) Iqbal also told me that Salam would usually find corners and places in the house where he would withdraw to be able to read in peace and quiet.

His daughter Aziza Rahman states:[16]

> My grandmother used to tell the story that my father would be so engrossed in studying that once, when he was very young he was having lunch and reading at the same time, when he looked up his plate was empty. He had been so engrossed in the book that unknown to him a pet chicken that was kept in the house that picked all the meat from his plate and departed! [17]

[15]Col.(R) G.M. Iqbal passed away in Lahore in the year 2010. Salam's first wife was Col. Iqbal's sister.

[16]Aziza Rahman: *My Father, Abdus Salam*; in Quarterly *Al-Nahl*, Special issue on Abdus Salam, Vol 8, Issue, Fall 1997, p 50.

[17]In the sub-continent it was, and still is, not usual for most families to sit at a table to eat. People usually sit on very low stool type objects, a foot or less in height and eat with their plates on the floor or placed on an object of similar height.

Salam faced very tough competition from two Hindu class-fellows and this competition made him work hard. From class fifth to eighth Salam secured the top position in his class. However, the class eight exam was taken province wide and in this exam Salam, though first in his class as well as the district, was fifth in the entire province. This made his father unhappy who sought out the answer sheets of the boy who had secured the first position and compared them with Salam's. He was satisfied that Salam's papers were not in any way inferior and that it was just a chance occurrence that Salam had missed the first position.

Salam's sister Hameeda Bashir Begum has described Salam as a school boy in the following words:[18]

> Education was Salam's life. He never wasted time. He would get up early and sleep early. In the morning he would read the Holy Quran after prayer. He would dress up after the breakfast and walk to school. He would learn arithmetic tables on his way to school, walking with friends sometimes. He was a humble, very obedient, very simple and studious student. He was helpful to the younger siblings but encouraged them to do their own

[18]Hameeda Bashir Begum: *My Glorious and Beloved Brother: Professor Dr. Abdus Salam*; translated by Dr. Rasheed Syed Azam, Quaterly Al-Nahl, vol 8, Issue 4, Fall 1997, p 58.

> homework. We played and enjoyed many children's games together including building clay soldiers and arranging our armies on the battlefield.

At the time Salam's schooling began, there was a high school in Jhang. However, at that time, i.e., 1934, the town of Jhang did not have any college. Fortunately, in the year 1938 this high school was upgraded to the status of an intermediate college, where the highest class is the twelfth, also known as the intermediate, or simply inter class. Salam studied at Government Intermediate College, Jhang from class nine to class twelve.

It appears that Salam's father wanted to bring the boy to a Lahore institution in 1938. Munir Ahmad Khan who eventually became Chairman Pakistan Atomic Energy Commission met Salam in 1942. He writes:[19]

> I could have met him four years earlier in the Central Model School, Lahore. However after having been selected for admission, the headmaster quietly advised his father to take him back to Jhang because the boy was wearing a red Fez cap and other students might make

[19]Munir Ahmad Khan: *Salam as I Knew Him* in *Science for Peace and Progress: Life and Work of Abdus Salam* compiled by Anwar Dil, publishers Intercultural Forum, San Diego and Islamabad (iforum@aol.com), 2008, p 599.

> fun of him. It was an advice the headmaster lived to regret.

Since Munir Ahmad Khan was to interact with Salam for the next five decades, this story most likely came to him from Salam. Salam's penchant for caps or hats never left him. Munir Ahmad Khan mentions that when he came to Vienna in the early 1960s to plead his case for an International Center for Theoretical Physics he was wearing a canvas hat that was "not only discolored but also rumpled out of shape". Munir Ahmad Khan somehow hid the hat (and also persuaded him to change his topcoat) so that he could look presentable before the Board of the International Atomic Energy Agency (IAEA). Munir Ahmad Khan seemed to have underestimated Salam's charisma and persuasive powers.

The matric exam was, and still is, generally considered a crucial exam in a student's career. Salam worked very hard for his matric exam.[20] In his book, Salam's younger brother Chaudhari Abdul Hameed states that their father had told him that Salam had prepared thoroughly for the exams and had revised and prepared the entire course at least twice, well before the exam date. Therefore, when his eyes went sore some days before the

[20] This exam may be considered similar to the O levels exams in Britain. At that time the University of the Punjab, Lahore, conducted all exams from matric upwards and its jurisdiction extended up to New Delhi.

exam it did not make any difference as he already had prepared well. Salam took the matric exam in March 1940 and stood first in the entire region covered by the University of the Punjab in undivided India.[21]

The results were announced on May 18, 1940. A day before the announcement of the result, a hairdresser had cut Salam's hair so short that he was forced to wear a traditional hat out of embarrassment. He had gone to his father's office outside Jhang when he found out about the result. He had secured 765/850 marks whereas the student who stood second obtained 733/850 marks. As Salam bicycled into town wearing the traditional hat, through one of the four gates of the city, he received a hero's welcome. He was only fourteen and in the hot summer afternoon the shops were usually closed. Siesta in such heat is a common practice and most shopkeepers were enjoying their afternoon nap. Most of the shops were owned by Hindus since the Hindus dominated business throughout the subcontinent. However, they broke their siesta and stood up for a non-Hindu who had beaten Hindus and Sikhs and had brought the somewhat remote town into limelight. It were usually Hindus who bagged the top honors. This warm reception also says something about the culture of the town - the town was proud of its

[21]The province of Punjab was divided into two halves, as were several other provinces, as a result of the creation of Pakistan in 1947.

son regardless of his faith. This was Salam's first brush with fame.

Salam's brother Abdul Hameed Chaudhari has described what happened on that day in Salam's own words. Abdul Hameed Chaudhari states in his book:[22]

> I remember the day the result was declared. I was sitting in my father's office. Father had sent someone to the Maghaiana[23] railway station to procure a copy of the result. When he brought the result my name was printed on the first page: "Abdus Salam, Roll No 14888, 765/800 has secured first position in the entire province." Father thanked Allah and went into *sajda*.[24]
>
> I remember that a day before the declaration of the result I had gone to the hairdresser for a haircut. He handed me over to an apprentice who cut my hair so short that it appeared that the head been shaved. In order to hide this

[22]This book is written in Urdu: Abdul Hameed Chaudhari: *Alami Shohrat Yafta Sciencedaan Abdus Salam* (World Renowned Scientist Abdus Salam); published by Ahmad Salam, 8 Campion Road, SW 15, 6 NW, London; 1998; p 31, 32.

[23]Maghiana is a town adjacent to Jhang.

[24]It is a posture in prayers where one prostrates oneself before Allah - one is on one's knees and the forehead touches the ground.

> I had to wear a turban. After the announcement of the result I got on my bike and went to Jhang. Jhang had four gates in those days, of which three remain today. To get home I had to go from Noor Shah Gate to Mumna Gate. The path went through the town center. All shops there were owned by Hindus. At the time it was extremely hot. I noticed that all Hindu shopkeepers were standing outside their shops to pay me respect. Usually at that hour they would be resting under the shades of their shops. It was an unusual sight.

Ram Prakash Bambah, who was Salam's contemporary at Government College, Lahore as well as at Cambridge, remembered Salam's emergence to lime light. In an article written after Salam's death, Bambah stated:[25]

> In the spring of 1940, the results of the MSLC[26] for that year were announced, and they carried the stunning report that a fourteen year old boy, from a remote place called Jhang, had not only topped the examination, but he

[25]Ram Prakash Bambah: *Together In Lahore and Cambridge* in *Science for Peace and Progress: Life and Work of Abdus Salam* compiled by Anwar Dil, publishers Intercultural Forum, San Diego and Islamabad (iforum@aol.com), 2008, p 575.

[26]Matric School Leaving Certificate.

> had also obtained a much larger score than all the previous ones. The next day the regional newspaper *Tribune*, with which I now have the privilege of being associated as one of its trustees, carried the picture of a small boy with a large turban. The turban that you saw Salam wearing at the Nobel Prize ceremony is similar to the one he wore in March 1940. And that is the picture that I carry of Salam as I saw him for the first time.

Taking advantage of his position as the current Vice Chancellor of the University of the Punjab, and recalling that during those years the University not only conducted exams for bachelors and masters degrees, but also for intermediate and matric, this author asked the office of the Controller of Examinations[27] to ferret out Salam's results. It was an exciting experience to see the original records. Looking at the detailed marks one finds that[28] Salam had secured 196/200 marks in mathematics, 143/150 in physics and chemistry, 171/200 in English, 111/150 in history and geography, and 144/150 in

[27]I am indebted to the Controller of Examinations, Professor Dr. Liaqat Ali, Additional Controller Mr. Ahmad Ali Chattha and their staff for digging out Salam's results from matric (1940) to M.A. (1946).

[28]This is probably the first time that the detailed marks of Salam's matric result are being published in a book.

classical languages (Arabic in his case, Sanskrit, Persian, Latin, Hebrew and Greek being the other options).

It is to be emphasized that at that time the jurisdiction of the University of the Punjab extended over a large part of the then North-West India. Its jurisdiction extended over most of present day Pakistan, the state of Jammu and Kashmir, Indian provinces of Punjab, Himachal Pradesh, Haryana and also the Union territory of Chandigarh. Salam had secured first position among all candidates appearing from such a large region.

According to the original Gazette, which contains the results of all candidates, and is present, in original, in the records of the office of the Controller of Examinations of University of the Punjab, Lahore, a total of 28,534 candidates appeared in the exam, of which 20,112 passed. The Gazette notification is dated 18th May, 1940, and was issued by S.P. Singha, the then Controller of Examinations. In the last line of the very first page of the Gazette notification, appears the following sentence:[29] "*Roll No. 14888, Abdus Salam of Govt. Intermediate College, Jhang, obtained the highest number of marks (765).*"

After this major success Salam never looked back. In his intermediate exam which he took as a student of the Jhang college he again topped in the entire region of jurisdiction of the Punjab University securing 555/650 marks.

[29]Emphasis added.

He had studied Mathematics, English, Physics, Chemistry and Arabic. The detailed marks obtained by Salam in the intermediate are as follows:[30] 150/150 in mathematics, 138/150 in physics, 111/150 in English, 47/50 in Urdu, 109/150 in classical languages (he chose Arabic out of the following options: Arabic, German, Latin, Persian and Sanskrit). It is evident from the detailed marks in both, matric and intermediate, that Salam had dropped only four marks in mathematics in the two exams (196/200 in matric and 150/150 in intermediate).

During his stay in the intermediate college at Jhang he was made editor of the college magazine *Chenab*.[31] Salam wrote an article in that magazine establishing the period when the foremost poet of the then India, known commonly as Ghalib, changed his poetic pen-name from Asad to Ghalib. Ghalib, it may be recalled, is one of the greatest poets in any language. Ghalib is a difficult poet, even for grownups and Salam's familiarity with Ghalib at such a young age is an exceptional thing. This was a topic for mature researchers of Urdu literature. He was at most fourteen or fifteen years of age at that time but his tendency to conduct high quality original research was already manifest. This piece of writing may well be

[30]This is probably the first time that the detailed marks of Salam's intermediate result are being published in a book.

[31]Chenab is one of the five rivers that flow through Punjab - the name Punjab literally means five waters. Jhang is located close to this river.

the first research publication of the versatile Salam, even though it pertained to a literary subject.[32]

Salam never forgot his alma-mater in Jhang and years later, when he had become a man of immense renown, he did whatever he could for the uplift of that institution. He arranged for donations of books for the library and equipment for the laboratories. The tendency not to break with, or forget, and to hearken back to, institutions where he studied and blossomed, was his characteristic. His school, upgraded as an intermediate college while he was a student there, at Jhang, Government College, Lahore, and finally Cambridge University, were the three institutions that molded him into what he became and he always recognized and acknowledged it.

[32]Professor Khwaja M. Zakriya, former Dean Faculty of Islamic and Oriental Learning, Punjab University, and former Principal of the Punjab University Oriental College, pointed out to me that Salam used to contribute to the weekly magazine *Urooj* of the Jhang District Board even as a school student. He gave me a copy of an article written by Salam on the great philosopher-poet Allama Muhammad Iqbal that appeared in weeky *Urooj* on January 16, 1938. His name appears as Muhmmad Abdus Salam, student class ninth. His Urdu composition is outstanding and he was only twelve years old then. I find it fascinating that the magazine was then edited by Majeed Amjad who was, later, to become one of the most original and deep poets of Urdu language.

Chapter 3

Government College Lahore

Salam passed his intermediate in 1942 and was granted admission in one of the finest colleges of the sub-continent, the Government College (abbreviated as G.C.), Lahore, as a student of B.A. In an article written for the College Magazine *Ravi* in 1989, Salam summed up his career in following words:[1]

> My ancestral home is in Jhang and before arriving at Government College, Lahore I was a student of Jhang College. I became a student of the College at Jhang at age 12, in 1938. In

[1] Abdus Salam: *Kuch yad e maazi, kuch guzarshat* (Some Reminiscences, Some Submissions) Ravi, Vol 77, December 1989, p 1.

those days this was an intermediate College. The basis of my academic career was laid in this College. I believe that I owe the humble successes in later life to the kindnesses of my teachers in these colleges.

In 1942 I was admitted to Government College as an undergraduate. I studied in Government College for four years and bid farewell to the College in 1946 after having secured the degree of M.A. in Mathematics.

I still recall unforgettable memories of those four years. I also remember its teachers, friends and fellows, who were Muslims as well Hindus and Sikhs. The English teacher was Professor Ish Kumar. He is now 80, is still alive and resides in Chandigarh, India. Professor Kumar used to recite verses from Iqbal very frequently ··· When I met him in Guru Nanak University in 1981 I enquired about his interest in Iqbal. He said that he had moved on to Ghalib and considered him the greatest poet of the world. He has authored an authentic book on Ghalib.

Another English teacher was Professor Abdul

> Latif who has now passed away. Professor Sirajuddin taught English to Honors classes and later became Principal of the College.[2] Mr S.M. Chowla taught Mathematics. He is probably associated with Kansas University now. The late Professor Abdul Hameed was also a mathematics teacher and there were others too.

Professor Shaista Sirajuddin, daughter of Salam's English teacher, and later Principal Government College, Lahore, gave me a written page describing her memories of Salam. She wrote:

> Dr. Abdus Salam was my father Professor Sirajuddin's pupil in the B.A. Hons English Literature class in the then prestigious Government College. The Honours class comprising a select group of young people with a 'genuine flair' for literature held a special place in the Professor's heart. Abdus Salam in par-

[2]Professor Sirajuddin became Professor and founder-Chairman of the Department of English Language and Literature at the University of the Punjab, Lahore and also served as Vice Chancellor of the University from January to October 1974. His daughter Shaista Sirajuddin subsequently served as Dean Faculty of Arts and Humanities in the same university, as Chairperson of the Department founded by her father, and as Professor against the same post her father once occupied.

> ticular, was one whom my father recognized at an early age as possessing not only a brilliant mind, but also a fine sensibility. In fact before seeking admission into a postgraduate programme he actually sought my father's advice about whether to continue literature or take up science. I wonder what he was advised to consider!

Munir Ahmad Khan has stated:[3]

> Having stood first in English and Mathematics his tutor wanted him to become an English teacher. But I suspect that he felt he could play chess better by sticking to mathematics.

Those who knew him well in those days were aware of his father's enormous influence on him. He also acknowledged this influence to this author while conversing with him in his Trieste office in the early 1990s. His father had forbidden him to play cards and so Salam never played cards in his hostel. He mentioned this to Syed Ghulam Sarwar while still a student at Government College, Lahore. He was highly respectful towards his father throughout his life.

---

[3]Munir Ahmad Khan: *Salam as I Knew Him* in *Science for Peace and Progress: Life and Work of Abdus Salam* compiled by Anwar Dil, publishers Intercultural Forum, San Diego and Islamabad (iforum@aol.com), 2008, pp 599-600.

Salam's father wanted Salam to become a civil servant by joining the prestigious ICS (Indian Civil Services). This required that Salam clear, with good marks, a competitive exam after his B.A. or M.A. To ensure success in this competitive exam the choice of subjects was important. The subjects that he would study in B.A. (or later in M.A.) would be his most likely subjects for the ICS entry exam. Salam's father therefore sought advice from a senior civil servant he knew. He advised that Salam take mathematics (A and B courses) and English Literature. Salam therefore took these courses in his B.A. He took Urdu as an optional paper.[4]

It was at Government College Lahore that Salam truly blossomed. Students from all over the province came to study at this prize institution. Living in a hostel brought him into contact with a wide variety of people. Lahore was, and still is, a great literary and cultural center of the entire sub-continent. The teachers at this institution were of a far superior quality compared to his earlier teachers.

[4]Salam's brother mentions in his book that his father sought advice from six people regarding the choice of subjects in B.A. The then Deputy Commisioner, Ludhiana, Hafiz Abdul Majeed wrote a letter to Salam's father on 13.8.1942 advising that Salam take mathematics A and B courses and English literature with Urdu as optional subject. His book is written in Urdu: Abdul Hameed Chaudhari: *Alami Shohrat Yafta Sciencedaan Abdus Salam* (World Renowned Scientist Abdus Salam); published by Ahmad Salam 8 Campion Road, SW 15, 6 NW, London; 1998; pp 37-38.

His mathematics teacher Dr. Chowla was particularly fond of Salam. Dr. Chowla was a dedicated mathematician who did nothing but mathematics and was considered unusual on account of having no interest other than mathematics. He used to pose an unsolved problem at the end of a class. He and Salam would try to solve such a problem independently after college hours, and compare their answers the following day. This sharpened Salam's problem solving abilities. He once told Syed Ghulam Sarwar[5] that his solution to a particular problem was just a few lines whereas his teacher's solution extended over a few pages.

One of the problems posed by Dr. Chowla[6] concerned four simultaneous equations in four variables - this was a problem due to Ramanujan, the great and raw mathematical genius from India, who ended up in Cambridge with Professor Hardy. Salam worked on this problem for

[5]Syed Ghulam Sarwar was a contemporary of Salam at Government College, Lahore, and a student of philosophy. He was a year senior to Salam who was a frequent visitor to his room in the New Hostel of G.C. Lahore. Mr. Sarwar served on the editorial staff of the daily *Pakistan Times* and, after retirement from *The Pakistan Times*, as magazine editor of the Daily *The Nation*. Mr. Sarwar, who turned 90 in August 2012, is still alive and well as these lines are being written. Very recently, on January 19, 2013, Mr. Sarwar also told me that Dr. Chowla used to obtain these problems from England.

[6]Dr. Chowla made a name as a number theorist after emigrating to US in the late 1940s.

a few days and came up with a solution. Salam's solution was sent by Dr. Chowla to a magazine. Thus, in the year 1943, Salam's first mathematical research paper titled "On a Problem of Ramanujan" was published in the March - July 1943 issue of *Maths. Student* (volume XI, Nos 1-2). Salam stated at the end of his paper that he had devised a method of solving these equations which was much quicker than Ramanujan's method. The concluding words were that Ramanujan's method is "a very laborious method." Salam was only seventeen then and his self-confidence oozes out of the concluding remark.

Salam became quite a celebrity in G.C. Lahore. He was elected editor of the college magazine. As mentioned in the previous chapter Salam had established the time period when the great poet Ghalib adopted the pen-name Ghalib. Salam submitted an article, establishing the time period of change of pen-name by Ghalib, to a highly reputed magazine.[7] The editor published this work. The late Professor Waheed Qureshi, a contemporary of Salam at G.C., and later Dean Faculty of Oriental Learning at the University of the Punjab, told this author that shortly after the publication of the article, Salam went to call on the editor along with him. The editor was very surprised when he saw that the author of the article was a young fellow in his teens. He said that he expected a maturer

[7]The magazine was *Adbi Dunya* - the name may be translated as Literary World.

person, a much older person, to be the author of that work.

About six weeks before the exams Salam used to have his room locked from outside with the help of a hostel employee so as to be able to focus on his studies undisturbed. In those days his father had been posted to Multan, known for its sweltering summers. During the summer break Salam used to go to Multan and stay with his father. However, his father ensured that he would be able to study during vacations and for this purpose a room had been arranged for him in the hostel of Government High School. According to Salam's brother Abdul Hameed Chaudhari, [8] the hostel superintendent, Chaudhari Rasheed Ahmad described Salam's conduct in the following words:

> I had given a room to Salam for study. The room had a bed, a table and a chair. Water and tea had been specially arranged for, and electric power was also available. Salam would come at 8 A.M., go back home at 12.30, return at 2.00 P.M. and then work till about 6 in the evening. He would not waste one moment. In my entire life I have never seen a

[8] His book is written in Urdu: Abdul Hameed Chaudhari: *Alami Shohrat Yafta Sciencedaan Abdus Salam* (World Renowned Scientist Abdus Salam); published by Ahmad Salam 8 Campion Road, SW 15, 6 NW, London; 1998; pp 41-42.

> student so deeply concerned about his studies. His residence was about two furlongs from the hostel. Around 5 P.M. Maulvi Nawab Din (M.A. Persian and Urdu and teacher of Government High School Multan) would come over. Salam would join us around 6 and spend an hour with us. He was never careless during those days. He was a different type of boy. He stayed aloof from other students and had a very good brain. Prayers of his parents were always with him. He kept coming to us till 1943 when he did his M.A.[9] He always had a smile on his face. He would listen attentively but quietly, and kept thinking whenever we discussed national and international affairs. His health was very good.

In the year 1944 Salam stood first in the entire region falling within the jurisdiction of the University of the Punjab (which extended well beyond the Province of Punjab)[10] in the B.A. examination breaking all previous recor-ds. He was awarded several medals on account of his performance. The Government of the Punjab awarded him a scholarship, in addition to a scholarship offered by his

[9] Salam actually did his M.A. in 1946.

[10] The jurisdiction of the University of the Punjab, at that time, extended over what is now Pakistan in its entirety (save Sindh), and parts of India, including Delhi.

own community. Salam told Syed Ghulam Sarwar that while he was taking one of his B.A. papers in mathematics he thought of leaving the examination hall since, at first sight, the question paper appeared difficult. There were twelve problems and the candidates were asked to solve any six. All the twelve problems were entirely new for Salam - he had not come across any one of those in the course of his studies. However he decided to try his luck. He was able to solve all twelve problems and wrote a triumphant note for the examiner on his script "See any six".

The details of marks secured by Salam were as follows: Maths 300/300, English (Hons) 121/150, Urdu (compulsory) 30/50. Salam told his brother that the script of his Urdu paper had been sent to someone in Aligarh University who apparently did not like his Urdu and gave him only 60% marks. Salam felt that he deserved 80% to 90% marks in Urdu. Despite his unsatisfactory marks in Urdu, Salam had broken all previous records in B.A.

Salam was awarded several medals and scholarships in view of his outstanding performance. He was awarded Nihal Chand Gold Medal for his English (Hons) result, and two silver medals for breaking previous records. The Government of the Punjab awarded him a scholarship worth Rs. 35 per month while his own community awarded him a scholarship worth Rs. 60 per month. In addition, the Head of his community gave him a monetary reward of

Rs. 200. The magazine *Arooj*, a publication of the District Board Jhang, published a poem in praise of Salam.

While a student of third year in college (i.e., the first year of his B.A.) Salam had apparently appeared in a test for engineering apprenticeship with the railways. He passed the test but did not join. A Chief Engineer of the railways told Salam's brother Abdul Hameed Chaudhari that it was a good thing that Salam did not join the railways. In that case "He would have remained a mere Chief Engineer like me", he said. Munir Ahamd Khan has however pointed out that Salam did not join the Indian State Railways because he had failed the medical test.[11] He writes: "The fact that he wore spectacles from an early age also saved him form from becoming an engineer and saved the Railways because he was no mechanical genius."

After his B.A., Salam toyed with the idea of pursuing studies in English literature. His father had always wanted him to join the Civil Services. On account of the World War the British authorities had suspended the Indian Civil Service exams. This meant a reorientation, not just for Salam, but for many bright and aspiring young

[11]Munir Ahmad Khan: *Salam as I Knew Him* in *Science for Peace and Progress: Life and Work of Abdus Salam* compiled by Anwar Dil, publishers Intercultural Forum, San Diego and Islamabad (iforum@aol.com), 2008, p 600.

men. Somehow Salam decided to do M.A. mathematics.[12] Salam did his M.A. in 1946, standing first and breaking records as usual.

In his M.A. Salam had scored 573/600 marks. The detailed breakup of marks was brought to this author's notice by the office of the Controller of Examinations of the University of the Punjab. There were a total of six papers, each carrying 100 marks. In three of these Salam had scored hundred percent marks whereas in the other three papers he secured 96, 89 and 88 marks respectively.[13]

Since the Gazette does not identify the names of the papers, this author sought the syllabus of the academic year 1945-46 from the records of the office of the Registrar

[12]Syed Ghulam Sarwar told me that at least on one occasion Salam had discussed this matter with him. Salam had told him that he could not make up his mind as to whether he should enroll for a masters in English Literature or Mathematics. Mr. Sarwar, who was deeply influenced by another Cambridge Wrangler, Inayatullah Khan (known as Allama Mashriqi, the founder of the Khaksar Movement), advised Salam to go for mathematics. Incidentally Mashriqi had the distinction of completing four triposes in five years - Wrangler 1909, First Class Oriental Languages Tripos and Natural Sciences Tripos, 1911, First Class Mechanical Sciences Tripos, 1912. See: *Al-Mashriqi The Disowned Genius*, by S. Shabbir Hussain; Jang Publishers, 1991, pp 9-12.

[13]The above and the following information about the details of Salam's M.A. results, has probably, never before, been brought to public knowledge.

(the academic section of the Registrar's office, headed by a Deputy Registrar Academics is the keeper of these records). According to the records the nomenclature and the numbering of the six papers in 1946 was as follows (the weight of each subject or component is indicated by the fraction written after the subject):

Paper I: Theory of Functions of a Real Variable (1/2); Infinite series (1/4) Differential equations (1/4). Salam secured 100/100 marks in this paper

Paper II: Plane Geometry, Pure (1/4); Plane Geometry, Analytical (1/4); Solid Geometry (1/4); Differential Geometry[14] (1/4); Salam secured 89/100 marks in this paper.

Paper III: Dynamics of a Particle (1/2); Rigid Dynamics (1/2); Salam secured 88/100 marks in this paper.

Papers IV, V and VI: Any three of the following:

A.– Theory of Functions of a Complex Variable (1/2); Elliptic Functions (1/2)

B.– Theory of Numbers (1/2); Algebra (1/4); Theory of Functions (1/4)

C.– Astronomy (3/4); Spherical Trigonometry (1/4)

D.– Attractions (1/4); Electricity (1/2); Magnetism (1/4)

E.– Statics (1/4); Hydrostatics (1/4); Hydrodynamics (1/2)

[14]The document mentions this part as 1/2 of syllabus of this paper but this is most likely a typing/printing error.

F.– Finite Differences and Statistics
It has not been possible to determine from the records as to which three options Salam took. However, according to the records, Salam secured 96/100 in paper IV and 100/100 each in papers V and VI.

In his valuable article on Salam in his book, K.K. Aziz has given a detailed description of his first introduction to Salam in the following words:[15]

> Dr. Abdul Hammed Siddiqui was lecturer at the Law College and I knew him through Shaikh Khurshid.[16] At some date in October 1944 when I was in third year and Salam in his fifth, Dr. Siddiqui entered the Coffee House with one of his friends, Professor Ganguli, who taught mathematics at the university and whom I had met a little earlier. With them was a well-built young man in double-

[15]K.K. Aziz: *The Coffee House of Lahore - A Memoir 1942-57*; Sang e Meel Publishers, 2008, p 209, 210.

[16]Author's note: Probably this is the same Shaikh Khurshid who, in the mid 1960s, was the Federal Law Minister of Pakistan during the regime of Field Marshal Ayub Khan. His brother Munir Ahmad Khan was appointed Chairman Pakistan Atomic Energy Commission by Mr. Z.A. Bhutto in the 1970s. Muneer Ahmad Khan, another Ravian (the usual name for a student of Government College, Lahore), was closely known to Salam, who worked in the IAEA Headquarters at Vienna, before Z.A. Bhutto appointed him Chairman PAEC.

> breasted suit and sporting thick moustaches. Led by Siddiqui they came to my table and I was introduced to the new arrival, who was Salam. He was well known to us because of his outstanding performance in the B.A. examination result, but I had not seen him before as he was reading mathematics at the university and rarely came to the College. He turned out to be very different from my imagined figure of a mathematician or scientist: a serious unsmiling, even surly, creature who knew nothing about anything outside his special field of interest. All such misconceptions melted away in the first half an hour. Salam smiled, joked, talked enthusiastically about things in general, and his bespectacled eyes sparkled with enjoyment. I found him genial, warm-hearted, approachable, witty and easy to make friends with.

K.K. Aziz has given us a valuable assessment of Salam's erudition as a College student. He writes:[17]

> On the subject of English poetry he ruffled my curiosity by his keen interest in the romantic poets because I knew the honors syllabus only

[17]K.K. Aziz: *The Coffee House of Lahore - A Memoir 1942-57*; Sang e Meel Publishers, 2008, pp 210-211.

> covered the metaphysical poets. He read my mind and with a smile said that he had read beyond the prescribed books, and advised me gently to do the same. Gradually I discovered other gifts in him: interest in Urdu poetry, curiosity about why historical events take place, a genial temperament, and a sense of humor which traversed the entire gamut of civilized jokes and titillating stories. I never heard him talk ill of anyone.

Air Marshal (R) Zafar Chaudhary was his contemporary at Government College. In an article published in 2010 he wrote:[18]

> I got to know Abdus Salam when we were students at Government College, Lahore in the early 1940s. We both lived in the New Hostel[19]; he was a year senior to me in class but, of course, aeons ahead in intellectual prowess. I remember he liked good food (Aloo gosht[20]

[18]Zafar Chaudhary: *The Friday Times*, Dr. Abdus Salam and his Love for the Country That Disowned Him; January 1, 2010.

[19]On the M.A. examination admission form, that exists in the records of the Controller of Examinations office of the University of the Punjab, Salam has written his current address as 30, New Hostel, Lahore. So he was residing in room number 30 at that time. His father's address is given as Inspector of Schools Office, Multan.

[20]Potato meat curry.

> being his favorite) and consumed it heartily. We often chided him about his hunger for food keeping full pace for his hunger for looks,[21] but he never minded our impudence. He had instructed his servant to put a lock on the door of his cubicle so that boys did not disturb him while he studied. The only relaxation he permitted himself was a game of chess in the Common Room with Khushia, the elderly keeper of this facility that housed several indoor games.

In the year 1989, the one hundred and twenty fifth birthday of G.C., Salam wrote an article in Urdu in the college magazine *Ravi* that he had edited while a student at G.C. He studied in G.C. for four years (1942-46) and wrote:

> During my stay at the Government College I was privileged to serve in many different ways. For example, in 1945 I had the honor of being elected President of the college union. Another good fortune was that I was the editor of both sections, Urdu and English, of the college magazine. During my stay in college I led a full life. My only regret is not being able to benefit from Professor Sufi Tabbasum's lec-

[21] I have copied this from the published text - the word is more likely books rather than looks.

> tures. He taught Persian. I did not opt for Persian and the practice of attending courses that one had not taken, did not exist. Like Cambridge, Government College ought to set up a tradition whereby a student may attend lectures of favorite teachers even if he has not opted for the course and is not going to take an exam in that course.

A string of coincidences took Salam from Lahore to Cambridge. A Punjabi landlord, Khizar Hayat Tiwana, had raised money for the war effort. The war ended in 1945 and the same landlord became Chief Minister of the Punjab in 1946. His coalition partner Sir Chotoo Ram persuaded him to use the money to institute scholarships for sons of small farmers. Salam's brother Abdul Hameed Chaudhari states in his book[22] that the amount collected by Khizar Hayat Tiwana was about 300,000 rupees. The fund was named *Punjab Peasant Welfare Fund.* Since his father owned a small piece of land[23] Salam was a natural choice on account of his outstanding career. Salam and

[22] This book is written in Urdu: Abdul Hameed Chaudhari: *Alami Shohrat Yafta Sciencedaan Abdus Salam* (World Renowned Scientist Abdus Salam); published by Ahmad Salam, 8 Campion Road, SW 15, 6 NW, London; 1998; pp 45-46.

[23] Actually Salam's father did not originally own any land. When he learned of the scheme, he requested his elder brother to transfer some of his own land in his name so that Salam could become eligible for the scholarship.

four others were selected for the award of these scholarships in 1946. The scholarship committee was headed by the then Vice Chancellor of the University of the Punjab, who was well aware of Salam's outstanding career. Salam was awarded a scholarship without being interviewed.

On the advice of the then Vice Chancellor (Mian Afzal Hussain) Salam had already applied for admission to various institutions in England. Although the scholarship was awarded a bit late, an unexpected vacancy had arisen at St. John's College and he was offered a place. In fact the cable offering Salam admission to Cambridge arrived on September 3, 1946. The Cambridge authorities asked him if he could come over in October. Salam immediately traveled from Multan to Lahore 300 kilometers north. He wanted to find out the status of the processing of his scholarship. He arrived in Lahore only to discover that the Government offices had been moved to Simla, a hill station 250 kilometers north, on account of the summer heat. So he took the train to Simla. He got the offer letter the very day he arrived in Simla.[24] He then had to book a seat on a ship for England. Apparently flights between India and England did not operate at that time.

[24]Apparently, in Simla, he asked someone on the road about the location of the office he wanted to go to. The person, instead, asked for his name. When Salam told him his name, the individual replied that he was going to the post office to post him a letter formally offering him a scholarship. Salam thus collected the letter of award of scholarship personally on the road! What a coincidence!

For this purpose he was advised in Simla to travel to Delhi. From Delhi he was referred to Bombay where he was finally able to book a seat on a liner for Liverpool with September 18th as the departure date. From Delhi he returned to Multan. The entire exercise had taken four days. Not much time was left before departure.

Salam's father borrowed nine hundred rupees from someone (a huge sum by standards of the day), the necessary purchases were done, and Salam traveled to Bombay. He put up in a hotel close to the harbor in view of the Hindu-Muslim rioting that had erupted in Bombay. At night he was woken up by the Royal Indian Military Police who had information that Salam was an absconder from the Royal Indian Navy and wanted to arrest him. Salam however kept his head and convinced them that he was a prospective student proceeding to England. They checked his documents and left.

In an ironic twist of fate the Chief Minister was replaced the following year, his successor canceled the scholarship scheme and the other four awardees therefore never went to England! Salam once quipped: "In the end all that effort to collect a war fund for buying munitions ended up in one thing alone: to get me to Cambridge". Salam's brother has quoted Salam as having said[25] that

[25]This book is written in Urdu: Abdul Hameed Chaudhari: *Alami Shohrat Yafta Sciencedaan Abdus Salam* (World Renowned Scientist Abdus Salam); published by Ahmad Salam, 8 Campion

had the war not intervened to thwart the desire of his parents, he would have, in all probability, joined the Indian Civil Service, where, the highest he could have achieved would be to rise to the position of Chief Secretary of a Province, or a Federal Secretary.

Cambridge was to change the course of Salam's life. The potential civil servant had no plans of taking up a scientific career at that time. Little did he know how his destiny was pushing him in the direction of deep creativity and fame. There is a chain of coincidences, each of which had a role in getting him to Cambridge. The World War led to a suspension of the Indian Civil Services exam, the end of the war led to the institution of a Peasant Welfare Scholarship scheme out of the war fund that was ended the following year with Salam being the sole beneficiary, the sudden availability of a position at St. John's, Salam's escape at the hands of the security forces who suspected that he was a deserter, his decision to pursue mathematics instead of English Literature, and so on. But all along it is also evident that Salam was seeking and getting the right guidance, was prompt in responding to situations that arose, such as his visit from Lahore to Simla without delay and then on to Delhi and Bombay for booking his seat, etc. Above all, he was keen to get to England, even though he had not yet decided to adopt a research career.

Road, SW 15, 6 NW, London; 1998; p 44.

However Salam never forgot Government College and his teachers. As Shaista Sirajuudin, the daughter of Professor Sirajuddin wrote:[26]

> Salam made a point of calling upon my father whenever he was in the country and in Lahore. The last time we met him was when we were living in our house in the cantonment. My father elderly now and almost a complete recluse, nonetheless invited him to tea, saying how touched and moved he always had been by the Doctor's affection and consideration for his old professor. The Pakistan government during that period had conferred certain honors upon Salam and unusually for him he arrived at our house with a cavalcade of official cars and security personnel. The neighbors were agog with curiosity and surprise at the unusual activity in the Professor's house. Dr. Salam be-speckled, soft spoken and genial was warmly embraced by my father. He was in no rush and spent the evening reminiscing and chatting quite happily and informally with us all. When the time came for him to leave both my father and he had tears in their eyes.

[26]Personal communication, dated August 23, 2012.

Chapter 4

Student at Cambridge

The journey to Liverpool lasted eighteen days. The ship on which he traveled was carrying around six hundred Italian POW's, and a similar number of British soldiers, mostly accompanied by their families.[1] In addition, it also carried around fifteen to twenty students. Salam had little idea of the cold in Britain and was inadequately dressed. Fortunately for him, a leader of his community, Chaudhri Zafarula,[2] was present. He had come to receive

[1]In his biography of Salam (*Cosmic Anger: Abdus Salam The First Muslim Nobel Laureate*; Oxford University Press, 2008), Gordon Fraser has put the number of British families aboard the ship H.M.S. *Franconia* at around six hundred whereas Salam's brother puts the number of British soldiers at around three hundred.

[2]Chaudhri Muhammad Zafarula Khan commonly known as Chaudhri Zafarula was, at that time, a Judge of the Supreme Court

his nephew. Chaudhri Zafarula then helped Salam by picking his heavy trunk from one side with Salam holding the other. Forty years later, in 1986, Salam wrote of the incident:[3] "This was an amazing reception for a humble student, who had never before encountered such gracious unself-consciousness on the part of a personage so highly placed." He traveled to London with Chaudhri Zafarula. Upon noticing Salam shiver Zafarula gave him one of his heavy winter coats, which Salam retained for decades.

4.1 Double Tripos

Salam had been admitted to St. John's College as a student of Tripos in Mathematics. In an article written for

of India. He later became Foreign Minister of Pakistan and subsequently President of the UN General Assembly. Chaudhri Zafarula was also knighted and retired as the President of the International Court of Justice. Salam first saw him when he was only eight years old. Subsequently, in response to a letter that the young Salam wrote to him at age fourteen, Chaudhri Zafarula advised him to take care of his health, go through the lectures the very day they were delivered and to prepare for lectures one day in advance. He also advised Salam to undertake educational travel to broaden his outlook.

[3]Abdus Salam: *Homage to Chaudhri Muhammad Zafarulla Khan*, Transnational Perspectives, Vol 12, No 2, 1986. The essay has been reproduced in Salam's book *Ideals and Realities: Selected Essays of Abdus Salam;* Editor C.H. Lai, World Scientific, 1987.

the college magazine the *Ravi* in 1989, Salam described aspects of his life at Cambridge in the following words:[4]

> I arrived at Cambridge in 1946 after having done M.A. from Government College, Lahore. In Cambridge classrooms, students sit in the same manner as those who sit in a mosque before prayers. There is complete silence before the arrival of the lecturer. You will see the English students using pens of four different colors and employing rulers for drawing lines properly during the lecture. My class-fellows had come straight from schools and were younger to me. It took me two years to attain the same level of self-confidence and aspirations that they possessed. They had come from an environment where, before despatching all good students to Cambridge, every school teacher would tell them that they were the sons of a nation that had produced Newton and that the knowledge of science and mathematics was their heritage - if they wished they too could become Newtons.

In the same article Salam stated that the kind of discipline that prevailed in Cambridge was a new experience

[4]Abdus Salam: *Kuch yad e maazi, kuch guzarshat* (Some Reminiscences, Some Submissions) Ravi, Vol 77, December 1989, p 1.

for him. Students could take the B.A. exam only once and if they failed that was it - one could never again sit for that exam. Students were not allowed to return to hostel after 10 pm without prior permission - in case of breach of the rule there was a fine of one penny for returning between 10-12 pm. Arriving later than midnight would incur a penalty called gating, for seven days. Three time gating meant expulsion from college. Salam stated that some of the punishments were "barabric" but the students faced them bravely. This kind of stringency in discipline was eased in 1968.

His friend K.K. Aziz has given a very valuable description of Salam's Cambridge days which is quoted here in full since it appears to have come to him directly from Salam. It is also of interest because it gives us a glimpse of the hardships of life in Britain resulting from the World War. He writes:[5]

> I was curious about Salam's student days in Cambridge and asked him many questions about his life in St. John's. Salam reminded me that he had come to Cambridge soon after the end of second World War and life in Britain was very hard: most things of necessary and daily use, like clothes, meat and eggs, were rationed. Hot water was scarce and taking a

[5]K.K. Aziz: *The Coffee House of Lahore - A Memoir 1942-57*; Sang e Meel Publishers, 2008, pp 212-213.

> bath was an ordeal. Heating in the college was intermittent because of the scarcity of coal and electricity. What really bothered him was taking notes in the classroom with nearly freezing fingers. So he practiced in his rooms to write fast with gloves on. He had to attend classes in heavy clothes and overcoat, which did not help concentration. The first winter was really a trail, he said. His Pakistani contemporaries like Javed Iqbal and Daud Rahbar in Cambridge and A.H. Kardar and Fazlur Rahman in Oxford were equally uncomfortable. But with the summer came heavenly release and he then realized why the Englishmen talked so much about weather and why the English poets sang so ecstatically of the sights and pleasure of spring and summer. He told me that my wife and I were lucky to have arrived in England just after the last war-time restrictions had been removed.

Mathematics Tripos was a three-year course that had three exams known as part I, II and III exams. The first exam was also called a prelim. Salam cleared the prelim in first class. Most of his classmates got a third division even though there were students from places like Eton and Harrow among them. When Salam asked one of his tutors as to why had so many students done so miserably in the prelims his tutor, Wordie, replied: "We set the exams of prelims so hard so as to make a distinction between just those boys and the people who are really serious." Fred Hoyle[6] was one of his teachers and had asked him how he had done? Salam said that he had made many mistakes and then went away laughing. Hoyle, however, saw the results when they were circulated among the examiners. In an article written after Salam's death, Fred Hoyle wrote that he remembered that Salam had over eighty percent marks and was probably third in the class. At Cambridge the students were not told of their positions in exams, but, from the the award of scholarships, one could judge that those awarded had done better than

[6]Fred Hoyle was a brilliant scientist who was, unfairly, not awarded the 1983 Nobel Prize in Physics even though his collaborator Fowler was. Robin McKie wrote in *The Observer* of 2 October 2010 that when Fowler was informed of the award he "was stunned, he later admitted. And so were other scientists, men and women who remain puzzled by the omission to this day. "I have no idea how the Swedes decided to make an award to Chandrasekhar and Fowler but not to Hoyle," admits astronomer Lord Rees, President of the Royal Society. "However, I think it would be widely accepted that it was an unfair misjudgment." Robin McKie adds: "Scientists' dismay at the refusal to give Hoyle a Nobel prize is understandable, although it should be noted that he could be cantankerous and opinionated and had offended a large number of influential colleagues unused to his Yorkshire bluntness." The article may be seen at http://www.guardian.co.uk/science/2010/oct/03/fred-hoyle-nobel-prize.

others.

During his very first year at Cambridge Salam realized that although his mathematical knowledge was excellent, his general knowledge was unsatisfactory. He, therefore, spent time in the excellent library reading about history of civilizations, particulary Islamic history, with special emphasis on the scientific achievements of Muslims. He also read about different religions and went through the eighteen religious books of Hinduism - the eighteen Shastaras. This kind of reading gave Salam's writings the depth and flow that makes them so powerful and convincing.

During his second year at Cambridge Salam prepared for his part II exam. He would sometimes attend lectures of part III which were then delivered by Paul Dirac. Dirac had won the 1933 Nobel Prize in Physics jointly with Schrodinger. Salam passed his part II tripos exam in 1948 securing a first class and qualifying for the title of Wrangler. It was exposure to Dirac that made Salam give up the aspiration to become a civil servant. He wanted to do a Ph.D. And it was probably exposure to Dirac that created in him a desire to do physics. This is confirmed by an interview that Salam gave to the *Illustrated Weekly of India* (February 1, 1981):

> Until 1948 I did mathematics. I had by then already listened to the lectures of Dirac and Pauli and had drifted more and more towards

> physics. In 1948, when I had finished my mathematics course, I still had one year's scholarship on and I had almost decided to do physics.

In order to finally make up his mind Salam sought the advice of Fred Hoyle who later became one of the most renowned astro-physicists of the twentieth century. Hoyle asked Salam as to what was it that he wanted to do. Salam told Hoyle that he wanted to do physics. Hoyle then advised him firmly to do experimental physics - otherwise "you would never be able to look a physicist in the eye." Hoyle then went on:

> You follow me? Physics is experiment, not theory. Science is experiment. You Indians are very good at theory. You must even if it kills you, take this last year for experimental physics".

Salam told Hoyle that he would get a first class if he did mathematics III but due to the fact that he had not done any physics experiments for the last five or six years he might just score a second class, if he opted for the physics course.[7] Hoyle simply told him that he must

[7] It is worth remebering that Salam had not studied physics either in B.A. or M.A. at Lahore. He had studied physics only up to intermediate, i.e., High School level of U.K. or U.S.

do the experimental course. The reason Salam sought Hoyle's advice had to do with his interaction with Hoyle as his student. In an article written after Salam's death Hoyle pointed out that he found it less strenuous to:[8]

> [...] tackle hard problems with a student like Salam than it was to be asked easier things by those chaps who sat there and stared out into space. With the latter you had to roll two stones uphill simultaneously. One stone was the problem itself, the other was to get the chap to understand. With Salam you had only one stone and he would do a fair amount of pushing.

Hoyle also wrote that between themselves, he and Salam managed to solve most problems set in various Tripos eaminations. Salam accepted Hoyle's advice and joined the physics course. In accepting Hoyle's advice Salam had taken up a challenge which few people had successfully met. It is not that Wranglers before him had not successfully completed the physics course in one year - the challenge was to secure a first class in physics in one year. His tutor J.M. Wordie also advised Salam that he

[8]Quoted in Abdul Hameed Chaudhari: *Alami Shohrat Yafta Sciencedaan Abdus Salam* (World Renowned Scientist Abdus Salam); published by Ahmad Salam, 8 Campion Road, SW 15, 6 NW, London; 1998; p 55.

should take physics so that Wordie could test his "theory". The "theory" was that it was possible for a Wrangler to secure a first in physics in one year even though some of the most intelligent people, G.P. Thomson (Nobel Prize 1937) and Neville Mott (Nobel Prize 1977) had only managed to obtain a second class in physics in one year. No wonder Wordie "rubbed his hands in glee" when he found out that Salam had opted for the Physics challenge. It was the acceptance of a very tough challenge that transformed him from a mathematician to a physicist, a transformation that led him to greatness and got him the Nobel prize eventually. But that was not foreseen at that time.

Years later Salam told Crease and Mann: "By God it was hard." He told them:[9]

> In Cavendish, there was the old equipment, ancient equipment, and nothing but. Rutherford's own equipment - and you were supposed to make it work. You had to blow glass tubes yourself and carry them three flights of steps. It was a torture. They wanted it to be torture and they succeeded.

Salam narrated two interesting incidents to Crease and Mann. He described one of these in the following words

[9]Robert P. Crease and Charles C.Mann: *The Second Creation - Makers of the Revolution in Twentieth Century Physics*; MacMillan Press 1986, pp 232-233.

> I remember the first experiment I was given. It took me four full days to complete. Basically rather simple, the experiment - you had to measure the difference of the two sodium D spectral lines, the wavelength difference, by an interferometer method. I took three days to set up the equipment, set it up properly, and then I took three readings. Three readings on the principle that I wanted to get a straight line - two points to determine a straight line and the third to prove it. I took this piece of work to Sir Denys Wilkinson, who is now vice chancellor of Sussex University and one of the brightest experimental physicists in UK. He was one of the supervisors who awarded marks on your write-up. He looked at this with a quizzical look on his face. He said "What is your background?" I said I came from mathematics. He said, "Oh I can see that. You realize you have to take *one thousand* readings before you have a straight line. This is just not worth grading. Go back!"

At the end of the year he took his exam. He did not do well in experiment and after the practical exam wrote to his father "My practical did not go well and I might not pass. If I pass it will be a miracle. Please pray for me."

His brother Abdul Hameed Chaudhari asked him in 1957 as to what was the background to that letter. They were living near Earl's Court subway station in London at the time and Salam was reminiscing with him. In his book Abdul Hameed Chaudhri quotes Salam's reply:[10]

> It was an eight hour practical. I had prepared chicken sandwiches for lunch which I enjoyed during the break and kept doing the practical. When I started looking at my data I discovered that my method was wrong. I grew really nervous. It was too late to redo the practical. That is why I wrote to father in my upset state.

According to his brother, Salam referred to this exam as "the hardest exam" of his life.[11] When his brother asked him how did he get a first class Salam told him that he had asked his practical supervisor a similar question - he had asked him as to how did he pass. His supervisor told him "You had done so well in all six theory papers that they (examiners) did not even ask for your practical result." Salam had been avoiding Denys Wilkinson ever

[10] Abdul Hameed Chaudhari: *Alami Shohrat Yafta Sciencedaan Abdus Salam* (World Renowned Scientist Abdus Salam); published by Ahmad Salam, 8 Campion Road, SW 15, 6 NW, London; 1998; p 59; this book is written in Urdu.

[11] *Ibid*, p 59.

since his disastrous encounter with him in the laboratory. He ran into Wilkinson while looking at the notice board outside the Senate Hall where the result had been posted. Wilkinson asked him what class had he obtained. When Salam said he had obtained a first class, Wilkinson was so surprised that he "turned a full circle" on his heels and then said, "Shows how wrong you can be about people!" Wordie's reaction has not been mentioned anywhere - perhaps Salam did not run into him after his result. Wordie's theory had been proven by Salam's results. Salam was to surprise more teachers and colleagues at Cambridge and elsewhere in the coming years.

Chapter 5

A Trip to Pakistan

When Salam arrived in Cambridge in 1946 India was a British colony ruled and administered by the British. In August 1947 the subcontinent became independent and two countries, India and Pakistan were carved out of it. Jhang, Multan and district Montgomery (Sahiwal), where his family and relations resided, were in the territory that came to be known as Pakistan. So in June 1949 Salam arrived in Pakistan for the first time in his life. Salam was now clear that he wanted to go for a research career in physics. But to pursue higher studies he needed a scholarship. This he planned to get from the Pakistani authorities.

Mian Afzal Hussain, who was the Vice Chancellor of the Punjab University when Salam was awarded his first Cambridge scholarship, was now the Chairman of the

Federal Public Service Commission. Mian Afzal Hussain was himself an former Cambridge graduate, having obtained a first in Natural Sciences at Christ College before Salam was even born. Mian Afzal Hussain had therefore moved to the then Federal capital, Karachi. Salam landed in Karachi and met Mian Afzal Hussain who agreed to help him. Mian Afzal Hussain was aware that funds from that very scheme, the Peasant Welfare Fund, that had taken Salam to Cambridge, were still not fully exhausted. He was delighted that Salam had done so well in his studies. After a two day stay in Karachi, Salam arrived in Multan by train where his brother received him at the station. His father had stayed back at home as he was not certain as to which train and on what day Salam was arriving.

After staying with the family for a few days Salam left for Lahore seeking a scholarship. He handed over a letter from Mian Afzal Hussain to the Director Education, Punjab. As advised by Mian Afzal Hussain he also met a senior officer of the Punjab government. Both officers agreed to help Salam and advised him to call on the Governor Francis Moody, himself an alumnus of St. John's. Hearing of this Salam asked his family in Multan to send him his college necktie. This shows the subtlety and sense of nuance of the young Salam. He called upon the Governor wearing his St. John's College necktie. Governor Moody immediately recognized the necktie and met him very affectionately. Impressed by Salam's performance he agreed to do whatever he could to get him a scholarship. Salam then wrote to Mian Afzal Hussain informing him of his meetings and thanking him for his support.

In his reply dated August 23, 1949 Mian Afzal Hussain expressed the opinion that a two year scholarship worth 600 pounds per annum would suffice. He also wrote that in his view the Punjab Education Department would agree to give him a scholarship only on the condition that Salam return after his Ph.D. and serve with them. He advised Salam not to worry about his job and instead return to Cambridge and do his Ph.D. first.

Salam's parents decided that his marriage be arranged while he was still in Pakistan. He had been betrothed to his first cousin, daughter of Salam's father's elder brother, at a very young age. Salam's father-in-law was the same individual who had transferred part of his agricultural land holdings to Salam's father enabling Salam to qualify for a scholarship meant for sons of small farmers. Salam was married to Amtul Hafeez on August 19, 1949.

Salam's brother Abdul Hameed Chaudhari has stated in his biography of Salam[1] that the formal religious contract of marriage (nikah) was conducted by the then Head

[1]This book is written in Urdu: Abdul Hameed Chaudhari *Alami Shohrat Yafta Sciencedaan Abdus Salam* (World Renowned Scientist Abdus Salam); published by Ahmad Salam, 8 Campion Road, SW 15, 6 NW, London; 1998; p 62.

of their community in Quetta, the capital of Baluchistan. This is quite far from Punjab where Salam's family and his in-laws resided. The reason for holding the nikah in Quetta had to do with the fact that the Head of their community had gone to Quetta which was less hot and humid compared to Punjab. The marriage procession however had to proceed later from Multan to Jhang as Salam's father was posted in Multan at the time. Six weeks later Salam departed for Cambridge after having secured a scholarship and a wife. He left his wife behind.

Chapter 6

Ph.D. Studies at Cambridge

Salam had the rare distinction of not only having secured first classes in mathematics and physics but also of completing the job in three years. The authorities at Cambridge knew that they had an unusual young man on their hands. The Cambridge tradition was to put first-class students into experimental physics and the inferior ones into theoretical physics. This was an odd tradition for an institution that had produced Dirac. Salam therefore started off as a research student in experimental physics in 1949. However, as he put it:[1]

[1]Abdus Salam: *Gauge Unification of Fundamental Forces*; Address delivered by Abdus Salam on the occasion of presentation of

> I knew the craft of experimental physics was beyond me. It was the sublime quality of patience - particularly patience with the recalcitrant equipment of the Cavendish - that I sadly lacked. Reluctantly, I turned my papers in, and started, instead on the Quantum Field Theory with Nicholas Kemmer in the exciting department of P.A.M. Dirac.

Salam's brother Chaudhari Abdul Hameed quoted Salam in an article written in 1997:[2]

> He once said that, "When you are in the hands of apparatus which you have to design yourself and if it does not work, you are frustrated and hit it with your fists. Therefore, I approached my supervisor and asked for his permission to switch over to Theoretical Physics. My supervisor was kind enough to grant such permission provided I could find another supervisor."

As Kemmer stated once, he "almost refused" Salam - he already had eight research students. The reason Salam

the 1979 Nobel Prize in Physics, 8 December 2009; reproduced in *Ideals and Realities: Selected Essays of Abdus Salam*; Editor C.H. Lai, World Scientific, 1987; p277-290; the quote appears on p 279.

[2]Chaudhari Abdul Hameed: *Abdus Salam, My Brother*; in Quarterly *Al-Nahl*, Special issue on Abdus Salam, Vol 8, Issue, Fall 1997, p 61.

was sent to Kemmer was simple - Kemmer was the only senior teacher then interested in Quantum Field Theory. He had done very creditable work in Quantum Field Theory and, after Yukawa, the Japanese Nobel laureate, had contributed the most to an understanding of the strong nuclear force. Kemmer was known to be a thorough gentleman. But Kemmer was probably too exhausted by the responsibility of supervising eight students and did not really want Salam. In his article *The Cambridge Days* written in 1990[3] Professor Kemmer states:

> ⋯ I was presented with a difficult personal problem. Some of my colleagues, both theoretical and experimental, approached me demanding, "You must accept one more research student," "Impossible! Not many have been as easy to cope with as Paul Matthews. He'll get his Ph.D. and will be off my hands!" "But this one has done better on his finals, both in Physics and Mathematics, than anyone we sent you before." "Who is he anyway?" "A Pakistani".

This was Kemmer's first introduction to Salam. Kemmer further writes:

[3]Reproduced in *Science for Peace and Progress: Life and Work of Abdus Salam* compiled by Anwar Dil, publishers Intercultural Forum, San Diego and Islamabad (iforum@aol.com), 2008; p 468-471.

> What I answered will remain a conjecture, but is bound to have expressed great doubt, about the man's qualifications being good enough. Anyhow, no doubt blaming myself for weakness in taking one more hard work, I accepted, but got myself out of immediate responsibility for devising a research problem for the new man by telling him that Matthews was the man who had made himself expert in problems he should study and sent him to consult Matthews.

Salam's own recollection of the days has been narrated in a talk that he gave at Fermilab, USA in 1985:[4]

> I said I started on theory research, but it was not easy. Those were the days of renormalisation theory with papers of Tomonoga, Schwinger, Feynman and Dyson providing feverish excitement. At Cambridge, Nicholas Kemmer was the only senior person interested in these developments. He had behind him not only the kudos of having tabulated all possible meson interactions, but also the reputation of being a prince among men - of

[4] *Physics and the Excellences of Life it Brings* in *Ideals and Realities Selected Essays of Abdus Salam*; Editor C.H. Lai; World Scientific 1987, p 297.

> generousness to a fault to his students. So I went to Kemmer and requested him to accept me for research. He said he had eight research students already and could not take any more. He suggested I go to Birmingham to work with Peierls. But I could not bear to leave Cambridge - principally because of the rose gardens at the Backs of my College - St. John's. (Incidentally Dirac was at St. John's College also). I asked Kemmer, "Would you mind if I worked with you peripherally for the time being?" He graciously assented. In my first interview with Kemmer, he said, "All theoretical problems in Quantum Electrodynamics have already been solved by Schwinger, Feynman and Dyson. Paul Matthews has applied their methods to renoramlise meson theories. He is finishing his Ph.D. this year. Ask him if he has any problem left.

So Salam went to Matthews asking him if he had any "crumbs" left.

Quantum Field Theory is essentially a framework into which any law purporting to describe a fundamental force of nature must fit. Certain new principles of physics, that go by the name quantum theory, were developed in the period 1900-1927 in order to correctly describe atomic and subatomic phenomena as the principles of Newton and Maxwell had failed in this domain. The basis of this theory had been laid by Dirac in 1927-28 when he discovered and wrote the law of electromagnetism in a form consistent with the new (Quantum) principles. Dirac's law goes by the name Quantum Electrodynamics (QED). Dirac showed that when solved approximately the fundamental equation of QED gave answers in reasonably good agreement with experiment. However, when precise solutions were attempted, one ended up with nonsensical answers - the answers came out to be infinite. The programme for obtaining sensible solutions by removing the infinities is known as renormalisation.

In his Fermilab lecture Salam summed up the situation at the time when he embarked on his Ph.D. One of the most difficult technical problems in renormalisation was known as the problem of overlapping infinities. He stated:[5]

> Matthews had at that time already tabulated which theories may be renormalisable with the techniques then known. He had come to the conclusion that no derivative coupling meson theory could be renormalised at all, and that among direct coupling theories with nucleons the only hopefuls were spin-zero, or the neutral vector meson theories with conserved

[5] *Ibid*, p 298.

> currents for nucleons. No charged vector meson theory (with massive mesons) could be renormalisable. He had also shown that the neutral vector meson theory with mass was a replica of electrodynamics and one could take over the work of Dyson more or less intact and show its renormalisability.

Now as regards the spin-zero theories Matthews had also shown that one had to introduce a new term that *could* represent a new fundamental interaction of nature.[6] It is quite amazing that Matthews did all that work while still a Ph.D. student. This tells us that Matthews was no ordinary physicist. He was seven years older to Salam and his research career had been delayed by the war. The framework of Quantum Field Theory required that this new interaction term should be such that the resulting theory should be renormalisable. But how to prove that?

When Salam went to see Matthews, the latter told him that he had a problem in "meson theories." This was the spin-zero theory referred to above. There was an expectation that meson theories would be relevant to the strong nuclear force in the light of quantum principles. Matthews told Salam that he was able to show that the first three terms in the solution of meson theories were finite. Actually he had shown that the "one-loop" cal-

[6]For those familiar with field theory this is known as the $\lambda\phi^4$ term.

culation, could be made to yield a finite answer i.e. was renormalisable. A "one loop" diagram depicts a process in which a traveling particle emits a force carrier and reabsorbs it as it moves on. Such emission and reabsorption of a force carrier (meson in case of nuclear force) by a neutron or proton, contributes to what is called self energy of the proton or the neutron. Such a process is one example of a process that contributes to the so called self energy of the nucleon - the generic name for a proton and the neutron. But then there were other processes in which the particle could emit more than one mesons and reabsorb them while traveling, etc. In an overlap case before the emitted meson is reabsorbed another one (or even more) is also emitted - they "overlap" in this sense - their fleeting existences overlap with each other - we have overlapping loops as it were, diagramatically and calculationally speaking. The precise solution, which would take account of all such processes, however, contained an infinite number of terms of increasing complexity. Even the one loop calculation is formidable.

Freeman Dyson, who incidentally never did a Ph.D. and went straight into high class research, was the external examiner for Matthews's Ph.D. defence. Dyson asked Matthews if he had encountered the infinities associated with the calculation of self energy diagrams, and if he did, what was his solution to the problem. Matthews simply referred to a recent paper by Dyson himself, in which

Dyson had *claimed* (not proved) that these infinities could be taken care of in QED (Quantum Electrodynamics). Matthews then said that he (i.e. Matthews) was simply following him (i.e. Dyson). As Salam said "No further question on these infinities was asked; both Dyson and Matthews kept silent after this brief exchange." The silence was understandable - neither had been able to *prove* that these complicated diagrams could lead to finite answers i.e. could be renormalised. Like two skilled hunters after the same trophy, they were not willing to expose their weaknesses to each other, and hence they did not discuss the matter further.

What was the detail regarding the problem that Matthews had mentioned to Salam? As Salam stated:[7]

> With characteristic generosity of which I became a life-long recipient, Matthews said to me "My viva is over. After my degree, I 'm going off, to take a few months holiday. And then I'll go to Princeton. You can have these problems of renormalising meson theories till I get back to work in fall. And if you don't solve it by then, I'll take it back."
> That was the sort of gentleman's agreement which we parted on. So I had to get to the bottom of the overlapping infinity problem before the fall.

[7] *Ibid*, p 299.

The difficulty was that in QED these overlapping infinities occurred only in the self energy calculations but in meson theories they were, as Salam put it, "everywhere". The first person Salam thought, could help him, was Dyson. So he phoned him in Birmingham. Dyson told him that he was to leave for Princeton the following day so Salam would have to come to Birmingham the next morning. Salam traveled that very day to Birmingham, stayed overnight at Dalitz's place and met Dyson the following morning. If he had thought that Dyson had dealt with the problem in QED he was wrong. Dyson told him that he had merely *conjectured* that the overlapping infinities could be taken care of - he had no proof. This disturbed Salam because he had hoped to seek some guidance from QED while dealing with these infinities in meson theories. However Dyson explained to him the basis of his conjecture and the two traveled back by train to London together. It was a most difficult problem whose complete solution had eluded both Dyson and Matthews. But Salam was able to tackle the problem with astonishing speed. To quote him:[8]

> At Cambridge, amid the summer roses at the backs of the Colleges, I went back to the overlapping infinity problem to keep tryst with Matthews's deadline. Using a generalization

[8] *Ibid*, p 300.

> of Dyson's remarks I was able to show that spin-zero meson theories were indeed renormalisable to all orders. At that time transatlantic phone calls for physics research had not been invented. So I had vigorous correspondence with Dyson, with the fullest participation of Kemmer, my supervisor. Exciting days indeed!

It was this work that brought Salam into limelight. It was thought that with his work physicists would be able to have the complete and correct law for the strong nuclear force that binds the nucleus together. However this was not to be. Almost at the same time as Salam another young man, Ward, also solved the problem of infinities by a different technique.

Professor Bambah, who knew Salam from his Government College days in Lahore, has narrated an interesting incident.[9] He writes that he came to Cambridge in 1948 and then went to Princeton in 1950. Salam asked him to convey the following message to Dyson if he happened to come across him in Princeton: "I have renormalised longitudinal photons". When Bambah conveyed Salam's message to Dyson he responded "I don't believe it, but if

[9]Ram Prakash Bambah: *Together In Lahore and Cambridge* in *Science for Peace and Progress: Life and Work of Abdus Salam* compiled by Anwar Dil, publishers Intercultural Forum, San Diego and Islamabad (iforum@aol.com), 2008, p 578.

he has done so he will be very famous". When Bambah commented that Salam had picked up the problem on account of a suggestion in one of Dyson's papers, Dyson responded by saying "I had said that it should be done and not that it could be done."

This was in 1950 and Salam had just turned 24. Although Salam's work on renormalizing meson theories was more than enough for a Ph.D., regulations required that he submit his thesis after completing the three-year period. So he went on to complete the renormalisation of the laws of electromagnetism where the problem of overlapping infinities stood in Dyson's way. With these contributions Salam joined the ranks of the world's foremost physicists. He was awarded the prestigious Smith Prize for the most outstanding pre-doctoral contribution and was sent to the Institute for Advanced Studies in Princeton, where Einstein worked. Salam told Akhtar Said that he met Einstein at Princeton but that Einstein had become too old by then. He spent one year at Princeton. Technically he could submit his thesis from anywhere so he decided to return to Lahore and teach.

It is interesting to note that by the end of 1950 there were six *young* theoretical physicists who dominated the scene of fundamental physics research. Their ages ranged between 24 and 32 years. These were Feynman (1918-1988) and Schwinger (1918-1984) in the US, Matthews (1919-1987), Salam (1926-1996) and Ward (1924-2000) in the UK and Dyson (born 1923) who worked at Birmingham as well as Princeton, but eventually settled in Princeton USA. Feynman, Schwinger and Salam won the Nobel Prize. Ward seemed to have dropped out mysteriously during the mid 1960s.[10] P.T. Matthews became Vice Chancellor of Bath University but died in 1987 in a most unfortunate car accident. Dyson went on to a most fruitful career at Princeton and made diverse contributions.

Kemmer's evaluation of Salam's thesis is most interesting. He wrote in his report on Salam's work:[11]

> ...I was quite reluctant to take him as I already had more research students than ideas. I anticipated that he would not give me much trouble for the first year as he had no previous knowledge of the field of research. ... How-

[10]Daniel Denegri of CERN solved this problem for me. He was a student at Rochester around the mid 1960s and Ward was teaching there. He said that Ward was an extremely shy person. In his class there appeared a gorgeous girl and soon after she fell in love with Ward, married him and took him away, to New Zealand, if my memory does not fail me. Had Ward stayed in the race he stood a good chance of winning a Nobel Prize. He and Salam had collaborated in some work on unification of fundamental forces.

[11]Quoted in Abdul Hameed Chaudhari: *Alami Shohrat Yafta Sciencedaan Abdus Salam* (World Renowned Scientist Abdus Salam); published by Ahmad Salam, 8 Campion Road, SW 15, 6 NW, London; 1998; pp 69-70 this book is written in Urdu.

> ever things developed very differently, within six weeks or so he had solved a problem which the best of my students had failed to solve and within another month I was going to him for clarification of details in the latest publication. The work he has done since, though based on recent ideas of Dyson and in more detail Matthews has been entirely his own and some of the details are to this day too complicated for me to follow, at least in the time I have hitherto been able to spare for it. Whenever I discuss any aspect of the work with him, I find complete clarity of ideas in his mind and profound understanding of what, after all, is one of the most difficult subjects at present being studied by theoretical physicists. Today I feel that I am very much more Salam's pupil than his teacher...I was not in the least surprised that Salam was gladly given membership at the Institute for Advanced Studies, Princeton less than one year after he began his theoretical research.

Kemmer narrates that before Matthews departed for Princeton:[12]

[12]N. Kemmer: *The Cambridge Days*; Reproduced in *Science for Peace and Progress: Life and Work of Abdus Salam* compiled by Anwar Dil, publishers Intercultural Forum, San Diego and Islam-

> Matthews came to me to say farewell and saying: "I had worked out a program of study for Princeton but this chap Salam had solved my intended problem!" So as early as that, Abdus Salam already made a mark among those contributing to the subtelties of Renormalisation ···

Dyson paid him a wonderful tribute:[13]

> He asked me for a topic for his research. I gave him the topic of overlapping divergences, a highly technical problem that had defeated me for two years. He solved it in a few months ··· When I first met Salam in 1950 I recognized him as an intellectual equal, a young man who could solve mathematical puzzles as quickly as I could. Ten years later I could see that he had grown over my head.[14]

abad (iforum@aol.com), 2008; p 470.

[13]Freeman J Dyson: *Abdus Salam* in *Science for Peace and Progress: Life and Work of Abdus Salam* compiled by Anwar Dil, publishers Intercultural Forum, San Diego and Islamabad (iforum@aol.com), 2008, p 618, 619.

[14]Mrs. Ray Chester, who was a Secretary to both, Professor Kemmer and his predecessor Professor Max Born, told me of an interesting incident about Dyson. She said that one day a young man, probably around twenty years or so of age, came to see Professor Born. Professor Born was busy so that he had to wait for

In the same article Dyson narrates an interesting incident from those years involving Salam and Pauli:[15]

> I met him a year later in Zurich. He came with a completed paper, a pioneering piece of work on scalar electrodynamics. He asked me to introduce him to Wolfgang Pauli, at that time the leading European expert on quantum field theories. I told Pauli who he was and Pauli agreed to see him.
> After the formal introduction, Salam said: Professor Pauli, could you please be so kind to look at this paper and let me know what you think of it." Pauli said, "I have to be careful not to use my eyes too much. I will not read your paper." That was the end of the conversation.
> Salam thanked Pauli and left the room show-

some time. He started helping Mrs. Chester. After a while the Professor was available and Dyson went in. After the meeting Professor Max Born came out with Dyson and saw him off in Mrs. Chester's office. When the young man had left Professor Born said to her "Mark his name - Dyson. He will become very famous one day." Mrs Chester remembered the incident in 1979 as I went to her place on one or two occasions - she was typing my thesis. She said she remembered Dyson because he had "the most beautiful pair of blue eyes I have ever seen". She also told me that Dyson went straight into research and did not bother about doing a Ph.D.

[15] *Ibid*, p 618.

> ing no trace of anger or disappointment. He knew his own worth. When I apologized for Pauli's rudeness, Salam said he was sorry for Pauli, not for himself. Pauli had missed the chance to learn something interesting.

Dyson has correctly remarked that Salam was aware of his own worth. His response shows his self-confidence and awareness that what he was doing was indeed interesting and valuable work. He was rubbing shoulders with giants like Pauli and standing on his own ground. The above quote also shows Dyson's generosity and awareness of his own worth too. Dyson (born 1923) and Salam (born 1926) were very young then.

Even though Salam's work was more than enough for a Ph.D. the degree could not be awarded before the end of a mandatory three year period. In the file of Abdus Salam at the Department of Mathematics, University of the Punjab, there is a "true copy" of a document related to his Ph.D. It is probably a typed copy of his Ph.D. degree and reads as follows:

SEAL

UNIVERSITY OF CAMBRIDGE

I hereby certify that

ABDUS SALAM

of St. John's College

in the University of Cambridge was at a full

Congregation holden in the Senate House on
29 November 1952 admitted to the Degree of

DOCTOR OF PHILOSOPHY

witness by hand this twenty-ninth day of November
one thousand nine hundred and fifty-two

Sd/ W.W. GRAVE
Registrary of the University

Sd/
Registrary's Clerk

One may therefore conclude that Abdus Salam became Dr. Abdus Salam on November 29, 1952.

In an interview given for a documentary being made on Salam's life, his and Dame Louise Johnson's son, Umar Salam, stated:[16]

> My father's accounts of Cambridge in the forties are full of the films he saw, *The Red Shoes* was his favorite - the experiences, it was full of life - everything touched him and everything reached him.

[16]http://vimeo.com/58447727; the documentary is being made by two young men Zakir Thaver and Omar Vandal.

Chapter 7

Back to Lahore

Freeman Dyson has written that Salam felt a compulsion to return to Pakistan. The country had paid for his studies and he wanted to repay.[1]

> He discussed his dilemma with me. I advised him strongly to come to America, to plunge into research for five years first, and then help his people afterwards. He thanked me for my advice and told me he was going home. Physics could wait but his people could not.

[1]Freeman J Dyson: Abdus Salam in *Science for Peace and Progress: Life and Work of Abdus Salam* compiled by Anwar Dil, publishers Intercultural Forum, San Diego and Islamabad (ifo-rum@aol.com), 2008, p 618.

In 1951 Salam joined Government College, Lahore as Professor of Mathematics. He was subsequently also appointed as Head of Department of Mathematics at the University of the Punjab.[2] From the world's foremost centers of learning he landed in a country where there

[2]There is a very interesting group photograph from the year 1952 which can still be seen in the faculty corridor of the Department of Physics of the University of the Punjab. In that year Professor G.P. Thomson visited the University of the Punjab. Everybody had noticed Professor G.P. Thomson sitting in the middle of the front row with the then Head of the Physics Department, Professor Beg, sitting next to him. However very few people noticed the young man seated next to Professor Beg. Even I did not notice it until 1993 even though I had been around since 1969! This was a rare photograph with the twenty six year old Salam seated one seat next to the Nobel laureate G.P. Thomson, son of another Nobel laureate J.J. Thomson who not only discovered the electron but also Rutherford, who was his Ph.D. student. It was the same G.P. Thomson who could not achieve the double first classes in Tripos Physics and mathematics! Who could have known then that Salam too would be a Nobel laureate one day!

I asked a photographer to take a picture of that photograph which would include only G.P. Thomson and Salam (and of necessity the person sitting in between). I then mailed that photo to Professor Salam's England address, as he had then moved to England on account of ill health and was living with his second wife Prof Louise Johnson. She wrote me a nice letter dated 17.10.1993, stating that she had been asked by Professor Salam to thank me and then added that the photograph had "brought tears to his eyes". She wrote that it was "historic picture". The photograph is printed in this book.

was not a single person with whom he could discuss scientific problems. Nor were any current scientific journals available anywhere. The nearest physicist in the region with whom Salam could engage in useful discourse was Bhabha - in Bombay, and that was another country. Wolfgang Pauli, the man whom Einstein considered his successor, planned a trip to Bombay in those days. He wrote to Salam about it and expressed his desire that Salam see him. So Salam traveled to Bombay. On return his explanation was called for having gone abroad without permission!

The above mentioned incident is well known but K.K. Aziz, who was Salam's friend and headed the Department of Political Science at Government College at that time, has narrated this incident in detail in his interesting book:[3]

> Professor Wolfgang Pauli, the 1945 Nobel Laureate of physics and a friend of Salam, was visiting Bombay on the invitation of the Indian Science Association. He sent a telegram to Salam wishing to see him and asking him if he could come to Bombay. Salam who had been craving to talk to a peer in his field, at once left for India and spent a week with Pauli. (Till that time traveling to India did not re-

[3] K.K. Aziz: *The Coffee House of Lahore - A Memoir 1942-57*; Sang e Meel Publishers, 2008, p 203, 204.

> quire long planning or visa). On his return to Lahore he was charge-sheeted for absenting himself from his station of duty without prior permission. Salam was shocked. He was used to European freedom of movement and had been part of Pakistani bureaucratic set-up for a mere three months. The Principal made so much fuss about the incident that Salam feared that he might be dismissed from the education service. At this point S.M. Sharif, the Director of Public Instruction of the Punjab, intervened and the period of Salam's absence was treated as leave without pay.

In a video-recorded interview conducted by Akhtar Said sometime near the end of 1987[4] Salam reminisced about the visit to Bombay in the following words:

> It was during 1952 (or 1951) $\cdots$ So Pauli sent me a telegram saying "I am very lonely. Can you come over to Bombay?" There was also an accompanying telegram from Bhabha stating that we are sending you a ticket and you come over. In those days there was no problem - I think I took the visa in half a day or so - no difficulty in those days. It was Christmas

[4]Personal record. I am indebted to Mr. Akhtar Said for providing me with a CD of the interview.

break. So I went straight and booked a seat. I traveled all night. The plane went from Lahore to Delhi. From Delhi we changed planes and went to Nagpur. In Nagpur four planes would meet. One came back to Delhi, one went to Bombay and two planes came to the west and the east (Calcutta). Nagpur was literally the meeting point of four planes. I changed planes to get to Bombay at about 7 A.M. I reached the Institute about 7.30 or 8.00. It was really hot even though it was December - it was very very hot. So I thought I will go and go to sleep in a hotel before I come back to the Institute but I thought I will say hello to Pauli - I was tired. So I went to Pauli's room and knocked. Pauli was there. He said come in. I went in. He did not, for one moment say what was new or that you have arrived or whether I was tired. He[5] straightaway said "Oh yes the problem

[5]Those who know Punjabi will appreciate this better - he actually referred to Pauli as "that *dalla*". The word *dalla* is a Punjabi word and is untranslatable. In this context it may be translated as rascal since it has been used affectionately. In the same interview he uses the word *dalla* in another place. He describes that Einstein had inserted a term in his equations to get a stable universe. When people told him that Hubble had discovered that the universe was expanding Einstein pointed out that had he not inserted that term,

> is if we take Schwinger's action principle ···"
> and so he went on to define his problem. I
> said "Pauli I am tired. Do you mind if I go
> away and sleep" and so on. Then he realized
> I was sleepy.

Professor Riazuddin, a prominent Pakistani physicist was a student of Salam in those days.[6] He writes:

> We were fortunate to learn from him some modern mathematical techniques in certain branches of applied mathematics in an environment where still some primitive mathematical methods were used. I also remember that he started an evening series of lectures on quantum mechanics, which was neither a part of physics curriculum nor was taught as a regular course. But soon the class disappeared, except, I believe, for two people.

M. Saleem Sheikh, currently in his eighties and still working as a prominent member of the Supreme Court of Pakistan Bar, started off his career as a lecturer of mathematics at Government College Lahore. He told me that since

---

his equations already had an expanding universe. Salam put it in Punjabi in the following words: "Einstein said Oh *dallas* I made a great blunder. If I had not put that term in there the universe would have expanded."

[6]Professor Riazuddin was elected Fellow of the American Physical Society in 2008.

many students could not follow Salam's lectures properly, Salam asked him to take over some of his classes, which Saleem Sheikh duly did. Perhaps Salam also needed time to devote to his research. He was probably the only physicist in a country which had tens of millions of people, who was doing the kind of high level abstract work. There was no research interaction with any other physicist in the country.

Salam's problems with the "administration" began soon after he joined the Government College. He had been directly appointed Professor at two institutions and his pay had been fixed at a much higher level than others who were his contemporaries. He was appointed Professor even though he had not yet formally acquired a Ph.D. degree. This was unprecedented and was probably, as remarked by Professor Bambah, the result of intervention on the part of Sir Zafarulla Chaudhri. Bambah's likely source was Salam himself. At that time Salam was only 25 years of age. In appointing him Professor the authorities had been magnanimous. However the sordid side of the administration was very much in evidence every now and then and that hurt Salam. The administration did not have any comprehension of the true stature of the man and could not care less. Its interests were non-academic. K.K. Aziz has mentioned an incident that he witnessed personally. He writes:[7]

> I think it was in October 1953 that the Punjab Education Minister, Chaudri Ali Akbar, paid an official visit to the college. The Principal and all heads of departments met to discuss several problems relating to appointments, teaching and syllabus. When the question of pass percentages of the College came up for the consideration of the Minister, after announcing that he was not concerned with the teacher's formal qualifications and academic achievements but only with the percentage of students who passed the university examinations every year, made the point that however highly qualified a teacher may be he would himself issue orders for his transfer to some God forsaken place if he failed to produce a satisfactory pass percentage. And then he turned to where Salam was seated, next to me, and staring at him said, "For example if Professor Salam's pass percentage does not please me I will send him back to Jhang." Most of us were stunned by this crude remark. Salam was the only teacher who was named, and he was the most brilliant member of the

[7]K.K. Aziz: *The Coffee House of Lahore - A Memoir 1942-57*; Sang e Meel Publishers, 2008, p 204, 205.

> teaching staff.
> When we were walking back from the meeting to the staff room Salam put his hand on my shoulder and whispered"I have made up my mind. I must get a job somewhere abroad."
> Who could blame him?

K.K. Aziz has also narrated an incident relating to Salam's difficulty in finding official accommodation. I have in my possession a copy of a letter[8] dated 24th June 1952, addressed to the Secretary, Allotment Committee, G.O.R.[9] Estate, Lahore. Salam writes:

> Sir,
> I returned from Cambridge last year in Septe-mber, to resume my duties as Professor of Mathematics at Government College, Lahore. It is about eight months now but in spite of my best efforts I have not been able to secure living accommodation in Lahore so far.
> I beg to apply for a house in the G.O.R. Estate. My basic pay is Rs.630/- p.m. and in addition I am entitled to draw Rs. 300/- per

[8]There exists an incomplete correspondence file in the Department of Mathematics of the University of the Punjab consisting of letters pertaining to Professor Salam. I had the documents in the file photocopied for my record.

[9]G.O.R. is an acronym for Government Officers Residences.

> annum from St. John's College, Cambridge as my Fellowship dividend and this makes to approximately Rs. 862 per mensem. My family consists of myself, wife and one child and two brothers studying in Lahore.
> I shall be most grateful.
> I beg to remain,
> Sir,
> Your most obedient servant
> (Abdus Salam)
> Head of the Mathematics Department,
> University of the Panjab, Lahore

K.K. Aziz narrates:[10]

> His problems began almost as soon as he took up his job at the Government College. Instead of honoring him for his brilliant achievements, he was humiliated by the College and the Education Department. He was not given an official residence, as was his right. Temporarily he stayed with Qazi Muhammad Aslam, the professor of philosophy at the College, and continued his efforts to get a house allotted to himself. Disappointed with the indifferent attitude of the officials he asked for

[10]K.K. Aziz: *The Coffee House of Lahore - A Memoir 1942-57*; Sang e Meel Publishers, 2008, p 202, 203.

> an interview with the Minister of Education, Sardar Abdul Hameed Dasti. Salam told him that he had a family to accommodate and was entitled to a residence. As Salam told me, the Minister brought the interview to an end by refusing any help and declaring: "*Pugdi e te kam karo warna jao*" (if it suits you, you may continue with your job; if not you may go). Salam was so frustrated that he was considering a resignation; but a house was soon found for him and he stayed on.

K.K. Aziz continues:[11]

> A little later, the Principal, Professor Sirajuddin, asked him to do something to earn his keep besides teaching. He was given three choices: to act as Superintendent of the Quadrangle Hostel or to supervise the college accounts or to take charge of the college football team. Salam chose to look after the footballers. Occasionally, at the end of the chore, he would drop in at Coffee House and tell me about the bitterness on being forced to waste his time. A man who had worked 14 hours a day at Cambridge as a student had

[11]K.K. Aziz: *The Coffee House of Lahore - A Memoir 1942-57*; Sang e Meel Publishers, 2008, p 203.

> now hardly any time to read new literature on his subject, and the facilities in the college laboratory were dust and ashes compared to the Cavendish Laboratories where he had worked as an undergraduate and a doctoral student. It was not difficult to take the gauge of Salam's frustration.

Air Marshal Zafar Chaudhary, who knew him from his student days, has given a valuable insight into the state of mind of Abdus Salam during the days he was working at Government College. He narrates:[12]

> I happened to meet Salam in Government College in the early 1950s where I think he was then the Head of the Department of Mathematics. He told me he was not making the best use of his time and was thinking of going back to Cambridge for further study. He said that he wasted a lot of time answering all kinds of objections raised by the university about some advance increments that had been sanctioned for him. Also, he had been made in charge of the college football team even though he knew nothing of the sport. He seemed quite determined to free himself of

[12]Zafar Chaudhary: *The Friday Times*, Dr. Abdus Salam and his Love for the Country That Disowned Him; January 1, 2010.

> the stifling environment of his job and dearly wanted to study further.

Salam could not continue in the kind of environment prevalent in Pakistan if he was to remain in the forefront. So he was forced to make a choice when offered a lectureship at Cambridge sometime during 1953.

An article that was to appear in the *Pakistan Times* on August 20, 1957 noted:[13]

> Returning to Pakistan with high hopes and still greater zest, he was appointed Head of the Department of Mathematics, at the Government College, Lahore, in 1951, and the following year he accepted the Chairmanship of the Department of Mathematics in the Punjab University.

[13]The article in the *Pakistan Times* introduced Salam to his countrymen as a scientist of great stature. It was filed by a Special Correspondent and carried the title: *A Pakistani Physicist Makes His Outstanding Contribution.* At the time Pakistan probably had three or four English language dailies with the *Pakistan Times* being the most important. The origin of this article has been described by Jagjit Singh in his biography of Salam (Jagjit Singh: *Abdus Salam A Biography*; A Penguin Book, 1992). Apparently Mian Iftikhar-ud-din, the owner of the paper "discovered" Salam during a visit to London and decided to bring Salam to the attention of his countrymen. This story seems reliable since Jagjit Singh apparently had the manuscript typed at Trieste (one of Salam's secretaries, Janet Hughes, typed it) and the story must have come to Jagjit Singh from Salam.

> However, for a person of Prof. Salam's ability, attainments and inexhaustible zest for work, Pakistan hardly offered any opportunity or conditions for the full play of his talents. He yearned for the opportunity, but none was visible within his limited horizon.

Professor Riazuddin remarks:[14]

> Obviously, in that environment where he could not interact with fellow scientists working on exciting cutting edge problems, his choice was starkly between intellectual death and migration to the West to work at an intellectually stimulating institution. He made the only choice available to an inquiring mind and left for Cambridge to take up a lectureship in mathematics at the end of 1953.

K.K. Aziz who knew him well and interacted with him for almost four decades in Lahore and abroad has summed it up very well:[15]

> When Salam was elected a Fellow of the St. John's College in 1951 he had accepted the

[14]Riazuddin in Foreword to *Science for Peace and Progress: Life and Work of Abdus Salam* compiled by Anwar Dil, publishers Intercultural Forum, San Diego and Islamabad (iforum@aol.com), 2008.

[15]K.K. Aziz: *The Coffee House of Lahore - A Memoir 1942-57*; Sang e Meel Publishers, 2008, p 205.

> honor on the condition that he would be allowed to go to Lahore and teach there and live in St. John's only during long vacations. St. John's was so anxious to have him that it made an exception and accepted his condition. This was a measure of Salam's love for Government College; he was prepared to forgo the considerable honor of a fellowship of St. John's for the sake of the prospect of teaching at the Government College. But he had been insulted and humiliated so often by the college he loved so much and for which he had sacrificed the full facilities of the St. John's fellowship, that he was now forced to look elsewhere for his professional future.

If one analyzes Salam's departure from Pakistan one can see that several factors, operating in concert, drove him back to Cambridge. Firstly he was genuinely frustrated by the fact that there was, literally, not a single individual in a country with such a large population with whom he could discuss research problems. He was completely alone and isolated as foreseen by his supervisor Kemmer. Such isolation, if sustained over a period of time, means certain death for a world class researcher. Secondly, the administration, both at the college and government levels, had no comprehension of the needs of a researcher. The environment was not only not conducive to research activity, it was at best indifferent, and in general hostile and negative out of sheer ignorance of the psychological and material requirements that enable a researcher to release his creative energies. Thirdly there had been a movement against his religious community in 1953 that must have disturbed him deeply. Contrasted with this the authorities at Cambridge, who were aware of his immense creative potential, and saw in him a leader of the community of physicists, wanted to salvage him, and to have him back in their fold. If the finest institution in the world wanted him as "the man for the post before anyone else in the world",[16] while those for whom he had shunned great opportunities, wanted him to under-perform, if at all, or to quit, what could a self-respecting Salam do? The competition was too one-sided - on the one hand was a society run by petty politicians and arrogant, and mostly empty, bureaucrats,[17] a society that had no desire to become knowledgeable, a society where religious intolerance had begun to take root, a society that had produced great poets but not a single great scientist, whereas, on the other side was a nation that had produced Newton and Darwin and had brought about the industrial revolution, a society that cared for talent and wanted to maintain

[16]Please see Kemmer's letter in the following chapter.

[17]Sheikh Imtiaz Ali, former Chairman University Grants Commission and a former Vice Chancellor of the University of the Punjab told me how the wife of a bureaucrat remarked that if Salam was so brilliant why could he not become a CSP, i.e., a bureaucrat.

its scientific and intellectual leadership. Above all, fate, or destiny, operates in its own inscrutable ways. Salam may have left Lahore with a heavy heart but his unhappy departure for Cambridge was to ensure his place in the history of twentieth century physics.

Chapter 8

Lecturer at Cambridge

At the end of 1953, N. Kemmer, Salam's supervisor, was appointed Tait Professor of Mathematical Physics at Edinburgh University. When I was doing my Ph.D. at Edinburgh University during the second half of nineteen seventies, Professor Kemmer told me that since his position at Cambridge was falling vacant he had suggested that Salam replace him.

Interestingly, in September 1997, Prof K.L. Mir, Head of the Department of Mathematics of the Punjab University at the time, and himself a theoretical physicist, showed me Salam's file which he had uncovered in the Departmental records. The file contained an undated and unsigned letter from Professor Kemmer. The language was indeed Professor Kemmer's whom I knew as a graduate student at Edinburgh. It appears that the letter was probably a typed copy made out of an original letter, since in those days there were no photocopying or xeroxing machines. On top of the letter, the following is written (italics mine): *From: N. Kemmer, Tait Professor of Natural Philosophy, Edinburgh, formerly Stokes Lecturer in Mathematics and Fellow of Trinity College, Cambridge.* It comprises six numbered paragraphs. The letter states:

> 1. I feel it is my duty to acquaint you with the circumstances of the offer of a lectureship at Cambridge University to Dr. Abdus Salam. I am on the Faculty Board of Mathematics and [member] of the Appointments Committee which has offered Salam the succession. In addition I am his former teacher and feel I can count myself as his friend. I know him not only as a great theoretical physicist but as a man and know very well that his strong sense of duty to his country is making it hard for him to decide to accept the post offered to him. That is why I feel I can be of some use in writing this letter.

In the next para Kemmer points out that "Dr. Abdus Salam's standing as a research worker in the most advanced, difficult and exciting field of modern theoretical physics is very high indeed." The letter further states that:

> 3. Lectureships at Cambridge are offered only partly to secure good teachers. We set much greater store on appointing leaders in their fields of research, and in this case opinion was unanimous that Salam was the man for the post before anyone else in the world. If he accepts it, I shall feel happy, when I leave to succeed Professor Max Born[1] at Edinburgh, that my former duties will pass into the best hands possible.

In the next paragraph Kemmer states that the appointment was initially for three years and that Salam might not accept it. Kemmer writes: "I respect his sentiments greatly but I think, and I have done my best to make Salam agree that it would really be in the interests of all concerned if he would accept." The letter then goes on:

> 5. Dr. Abdus Salam is at present at the age of greatest scientific productivity and given

[1]Max Born was the Ph.D. supervisor of Werner Heisenberg who discovered quantum mechanics at age 24. Max Born took active part in the creation of quantum mechanics and was belatedly awarded the 1970 Nobel Prize in Physics. He had to leave Germany during the Nazi regime but decided to return to Germany in the early 1950s.

> the stimulus of close contacts with workers in allied fields he is certain to increase his reputation from year to year and, in due course, can become one of those few to whom advanced students from all over the world come to learn, wherever he might be. In a few years he would then be capable of going back to Lahore or wherever he pleases and, with the necessary financial backing, establish his own school of theoretical physics with the highest international reputation. However, if he were to stay at Lahore now, scientifically isolated and inevitably burdened with very elementary teaching he would certainly lose the chance of any great scientific and educational achievement later on, for even the best of the young scientists in a field such as ours cannot be expected to thrive without concentrating on advanced work and constant stimulus from others of similar intellect and interests.

The letter concludes with the plea:

> 6. I hope very much that you will help to make it possible for Abdus Salam to take up the appointment in Cambridge. You would be acting in the interests of international science, of one of your greatest citizens and your country.

This letter reveals several things. Firstly Salam's teachers were aware of his outstanding potential to become a world leader in his field. Secondly they did not want Abdus Salam to go waste by taking a wrong decision to continue to stay on in Pakistan. They were aware that it would be a loss for the world, for international science, for their institution, for Pakistan and for Abdus Salam himself if he stayed on in Pakistan. One is touched by the concern, free of all prejudice, to salvage genuine world class talent. There is a lesson for the leadership of developing countries in this.

When he received the offer he had to think about it as family pressures and his commitment to the country might have pulled him in another direction. However everyone, including Kemmer as well as the then Secretary Education Punjab, S.M. Sharif, advised him to accept the offer. In fact when S.M. Sharif learned of this offer, he advised Salam to accept it since it was a great honor for the country.

Salam decided to accept the offer but never forgot his country nor the plight of the tiny community of scientists trying to survive in the intellectually barren environments of the Third World. This led to the idea of the International Center for Theoretical Physics. This Centre, established in 1964, survives him and is now renamed as Abdus Salam International Centre for Theoretical Physics, thanks to the courtesy and good sense of the Italian Government.

As Professor Riazuddin notes:[2]

> I believe that this choice left a deep impression on him. His enforced exile lay behind his determination to do something for physicists working in developing countries under difficult conditions so that they would not be forced to make the choice he was forced to make.

It was at the end of 1953 that Salam traveled to England with his wife and two and a half year old daughter. He was to join Cambridge as Stokes Lecturer in Mathematics with effect from 1st January, 1954. His daughter Aziza Rahman wrote of those days in an article published in 1997:[3]

> My earliest memories of my father date back to when my mother moved and I moved to Cambridge with him. I was three and a half years old at the time. Cambridge is a beautiful university town on the edge of river Cam. We lived in a small apartment near St. John's

[2] Riazuddin in Foreword to *Science for Peace and Progress: Life and Work of Abdus Salam* compiled by Anwar Dil, publishers Intercultural Forum, San Diego and Islamabad (iforum@aol.com), 2008.

[3] Aziza Rahman: *My Father, Abdus Salam*; in Quarterly *Al-Nahl*, Special issue on Abdus Salam, Vol 8, Issue, Fall 1997, p 50.

> College, where my father was working., because the gardens of St. John's were the prettiest in Cambridge. He had chosen to work at St. John's turning down an offer from the more prestigious Trinity College. One of his favorite pastimes was "punting" on the river. A punt is a small boat which is pushed along by one person standing in the back with a large pole, rather like a gondola. My mother and I would sit in the front, while my father would manage the pole. Sometimes the pole would fall in the water and we would use a small paddlle to reach the shore.

Jagjit Singh mentions that at Cambridge Salam's total income was around 950 pounds per annum. He has also given a break up of his teaching responsibilities. He was to teach both graduate and undergraduate students. He was to teach for 12 hours per week, nine hours for undergraduates and three hours for graduate students undertaking Ph.D. work. Of these six hours were for actual lecturing and the remaining six for research guidance. As Jagjit Singh writes:

> In his first year at Cambridge he taught the "Dirac Course" on quantum mechanics to the graduate class (so called because he substituted for P.A.M. Dirac who had left Cam-

> bridge on leave of absence that year.) According to an old tradition at Cambridge, mathematical topics are taught to undergraduates simultaneously in two separate classrooms by two lecturers. The students are free to choose which of the two to attend. It is said that Salam's lectures on electricity and magnetism became so popular with students that nearly two-thirds of them flocked to his class. What attracted them was his ability to share his own problems in the topics he taught.

At Cambridge Salam continued to work in renormalisation theory apart from becoming an expert on dispersion relations.[4] Dispersion relations are mathematical relations which incorporate causality i.e. cause must precede effect. As noted by editors of *Selected Papers of Abdus Salam*:

> In 1955, Salam made a key contribution to the development of dispersion relations extending the relations previously obtained in

[4]One of his papers on dispersion relations was coauthored with a Ph.D. student named Walter Gilbert. At that time Gilbert was a neighbor of Watson who discovered the structure of DNA with Crick. Subsequently Gilbert emigrated to the US where he devised a technique for deciphering the genetic code. In 1980 he received the Nobel Prize in Chemistry for his work.

> the case of forward scattering to arbitrary momentum transfer. Then with his student Walter Gilbert (later a distinguished molecular biologist), he enlarged their scope further to include spin-flip amplitudes.

At Cambridge, he had also supervised an extremely important thesis which contained the idea of what is technically called non-abelian gauge invariance. The same year (1954), Yang and Mills independently invented the same thing. This concept is now the basis of constructing all the laws for various fundamental forces. What it essentially does is to impose a very severe restriction on the possible form of these laws; it is in essence a highly restrictive symmetry.[5] The Ph.D. student who generalized gauge symmetries to the non-abelian case at Cambridge was Ronald Shaw. The story of Shaw's work on non-abelian gauge theories is both interesting and important and Gordon Fraser's research has thrown light on

[5]In his unfinished memoirs John Ward wrote: "Oscar Klein in 1939 had invented general gauge theories as classical fields. He had the misfortune to publish in the *Acta Physica Polonica* late in the year. Frank Yang rediscovered them after the war, as did a student of Abdus Salam, a Dr. Shaw. When I remarked to Abdus in 1957 that there must be a generalization of the Abelian theory to the non-Abelian case, Abdus at once said that this was in fact the subject a student's Ph.D. thesis." *Memoirs of a Theoretical Physicist*; J.C. Ward; http://www.opticsjournal.com/JCWard.pdf

the issue in great detail.[6] Shaw completed his work on non-abelian gauge theories in January 1954 (Salam had inherited Shaw as a research student from Kemmer) but did not publish it. He submitted his thesis in September 1955 and included this work as a part of his thesis among other things. When Yang and Mills published their work in October 1954, Salam showed it to Shaw and insisted that Shaw too submit his work to a journal for publication. But Shaw was reluctant. Sometimes Salam would refer to the Yang-Mills theories as Yang-Mills-Shaw theories - he referred to Shaw's Ph.D. thesis in his Nobel Prize lecture too. But people were sceptical. Now with the effort of Gordon Fraser the situation has become quite clear. Let us quote directly from Gordon Fraser (p 117):

> Shaw submitted his thesis in September 1955. It consisted of two parts, each self-contained. The first was about the mathematics of special relativity and its possible implications for the types of elementary particles that could exist. The second part 'Some Contributions to the Theory of Elementary Particles' was easy to overlook, because its contents were only listed after the end of part I, and itself was split into three parts, the third being called 'Invariance under isotopic spin trans-

[6]Gordon Fraser: *Cosmic Anger: Abdus Salam The First Muslim Nobel Laureate*; Oxford University Press, 2008.

> formations.' A footnote in the dissertation reads: 'The work described in this chapter was completed, except for an extension in Section 3, in January 1954, but was not published. In October 1954, Yang and Mills adopted independently the same postulate and derived similar consequences. But although their publication date was in 1954 Yang and Mills must have priority since it seems that their research was completed in 1953. My idea came to me in a flash while reading a manuscript of Schwinger's in the Philosophical Library in Cambridge. I showed my generalization to Salam in early 1954, but in a rather disparaging way. Later in 1954, Salam showed me the paper by Yang and Mills. Salam still wanted me to publish my contribution, but I never did.'

One is reminded of Dirac whose papers were published in the *Proceedings of the Royal Society* very speedily so as facilitate him in having priority in case any disputes arose. Had Shaw agreed to submit his work, and had his submission then received similar treatment, it would have been Shaw's theories instead of Yang-Mills theories.

Professor Riazuddin, who was doing his Ph.D. at Cambridge in those days, has given a first-hand account of Salam at work in Cambridge:

> The atmosphere at Cambridge was informal particularly with Professor Salam. One could always knock at his door at St. John's College, where one would always find him absorbed in his work. But he would immediately set aside his work and start discussing with you: and when you left, one would find him again absorbed in his work as if nothing had disturbed him.

John Polkinghorne was another important Ph.D. student at Cambridge when Salam joined. Polkinghorne himself became a Professor at Cambridge. He resigned his chair at Cambridge and went into a religious career - he was ordained as an *Anglican* priest in 1982. He has written several outstanding popular books on 20th century physics. He summed up Salam at Cambridge in the following words:

> Salam had about him an air of uncontrolled fertility. Some of his ideas have been very good indeed ··· but some of them have been ··· less inspired ··· This fecundity did not impinge on me very much when I was a research student. Salam mostly left me to pursue what interested me ··· Salam's exuberance extended to his lecturing style ··· One got an impression of excitement of not always

> a clear notion of exactly what the excitement was about.

A valuable glimpse of Salam's life in Cambridge as a teacher has been provided by Moffat. Moffat was temporarily assigned to Salam as a Ph.D. student after his Ph.D. supervisor Fred Hoyle, who had taught Salam as an undergraduate, left for the United States in 1955. Moffat was then working on relativity and gravitation whereas Salam's interests lay in quantum field theory and particle physics. Moffat writes:[7]

> Consequently, my supervision under Abdus Salam turned out to be as haphazard as it had been with Fred Hoyle. A session most often consisted of my meeting Abdus at the Arts School on Benet Street and striding at breakneck speed through King's Parade and Trinity Street on the way to St. John's College, black gowns flapping, with me breathlessly explaining my pursuits in relativity and gravitation, to a silent Salam. We would part at the gates of St. John's College and Salam would dart in to undergraduates in his rooms. ··· It was inspiring to see how passionate Salam was about physics. During my time at Cam-

[7] John W. Moffat: *Einstein Wrote Back*; Thomas Allen Publishers, Toronto, pp 139-142.

> bridge, he gave a series of lectures on the strong force in particle physics and what is called dispersion relations ··· I spent a lot of time in those days in the upper gallery at the Arts School library, poring over microfilms, turning a little wheel to read them. These microfilms were a preliminary copy of *The Theory of Quantized Fields* by the Russian physicists Nikolay Boguliubov and Dmitry Shirkov, which was Salam's holy book on the subject. At one classroom session when Salam was lecturing and writing on the blackboard, he kept ignoring certain mathematical factors, which made the calculations hard to follow - and I knew what those factors should have been, from reading the Bogoliubov-Shirkov book. I stood up half way through Salam's lecture and complained to him about the lack of rigor in his calculations, turned my heel and walked out. Salam never showed any anger at me for this arrogant behavior. In fact, it seemed to me that I had won more respect from him as a physicist.

Salam's response to Moffat's outburst is consistent with his response to those who differed with, or criticized him on good grounds. If you could stand your ground in a difference of opinion with him he would respect you for it.

Air Marshal (R) Zafar Chaudhary[8] has written:

> I happened to visit Cambridge in 1956 as a guest of Mr. Ian Stephens who had been the editor of *The Statesman* in India; he had visited the Pakistan Air Force a few years earlier and I had flown him in a dual seater fighter aircraft at Peshawar. He was now a don at Cambridge. He asked me if he knew a young man by the name of Salam from Pakistan who had made quite a mark at Cambridge and was thought of very highly by his teachers. I said I knew him well and that we were good friends. He also told me that I was to attend a formal dinner that evening where I would be sitting next to E.M. Forster, the author of *A Passage to India*. However, I needed to wear a dinner jacket and a bow tie for this formal occassion, which I was obviously not carrying with me. As Salam had about the same physique as I did, I visited him and borrowed his clothes for the evening function. He told me that he received an offer of a chair at the Imperial College of Science and Technology, London, which he was planning to accept.

[8]Zafar Chaudhary: The Friday Times, *Dr. Abdus Salam and his Love for the Country That Disowned Him*; January 1, 2010.

Salam, like all renowned young researchers, had been looking for a better opening in his career. Fred Hoyle wrote after Salam's death that he did not want Salam to leave Cambridge. Hoyle wrote that when Salam left Cambridge he had hoped that Salam would, one day, return to Cambridge. As he wrote:[9]

> I think that an offer of a chair in Theoretical Physics would indeed have brought him back. There were two chances in the 1960's. But on both occasions the Faculty of Mathematics instructed the electoral board that there was a greater need for an appointment in Quantum Mechanics than in Theoretical Physics. This I did not believe myself and it was one of the reasons why from the 1960s my relations with the Faculty fell to zero.

There is something sad about the entire affair. It is particularly touching that after Salam moved to Imperial, he did not vacate his Cambridge residence for another six months. He found it difficult to break ties with Cambridge! In fact he had refused an offer of fellowship at Trinity on one occasion, after he had become famous.

[9] Quoted in Abdul Hameed Chaudhari: *Alami Shohrat Yafta Sciencedaan Abdus Salam* (World Renowned Scientist Abdus Salam); published by Ahmad Salam, 8 Campion Road, SW 15, 6 NW, London; 1998; p 56; this book is written in Urdu.

And when his brother queried him he did say that he liked the rose gardens and lawns of St. John's better and then added "After all loyalty is something" - he said he had spent three years at St. John's at that time. It also appears that with Dirac, whom he rated higher than Einstein, at St. John's, Salam would have preferred to stay at Cambridge. He was loyal to St. John's and the knowledge of that loyalty makes one more sad at the attitude of the Faculty of Mathematics at Cambridge. History does, many a time, sift things and expose events in their true light. This goes to show that even the greatest of institutions are not immune to the pettiness of human nature.

8.1 Two-component Neutrinos

It was during 1956 that Salam made another astounding contribution. He was at Cambridge at that time. There is a law known as the law of conservation of parity. It essentially states that if a particular process occurs in nature with a certain probability then its "mirror image" also occurs in nature with an equal probability. The phrase "mirror image" means that quantities pertaining to the process become "inverted" - left becomes right, up becomes down, an object moving in one direction starts moving in the opposite direction with the same speed, etc.[10]

In 1956, Chinese-born American physicists Lee and Yang propounded the shocking hypothesis that left-right symmetry was violated in certain processes governed by the weak force. This hypothesis is commonly called parity violation or the failure of the law of conservation of parity in weak interactions. Salam was present at the conference which was held in Seattle, USA at which Lee and Yang presented their thoughts on the subject. Somehow Salam flew from US to London on a US Air Force transport plane carrying families of US soldiers. During the course of an uncomfortable flight during which a lot of children were crying, he thought about the whole thing and came to a fascinating conclusion.

Pauli had postulated the existence of a massless particle to save one of the most important principles of physics - the law of conservation of energy. In 1930, he had conjectured that whenever an atom decays via beta radioactivity, it not only emits an electron but also a mysterious particle which he named neutrino. The elusive particle could not be discovered for another quarter of a century. Salam was able to prove that the violation of left-right symmetry in beta radioactivity was intimately connected with the zero mass of the neutrino. It was a most beau-

[10]It is also simplistically called the law of left-right symmetry. It may, however, be kept in mind that there are quantities like energy, etc., which remain unaffected by this inversion.

tiful connection and in establishing it he introduced a new type of symmetry that is now called "chiral" (from handedness) symmetry. It is now part of all graduate textbooks on the subject.

The publication of this theory however was delayed due to the negative reaction of Peierls as well as Pauli. Actually Peierls had asked a question from Salam during the latter's Ph.D. defence. Peierls had asked Salam as to why was the neutrino massless? The photon, the particle of light that carries the electromagnetic force is massless because of a certain symmetry principle, the gauge symmetry known by the name $U(1)$. At that time no one knew as to what symmetry, if any, made the neutrino massless.

Since Peierls had asked the original question, Salam went to Peierls in Birmingham with the idea that chiral symmetry made the neutrino massless. Since chiral symmetry implied non-conservation of parity, and Peierls believed that parity conservation would not be violated, he did not approve of Salam's ideas. In fact in his Nobel Prize lecture Salam stated that he had taken traveled to Birmingham to discuss the idea with him but Peierls did not approve of it. After looking at documents in the the Trieste archives, Fraser[11] has pointed out that Peierls wrote to Salam stating that his Nobel Prize lec-

[11]Gordon Fraser: *Cosmic Anger: Abdus Salam The First Muslim Nobel Laureate*; Oxford University Press, 2008.

ture version did not agree with what had actually happened. What Peierls had refused was the idea of a joint publication on the implications of massless neutrinos before the discovery of parity nonconservation. While this appears to be correct, refusal on the part of Peierls was most likely due to his belief in parity conservation.

Salam then sent his manuscript to Pauli, who has been perceptively referred to by Gordon Fraser, as the Chief Justice of physics. Salam referred to him as the "Oracle". After all Pauli was the father of the neutrino - he had postulated its existence. Salam gave his manuscript to Professor Villars of MIT, who was traveling to CERN, so that he could give it to Pauli. Pauli's reply was brought back by Professor Villars: "Give my regards to my friend Salam and tell him to think of something better". Salam therefore withheld publication of the paper. This was a mistake.

As pointed out by Gordon Fraser, Salam agonized for two months over whether or not to publish the paper. In doing so he lost precious time. Salam subsequently submitted his paper to the Italian journal *Il Nuovo Cimento* where, it was received on 15 November, 1956. The paper appeared in the January 1957 issue of *Il Nuovo Cimento.* Soon afterwards Lee and Yang propounded identical ideas although they did mention in their paper that they had come across Salam's work whose conclusions were similar to theirs. In fact in his *Collected Papers (1945-1980)*

With Commentary, Yang states:[12]

> In November 1956, A. Salam had distributed a preprint discussing the two-component neutrino theory. His preprint was written before any experimental evidence for parity non-conservation existed. In January, 1957 Landau also distributed a manuscript on the two-component neutrino theory.

It is of interest to quote Gordon Fraser:[13]

> Lee and Yang's achievement was startling by its promptness. The Nobel had been awarded to Lee and Yang for setting the scene for parity violation in weak interactions. Salam had entered only in Act II, realizing why parity should be violated before any effect had been seen, and that it should be a big effect. He had not waited for proof from experimental discovery to emerge. Had he not been muzzled by Pauli he would have published months earlier. Some gossip and garbled reports of the Nobel award even mentioned Salam's name. Friends sent Salam their congratulations

[12]World Scientific, 2005 Edition, pp 35-36.

[13]Gordon Fraser: *Cosmic Anger: Abdus Salam The First Muslim Nobel Laureate*; Oxford University Press, 2008.

> and looked forward to a share of a Nobel Prize. The Prize for physics can be awarded up to three people. By now many people were on the scene, but clearly Lee and Yang had made the first move.

In an interesting article[14] Norman Dombey, who had looked at Salam's archives, pointed out that Paul Matthews wrote to Salam from the US: "You have really hit the jackpot this time." He also points out that John Ward wrote: "So many congratulations and fond hopes for at least one third of a Nobel prize."

Fraser further adds:

> Salam resolved not to make the same mistake again. There was no harm in submitting revolutionary new ideas for publication: if they were not right they could still influence others ··· Salam realized that the Nobel Prize for physics was within his reach. 1957 was one of the few times that it had gone to researchers who had not been born in Europe or the United States. Asians could go to Stockholm. Salam had almost got the prize with the massless neutrino: all he had to do now

[14]Norman Dombey: *Abdus Salam: A Reappraisal; Part I - How to Win the Nobel Prize*; arxiv.org/pdf/1109.1972.pdf; September 24, 2011.

> was to follow Pauli's advice - 'think of something better'.

As we will see Salam was to make a similar mistake again with the $V - A$ theory of weak nuclear interactions, but in the case of $V - A$ theory he had only himself to blame.

Salam was to join Imperial College, soon afterwards, in January 1957. In his memoirs John Moffat wrote about Salam's reaction to having missed the chance to get a Nobel prize:[15]

> At this time, in the late 1950s, Salam was upset about having missed the Nobel Prize for proposing the left-right parity symmetry violation in the weak interactions of particles, and he would frequently complain about it $\cdots$ At our Imperial College lunches Salam would occasionally display his frustration at having missed this Nobel Prize. The fact that he had not published his ideas about parity violation set a rule in his mind for the future. Henceforth he would always publish any idea that seemed reasonably worthy of attention, regardless of whether he was sure it was right. He demanded the same of us in research, chiding us to publish our ideas, on the off chance

[15]John W. Moffat: *Einstein Wrote Back*; Thomas Allen Publishers, Toronto, p 155, 156.

that they would turn out to be important.

It another interesting episode a Russian physicist, I.S. Shapiro, lost the chance to win the Nobel Prize for parity violation because he had been muzzled by Pauli's counterpart in Soviet physics, Lev Landau. Such was Landau's grasp of all areas of theoretical physics, and so profound was his insight, that it was extremely difficult for most people around him to defend themselves against his attacks. This had the most unfortunate consequences in case of Shapiro, who lost his chance of winning a Nobel Prize because of his inability to take a stand against Landau.

While investigating the problem of the decay of what were then thought to be two different unstable particles (called theta and tau). Shapiro came to the conclusion that the tau and theta were actually identical particles but that a well-established law, the law of conservation of parity, was violated in the process. Since the above decay process is caused by the weak nuclear force, Shapiro made some further calculations, indicating that the law of conservation of parity is violated in processes controlled by the weak force. Landau, when presented with Shapiro's results, laughed at the revolutionary idea of parity violation. And it is said that since Shapiro's work could not be published without Landau's consent, he was unable to do any thing further. Janouch, a Czech physicist, has stated that he saw the manuscript at Landau's table many months before the same idea was published independently by Lee and Yang in the USA. For this very idea Lee and Yang got the 1957 Nobel Prize in Physics and Shapiro thus suffered badly.[16]

The two-component neutrino theory makes very specific predictions about various processes involving the weak force, all of which were experimentally verified. One of these predictions is that the neutrino always spins in one particular manner instead of the two possibilities expected on the basis of quantum principles. If a neutrino is coming towards you, it will always appear to spin in a clockwise direction with respect to its line of travel. An easy way to remember this correlation between its direction of motion and spin is as follows: extend the thumb of the left hand in the direction of motion of the particle, then curl the fingers of the same hand into the palm; the particle will always spin in the same sense in which the fingers of the left hand curl. That is why a neutrino is called a left-handed particle.

According to Salam's two-component theory right-handed neutrinos do not exist in nature.[17] If one were

[16]F. Janouch: *Lev. D. Landau: His Life and Work*; CERN preprint 28 March 1979; also accessible at: http://image.sciencenet.cn/olddata/kexue.com.cn/upload/blog/file/2010/6/20106212148213857 23.pdf

[17]In recent years it has been revealed that neutrinos are not massless but possess a very tiny mass. This has been revealed through the phenomenon of neutrino oscillations in which one type of neu-

to look at a mirror image of a left-handed particle, it would appear to be a right-handed particle. Since right-handed neutrinos do not exist in nature one would not find the mirror image of a neutrino in real life! The world of subatomic particles is indeed baffling.

For people who have little interest or aptitude for sciences but have an interest in literature Salam had described the absence of a mirror image of a left handed neutrino (i.e., a right handed neutrino) by referring to the one eyed mythological giants - the cyclops. He said that it is as if only if left-eyed cyclops existed (assuming that the eye of a cyclop is not in the middle of the forehead). Then if a cyclop looked at into a mirror it would have to appear right-eyed of necessity since in the mirror left and right get interchanged. But since right-eyed cyclops would not exist it would not see any thing in the mirror! This is of course just an interesting imagery for those with a background of literature.

---

trino (there are three types known) transforms into another. Such a transformation would not be possible if the neutrino mass were precisely zero. This implies the existence of right-handed neutrinos as well.

Chapter 9

Imperial College

In 1957, at the young age of 31, Salam was appointed Professor and first ever Chairman of the Theoretical Physics Department at the Imperial College, one of the world's foremost scientific institutions. The Physics Department at Imperial College was then headed by Professor Blackett. Blackett was one of Rutherford's "boys" and was an outstanding experimentalist. It was felt that Imperial College should have a Department of Theoretical Physics and therefore the authorities were in search of a suitable choice. Salam's brother has remarked in his book that the post offered to Salam was once occupied by the philosopher-mathematician Alfred North Whitehead.[1]

[1]This could be true because, according to several web sources, Whitehead was at University College London and Imperial Col-

The story of how Salam got an offer of Professorship at Imperial is quite interesting. It is said that Professor Blackett was visiting Cambridge and happened to meet Bethe, the Nobel laureate who first discovered how the sun shines. The two had known each other from the war days. Blackett asked Bethe to suggest a suitable person for a chair of theoretical physics. Bethe immediately suggested Salam's name. Professor Blackett, a Nobel laureate and a most influential figure in British science, knocked at Salam's door, and without waiting for his response, just walked in. Salam told his brother that he was a bit startled and disturbed at the sight of the formidable Blackett. He straightaway asked Salam if he would like to be appointed as a chair at Imperial? Salam immediately said "Yes sir". Blackett simply replied that he could have the job. Salam had to appear for a formal interview before Professor Temple who was a great admirer of Sir Arthur Eddington. The only question Temple asked from Salam was as to what was Salam's opinion about Eddington's book. It was a difficult question because Salam did not have a high opinion of that book. However he was sensible about it and said that he had not read it with a free mind (i.e. objectively) to which Temple responded that Salam should be in the diplomatic service. His diplomatic skills, noted so early by Professor

lege London between 1910 and 1926. He was Professor of Applied Mathematics at Imperial College.

Temple, stood him in good stead when he embarked on the task of setting up and sustaining the International Center for Theoretical Physics. He could be diplomatic whenever he needed to be.

When Salam joined Imperial College he delivered his inaugural lecture. Professor Blackett described Salam's inaugural lecture as the most eloquent of inaugural lectures he heard at Imperial.[2] Professor Riazuddin who was present at the lecture states that Salam concluded the lecture by quoting the following verse from the Holy Quran:

> Thou seest not in the creation of the All-Merciful any imperfection. Return thy gaze; seest thou any fissure? Then return thy gaze again, and again thy gaze comes back to thee dazzled, aweary.

We have already quoted Polkinghorne on Salam's lecturing style at Cambridge. Robert Delbourgo, who, with Salam and Strathdee, developed the well known Delbourgo-Salam-Strathdee method, was a student at Imperial College. He writes

> My first contact with him was as a teacher. Even though Salam did not relish lecturing, I found him to be one of the most inspiring

[2] He made this remark during a visit to Pakistan.

> teachers, his breakneck pace notwithstanding. And he mixed well with students at Imperial··· Naturally he was a great source of inspiration to the students who had somehow got wind of this brilliant, charismatic professor who had been recruited by Blackett and who inhabited the Huxley Building. It was the basic reason why I chose to study theoretical physics at Imperial under his tutelage··· I vividly remember the verbal slanging matches between Salam and Ne'eman during early exploration of the eight-fold way. You must realize that Salam was a formidable task master and not many persons survived his scrutiny: he was ever impatient for quick progress and his fertile mind kept on exploring new avenues or angles - far too disconcerting for a budding postgraduate. Each day he would come into my room, rub his hands together and inquire if the problem was "all done" even when the calculations could be pretty gruesome. With Salam you either learned to swim well or sank: no snorkeling allowed.

This reminds one of Rutherford in his laboratory where he wanted results from his students and would not stand any nonsense.

Professor G. Murtaza also did his Ph.D. with Salam.

He has written interesting articles on Salam. In one of these he describes him as a teacher. He states:[3]

> Salam Sahib was not one of those who put in a lot of effort in preparing their lectures and try to make the lecture easy to understand - this was P.T. Matthews's style, but not Salam's. Salam Sahib was also not one of those lecturers who prepare systematic lecture notes and then transfer them in a beautiful manner on to the blackboard so that what is written on the blackboard becomes a picture of a book - this was Kibble's style not Salam's. Salam Sahib was different. He had his own distinct and unique style. The aforementioned things did not appear to have much importance for him. From his attitude it appeared that these were things for lesser mortals. Not that he was incapable of these things. We saw and heard him in numerous conferences where he would be invited as a VIP speaker. People would be impatient to hear his lecture, halls would be packed, spellbinding physics was dealt with in a literary

[3] I have translated this from an Urdu article of his, a copy of which he kindly gave me. The article is titled: *Professor Abdus Salam - Ehad Saaz Shakhsiat aur Azeem Ustad*; (Epoch-making Personality and Great Teacher).

> manner, his command over language would draw praise, and then this incarnation of knowledge and intelligence would receive standing ovations, as if what he had said reflected what was in the hearts of the audience.

Murtaza also wrote that when Salam entered the classroom he would have several volumes of journals in his hand with page indicators. The Diploma[4] lectures were more of a presentation on Frontiers of Physics, where research problems were analyzed in the class. A lot of the stuff went over the heads of students but it was an "exciting experience" that would motivate and inspire students. " He appeared to be in a hurry and wanted his students to move ahead speedily. It appeared as if he was short of time and a lot needed to be done."

In his memoirs John W. Moffat has described the inexhaustible fecundity of Salam's mind and his interaction with his colleagues in the following interesting words:[5]

> Almost every day at lunchtime, Matthews, now a Professor in the Mathematics Department, John Taylor and I would meet at the faculty restaurant at Imperial. At some point during the lunch, Salam would appear, and

[4]DIC - Diploma of Imperial College.

[5]John W. Moffat: *Einstein Wrote Back*; Thomas Allen Publishers, Toronto, p 154.

> while eating a sandwich, would excitedly tell us about his latest physics idea. He had new ideas daily, and would use the three of us as his sounding boards. After listening carefully to the daily idea, the Matthews-Taylor-Moffat trinity would proceed to demolish it. We almost always succeeded. But Salam, undeterred, always appeared the next day with another idea. However, now and then one of Salam's ideas would survive the lunch, and he would then dash off and pursue it further with great intensity. It would eventually surface in a physics journal as a joint paper with Matthews, who would have worked out many of the technical details. This partnership - with Salam usually providing the motivating idea and Matthews working out all the tedious calculations with the correct numerical factors - was an ideal collaboration.

One may note Salam's passion, his inexhaustible creativity, and his persistence in the above description. It also shows that he had the courage, not only to face almost daily rejection of his ideas, but to come back with new ones. His total commitment to physics comes through very clearly. Nothing could deter him from his goal.

9.1 $V - A$ Theory

The next step in the search for the law of the weak force was the so-called V minus A (written as $V - A$) theory for particles like the electron, neutrino and the muon (collectively called leptons). It always baffled me as to how could Salam have missed arriving at the V minus A theory. So in summer 1990 I asked him in his office at Trieste as to what happened. He pulled out a copy of a manuscript from his drawer and gave it to me. These were the galley proofs of a paper that had been accepted for publication in the prestigious American journal *Physical Review.* It carried the handwritten date February 1957, which was the month during which the work may have been submitted and/or accepted for publication. The paper was titled "*On Fermi interactions*". Riazuddin, who along with Marshak and Ryan wrote a comprehensive book on weak interactions in the late 1960s, has also narrated the incident. He states that on one of the weekends in February 1957 Salam came to pick up his luggage from his flat near St. John's in Cambridge.

> With him was a preprint just written from Imperial College, the content of which I could not comprehend at that time due to my poor background. My memory, however, was good and when Marshak, Ryan and myself were writing our book on weak interactions in mid

> 1960s, the memory of that preprint came to me in connection with my writing of my share of chapter 2 on chirality or γ_5 transformation. I searched for a reference for that preprint in the issues of leading journals of Physics of that period, but could not find it.

Riazuddin therefore contacted Salam when the final touches were being given to their book and found out. That paper was then included as a reference in chapter 2 of that classic book.

In this paper he had clearly arrived at the V minus A hypothesis for particles like the electron, neutrino and the muon (collectively called leptons). Unfortunately at a conference soon after the paper had been accepted Madame Wu claimed that experiments ruled out this type of theory for the weak force. Since Madam Wu had recently made headlines by establishing that the Yang and Lee hypothesis of parity violation, her words carried great weight. Salam hastily withdrew the paper lest he be proved wrong. The irony was that Salam was right and the experiments were wrong! Gell-Mann and Feynman, and independently Marshak and Sudarshan made the same hypothesis extending it to include other particles such as the proton and neutron (collectively called hadrons). It may also be mentioned that in the same paper Salam had also dealt with what is now called breaking of chiral symmetry to generate masses of the electron and the muon. This in itself is a novel idea which, in a different way, has deep implications for the unification of the weak nuclear force with the force of electromagnetism.

9.2 Unitary Symmetry

In 1961, Salam and Ward made an important discovery pertaining to particles that can feel the strong nuclear force (hadrons). By use of symmetry arguments they were able to predict the existence of a group of eight hadrons with specific properties (they are called spin one mesons). The existence of this octet was subsequently confirmed experimentally. His research student Ne'eman also used the particular type of symmetry argument, known as unitary symmetry,[6] to predict the existence of a set of ten hadrons - one of these was missing and was subsequently found. Gell-Mann also made the same prediction independently.

Salam was elected a Fellow of The Royal Society in 1959. He was 33 at the time and was perhaps one of the youngest-ever scientists to be elected on this most

[6] Unitary symmetry refers to invariance of the fundamental equations for an interaction (strong nuclear interaction in this case) under an infinite set of transformations. The letter U in $U(1)$ or $SU(2)$, etc refers to unitary while the letter S denotes an additional condition for which the word special is used. Thus $SU(2)$ denotes the special unitary transformation group in two dimensions, etc.

prestigious body.[7] In 1964, he was awarded the Hughes Medal. Commenting on this award, the journal *Nature* (December 13, 1964 issue) refers to Salam's work on the two-component theory and unitary symmetry as contributions "in the absolutely highest class." Salam's Ph.D. work had already earned him prestige and respect. Budding physicists assembled around him. Weinberg, who later shared the Nobel Prize with him, spent some time at the Imperial College; Higgs, whose famed Higgs mechanism paved the way for unification, was a post-doc at Imperial College; Kibble, who made significant contributions of the first order, came to Imperial College, Ward and a host of other leaders in the field interacted with Salam. Under his leadership the Imperial College joined the forefront of theoretical research in the field of elementary particle physics, also known as high energy physics.

At Imperial College Professor Salam also made important contributions to the field of particles that feel the strong nuclear force, hadrons as they are called. The number of hadrons had steadily proliferated after WW II as a result of experiments with new machines called particles accelerators. In order to put some order in this

[7]Not many foreigners were elected Fellows of the Royal Society. For instance when Kapitsa was elected FRS, he was the first foreigner to receive such an honor in approximately two hundred years.

plethora of unwanted hadrons[8] the idea of unitary symmetry was invoked (more about unitary symmetry groups later). Salam's research student Y. Ne'eman (who later became a minister in the Israeli cabinet) used this symmetry to develop what is known as the eightfold way in which hadrons get grouped together on the basis of common properties (all particles in the same multiplet have close masses and identical values of spin and parity).[9]

How did Ne'eman get Salam as a thesis supervisor? He writes:

> My choice for a supervisor for my thesis was somewhat incidental. I consulted the College prospectus and approached one of the professors whose name appeared under 'Theoretical Physics'. I told him about my interest in Einstein's unified field theory, to which he replied that he did not know if anyone was still working on that, but Abdus Salam and his group in the Mathematics Department were working on Field Theory.

[8]The appearance of a large number of hadrons led to Salam's famous adaptation of George Orwell "*All particles are elementary but some are more elementary than others*!"

[9]Ne'eman describes his first interaction with Salam in the following words: "I came to Salam, presenting the only letter of recommendation I had, which was from Moshe Dayan. Salam laughed and commented: "What can a General know about scientific abilities."

Regarding his working with Salam, Ne'eman, who was to make a highly important discovery eventually, has given interesting insight in his book:[10]

> When I first showed him my suggestions, Salam told me that they had already been attempted five or six years previously. My next proposal, he told me, had been suggested by others two or three years before. I felt I was getting nearer to the present. Salam was skeptical.
> He proposed another subject, and when I insisted I wanted to classify the hadrons, he said: "I wanted to assign you an easier problem, on the assumption that it would be better for you to produce a complete work during one year of leave from the army. However, since your mind is made up, do it your way, but you should know that you are embarking on a highly speculative search. If indeed you have already decided, at least do it properly. Learn group theory thoroughly."

Salam recommended Dynkin's book which Ne'eman studied thoroughly and then began trying various groups for

[10] Y. Ne'eman: *The Particle Hunters*, Cambridge University Press 1986.

classification of hadrons (according to strangeness and isospin). He writes:

> I found that only four groups might do the job, and began to examine each of these separately.
> I remember that one of them (called *G2*) yielded diagrams in the form of the Star of David, and I hoped that it might be the correct one - but it was not. On the other hand *SU(3)* gave a perfect fit.
> I finished my work in December 1960 and discussed it with Salam. I then submitted a paper for publication, early in 1961, and it appeared shortly after.

The *SU(3)* classification of hadrons, now part of graduate textbooks, is also called the eightfold way. The eightfold way of classification led to the discovery of a new particle, the omega minus as it is called, as a result of prediction made by Gell-Mann who independently developed the eightfold way. Salam and J.C. Ward used what is known as $SU(3)$ flavor symmetry to predict a set of nine hadrons each carrying a spin of one unit. These particles were observed later. In what is known as the Standard Model of Particle Physics, $SU(3)$ color symmetry, an exact symmetry discovered in the 1970s, unlike the approximate $SU(3)$ flavor symmetry, is employed.

9.3 Glimpses of Life at Imperial

Salam was incredibly dynamic and interactive. Under his leadership, Imperial College, without any doubt, became one of the foremost centers of research in Quantum Field Theory and Elementary Particle Physics. It was visited by most important physicists. Promising young men came to Imperial as Ph.D. students. Peter Higgs, who has hit headlines world wide after the recent discovery of the Higgs or God particle, was my teacher at Edinburgh University and told me that he had worked as a post-doc at Imperial with Salam.[11]

Weinberg, Golstone, Glashow and many other famous names, or names in the making, spent time at Imperial, Salam's "London haunt", as Glashow once described it. Weinberg and Glashow shared the Nobel Prize with Salam in 1979 for their unification of the weak nuclear force with the electro-magnetic force. Weinberg narrates:[12]

[11]Higgs also told this author that he did his Ph.D. in theoretical chemistry. He said that one of his professors said to him that Quantum Field Theory was in a state of mess and that one could sink in this complicated field and therefore it was safer to go into an area where Ph.D. was assured. Higgs said that, retrospectively, it was not good advice because one could make important contributions at the time. Peter Higgs however should have no regrets - his contribution has made him much more famous than most of the prominent twentieth century physicists.

[12]This has been taken from Weinberg's contribution to *Salamfestschrift: A Collection of Talks from the Conference on Highlights*

> I first met Abdus Salam in 1960, when he knocked at the door of the little cubbyhole that I had for an office at the Rad Lab in Berkeley. I had spent a fair fraction of my time as a graduate student in mastering Salam's analysis of overlapping ultraviolet divergences, and then as a post-doc at Columbia in using Salam's result, that renormalisation makes all integrals and subintegrals however chosen superficially convergent, to show that the integrals actually converge $\cdots$
> I think it was then that I proposed that I use a Sloan Fellowship to make a visit to London for several months the following year. Salam was good enough to offer the hospitality of his department at Imperial College, and I arrived in October 1961.

In his contribution to *Salamfestschrift* Mike Duff gives us a glimpse of life at Imperial College in Salam's department:

> When the deeds of great men are recalled one often hears the cliche "He did not suffer fools gladly." But my memories of Salam at

of Particle Physics and Condensed Physics at ICTP, Trieste, Italy, March 8-12, 1993; Editors A. Ali, J.Ellis and Randjbar-Daemi, World Scientific, 1994; p 4, 5.

> Imperial College are quite the reverse. People from all over the world would arrive and knock at his doors to expound their latest theories, some of them quite bizarre. Yet Salam would treat them all with the same courtesy and respect. Perhaps it was because his own ideas always bordered on the outlandish that he was tolerant of eccentricity in others, he could recognize pearls of wisdom where the rest of us were only irritating grains of sand.

Glashow has mentioned his interactions with Salam in his book *Interactions - A Journey Through The Mind of a Particle Physicist and the Matter of This World*[13]. He went to Copenhagen, at Niels Bohr's institute, in 1958 and stayed there for 27 months visiting various places outside Denmark as well. He writes of his encounter with the crowd at Imperial College:

> In the early spring I was invited to speak about my work at Imperial College, the London haunt of Abdus Salam, with whom I was to share the Nobel Prize twenty years later. Then, as now, Salam had the presence of an oriental potentate with a Cambridge education and the gift of speaking perfect English.

[13]Sheldon L. Glashow with Ben Bova; *Interactions: A Journey Through the Mind of A Particle Physicist and the Matter of This World*; Warner Books, 1988, p 140.

> A practicing Muslim, he neither drinks nor smokes.
> I explained what progress I had on the electroweak synthesis and why I believed that the theory was renormalizable. I was received politely but coolly, as one might expect in England. Some months later, Salam and his cronies published a paper showing that my arguments were hopelessly naive and dead wrong. Boy, was I ever stupid! I didn't get any sympathy from my friends at the Institute - there was no reaction at all. Nobody cared about the work I was doing.

Tom Kibble, one of the most prominent theoretical physicists of those days, a former student of Professor Kemmer at Edinburgh,[14] the man who generalized Higgs mechanism, and who, as Salam mentioned in his talk on the occasion of award of the Nobel Prize, tutored him on the Higgs mechanism, has the following to say:

> I had the good fortune to join the Imperial College Theoretical Physics Group in 1959, two years after it was set up by Professor Abdus Salam accompanied by his erstwhile supervisor Paul Matthews. It was a time of

[14]Professor Kemmer once told this author that Kibble had achieved a double, graduating simultaneously in physics and mathematics.

> tremendous excitement and rapid progress, and Imperial was I believe one of the best places to be ···
> One of the great things about our group in those early days was that we always had lots of visitors, both long- and short-term. Our guests included Murray Gell-Mann, Ken Johnson, John Ward, Lowell Brown, Gordon Feldman and Steven Weinberg. Overseeing us all was Professor Salam's formidable secretary Bridget of whom we were all terrified - all that is, except Professor Salam

A similar and interesting picture of life at Imperial in those days has been drawn by G. Murtaza.[15]. He writes:

> It was characteristic of Salam - whether or not one understood him, one would be inspired. He was always in an excited state. Wherever he went he created ripples. New ideas would create the impression as if a revolution was at hand. The Department was in such a state that there was a continuous stream of visiting scientists. Seminars were

[15] I have translated this from an Urdu article of his, a copy of which he kindly gave me. The article is titled: *Professor Abdus Salam - Ehad Saaz Shakhsiat aur Azeem Ustad*; (Epoch-making personality and Great Teacher).

> held frequently. Physicists from US and Europe were all drawn to South Kensington as if on a pilgrimage. One day Julian Schwinger would be giving a seminar, on another Steven Weinberg. Today it is Feldman, tomorrow J.C. Ward. The Department was inundated with literature. Every day heaps of preprints would arrive from four corners of the world. As a teacher Salam would not spoon-feed you but would provide you with an ideal environment in which, using your abilities, you could reach the skies.

The above sample of quotes gives us a flavor of life at the Department of Theoretical Physics at Imperial College. Until he set up the International Center for Theoretical Physics (ICTP) at Trieste in 1964, Salam was fully committed to Imperial where a lot of new contributions were made. Once the ICTP was set up he had to divide time between the two institutions.

Chapter 10

Electro-weak Unification and Nobel Prize

Salam never wavered in his conviction that the unification of fundamental forces was inevitable. He pursued this goal ceaselessly for over four decades. Even as a young physicist Salam stuck to this conviction despite the fact that men of the caliber of Dirac and Pauli despaired of the task. When, in 1957, Salam sent one of his papers to Pauli he received the following reply:

> I am very much startled on the title of your paper 'Universal Fermi interaction ⋯'. For quite a while I have for myself the rule if a

> theoretician says universal it means pure nonsense. This holds particularly in connection with the Fermi interaction, but otherwise too, and now you too, Brutus my son come with this word · · ·

Interestingly this response came months after Pauli had apologized publicly and graciously to Salam for being responsible for the delay in the publication of Salam's two-component theory. Nothing could dent Pauli's sarcasm and he would not even spare his own self.[1] Salam however remained undeterred and kept on pursuing the problem of unification of forces of nature.

John W. Moffat, who was at one time assigned to Salam as a Ph.D. student at Cambridge, and subsequently joined Salam's group at Imperial College, published his memoirs in the year 2010. He wrote about Salam's overwhelming preoccupation with the problem of unification

[1]When Pauli was proved wrong in his conviction that parity (i.e. left/right symmetry) is always conserved he wrote an interesting letter to Weisskopf. He wrote: "It is good that I did not make a bet. It would have resulted in a heavy loss of money (which I cannot afford). I did make a fool of myself, however (which I can afford to do). What shocks me is not the fact that God is just left-handed but the fact that in spite of this He exhibits Himself as left-right symmetric when He expresses Himself strongly." He was referring to the fact that left-right symmetry is observed in strong nuclear interactions but violated in weak nuclear interactions.

of forces in the late 1950s:[2]

> All of us would orbit Salam's grand office, attempting to meet with him to plan future research projects. We expected Salam to provide us with research guidance, but as it turned out, our sun had only one stock-in-trade problem, which he handed out to graduate students and post-doctoral fellows. This consisted of following a suggestion of Julian Schwinger, a Nobel Prize winner at Harvard University, who had formulated a way of engendering masses of elementary particles.

This was the problem that eventually led to the work of Higgs, who was also a post-doctoral fellow at Imperial. The famed Higgs or "God" particle was discovered in 2012.

In order to understand what electro-weak unification is and how it was brought about we will have to summarize a bit of relevant physics along with the major steps in the unification process.

A) The concept of symmetry can be given a precise mathematical formulation. There exist many symmetries but the whole subject is dealt with in a most systematic and beautiful manner in a branch of mathematics called

[2] John W. Moffat: *Einstein Wrote Back*; Thomas Allen Publishers, Toronto, p 152, 153.

group theory. It is a conviction, shared by most physicists, that fundamental laws of physics must satisfy some symmetry requirements. A-priori it is not possible to tell what symmetry is relevant. But in the late 1950s a feeling developed among leading physicists that a type of symmetry known as gauge symmetry must be the one relevant to all basic forces of nature and to unification. Salam was among the very first people to realize this.[3]

B) The framework of Quantum Field Theory views all fundamental forces as arising out of the exchange of messenger particles between the interacting particles (something akin to an unending series of incredibly swift volleys between two tennis rackets, the ball acting as messenger that transmits energy and momentum from one side to the other). The range of the force depends upon the mass

[3] In his 1993 lecture, *The Dawning of Gauge Theory*, O'Raifeartaigh states:

> Although Professor Salam has been active in many areas he will perhaps best be remembered for his work on non-abelian gauge theories, first for promoting them in the late fifties and early sixties, when it was neither popular nor profitable to do so, and then for bringing this work to a successful conclusion in 1968.

Quoted from: A. Ali, J. Ellis and Randjbar-Daemi (Editors): *Salamfestschrift: A Collection of Talks From the Conference on Highlights of Particle and Condensed Matter Physics; 8-12 March 1993, ICTP, Trieste*; World Scientific Publishing Co 1994, p 577.

of the messenger particle - the heavier it is the lesser the range. A massless particle gives rise to a force of infinite range.

C) Gauge symmetry automatically forces the introduction of messenger particles (that is why they are called gauge particles in technical jargon). This symmetry further requires that gauge particles be massless and carry one unit of spin (most particles in nature are found to spin like a spinning top - like mass or charge spin is an inherent and ineradicable property of these particles). Gauge symmetry further tells us how many types of messenger particles will there be.

D) The fundamental equations of electromagnetism satisfy a gauge symmetry known as $U(1)$. $U(1)$ requires only one massless messenger particle which can be identified with the photon - the massless pellet of electromagnetic energy emitted and absorbed continually by electrically charged particles. Because of the zero mass of the photon the electromagnetic force has, like gravity, an infinite range. The photon is electrically neutral. The electromagnetic force is left - right symmetric (i.e. parity is conserved in electromagnetic processes).

E) The weak force is apparently very different from the electromagnetic force. It is, roughly speaking, ten thousand times weaker in strength and its range is incredibly small (millionth part of a billionth of a centimeter!). Also the particles capable of feeling the weak force feel it only when they are spinning in the left-handed state In elucidating this aspect of the weak force, Salam, with this two - component theory, had already played a leading role.

F) Salam was among the very first people to realize in the late 1950s that a gauge symmetry known as $SU(2)$ could be relevant to weak forces and to unification. $SU(2)$ requires the existence of three massless messengers. For the weak force two of these messengers should be electrically charged and the third neutral. These three particles are denoted as W^+, W^- and W_0. But massless messengers give rise to forces of infinite range, as pointed out in (B) above, whereas the weak force has a very short range. The problem of generating masses of messenger particles while preserving gauge symmetry of the fundamental equations was not fully solved until 1967 by Weinberg. (Incidentally the adaption of $SU(2)$ as a gauge symmetry was in itself a difficult problem which was solved in 1954 by Yang and Mills, and independently by Salam's Ph.D. student R. Shaw).

G) Salam and Ward (and independently Glashow) wrote papers in the period 1959-61 using $SU(2)$ to treat the weak force and to unify it with the electromagnetic force. Schwinger (Glashow's Ph.D. supervisor) had suggested that one should regard the photon as the neutral member of the triplet of weak messengers required by $SU(2)$. It was this suggestion that had opened a possible avenue to electro-weak unification. However even after having suggested this Schwinger did not pin much hope on gauge symmetry. In these papers Salam and Ward forged a fundamental link between the strength of the weak force, the electric charge to which the photon couples in electromagnetism and the electric charge of the two W particles. In this manner they reconciled the differing strengths and ranges of the weak and electromagnetic forces. However, the mass of the W particles and the problem of different left-right behavior of the two forces remained a problem.

H) In a paper published in 1964 Salam and Ward introduced a still heavier particle, the Z_0, and by considering the third (electrically neutral) member of the weak triplet as a mixture of the photon and Z_0 , showed how to account for the parity conserving behavior of the weak force. The Z_0 accounted for the left handedness of the weak force. Further Salam and Ward were able to achieve a delicate elimination of certain inconsistencies. But the problem of generating masses of the (two) W and (one) Z_0 particles remained unsolved. Glashow had also mixed the photon and the electro-weak messenger in a paper in 1961 of which Salam and Ward were unaware. The same was done by Weinberg in 1967 and he too was unaware of the work of Glashow although both worked at Harvard. It must be emphasized that *the intertwining of the messengers for the two forces had become a necessity in order to get rid of inconsistencies.*

I) A mechanism called *spontaneous symmetry breaking* was developed in the period 1961-64. In spontaneous symmetry breaking the fundamental equations of the theory continue to satisfy the requirements of gauge symmetry but the state with the lowest possible energy (technically known as ground state or vacuum) violates the symmetry. In important papers Nambu and Goldstone presented this novel idea which was explored further by Goldstone, Salam and Weinberg. It was in 1964 that Peter Higgs of Edinburgh University (in the 1950s he worked as a post - doctoral research fellow with Salam) made the decisive breakthrough. Peter Higgs was able to show how, using a mathematical trick, one could use spontaneous symmetry breaking to generate messenger particles[4] with

[4]In this mechanism the fundamental equations of motion are unchanged by the gauge transformations imposed on them but the vacuum state, the state with the lowest possible energy, is changed by the transformations. In technical language we say that the equations of motion are invariant under the transformations but the vacuum state is not. This subtlety had been overlooked by previous investigators because if both, the equations of motion and the vacuum state are invariant, then the gauge symmetry automatically leads to massless messenger particles. To reveal this Higgs had to introduce a new field known as the Higgs field. The quantum of the Higgs field is a particle whose mass was not fixed by theory. This made the search for the Higgs particle extremely difficult. After a marathon search spanning almost three decades, the Higgs particle was finally nailed down at the CERN (European Organization for

non zero masses! (Englert and Brout also arrived at the same result independently and almost simultaneously). It gradually became obvious that this would be highly relevant to all short range forces viz the weak and strong nuclear forces because a short range force requires a messenger particle with non zero mass (see B above). At Imperial College Tom Kibble (another former student of Salam's supervisor Kemmer and a graduate of Edinburgh University) generalized the Higgs mechanism to take account of the requirements of the theory of relativity and tutored Salam about it. Incidentally Glashow and Higgs were together at a summer college in Scotland in 1961. Glashow was pursuing unification and Higgs was interested in spontaneous symmetry breaking. Glashow states in his autobiography:

> Peter and I at Newcastle Abbey should have put it all together there and then. Instead we flirted with secretaries, hiked in highlands and drank many liters of fine Hungarian wine,

Nuclear Research) LHC (Large Hadron Collider) machine. Its momentous discovery was announced at CERN on July 4, 2012. It has a mass of 126 GeV i.e. it is about 134 times heavier than the proton. The Higgs particle became known as the God particle, partly because of its elusiveness and partly because it was responsible for giving mass to messenger particles. The mass of the messenger particles determines the range of the force they carry or give rise to.

courtesy of NATO grant that supported the school.

Weinberg and Salam independently arrived at the conclusion that the gauge symmetry relevant to electro-weak unification was $SU(2)_L \times U(1)$ where L stands for left handed. In this model the photon is not directly identified as the $U(1)$ messenger. Instead one interprets the $U(1)$ messengers as a particle called the B. The B and the W_0 are not observed in nature. One then regards the photon as well as the Z_0 as physically observable combinations or mixtures of these unobservable particles (electro-weak mixing). Application of spontaneous symmetry breaking to this gauge symmetry then leads to a prediction about the masses of the W^+, W^- and Z_0 particles (the symbols $\pm$ and 0 refer to the electric charge on these particles). The two W particles are oppositely charged, and have an identical mass. As shown by Weinberg, theory predicts their mass as being about 80 times that of the proton. The electrically neutral Z_0 is predicted to be about 90 times heavier than the proton. Further the existence of the Z_0 implied the existence of hitherto unobserved processes known as neutral current processes i.e. when a particle emits or absorbs a Z_0 its charge does not change (charge must be conserved in every emission or absorption).

When the theory was first presented in 1967-68 it remained completely ignored. As Sidney Coleman put it

"Rarely has so great an accomplishment been so widely ignored".[5] For almost three years not a single paper cited the work of Weinberg and Salam. In fact Gordon Fraser[6] has given the following count of the number of citations the Weinberg paper: 1967, 0: 1968, 0: 1969, 0: 1970, 1. He writes: "Weinberg was not even referring to his paper and the single hit in 1970 was Salam!"

There were several reasons for this neglect. A major cause of this neglect was aesthetic. There is a sort of implicit but deep conviction shared by most great physicists that the physical laws must be 'simple' and 'beautiful'

[5]Professor Sir David Wallace, who did his Ph.D. with Peter Higgs, told me in 1979 that even Peter Higgs had failed to notice the important paper of Steven Weinberg in which he had carried out electro-weak unification. Professor Wallace was appointed Tait Professor of Mathematical Physics and Head of the Physics Department at Edinburgh University in the latter part of 1979, just as I was about to leave. He replaced Salam's supervisor Professor Kemmer. Talking to me (I was just a graduate student) in the Library of the James Clerk Maxwell Building, which housed the Department of Physics and Astronomy along with a few others, he remarked that while he was a Ph.D. student under Peter Higgs he was referred to a paper right next to Weinberg's paper in *Physical Review Letters* but not to the Weinberg paper. Professor Wallace remained Head of the Physics Department till 1993, then became Vice Chancellor, Loughborough University, and Director of Institute of Mathematical Sciences as well as well as N.M. Rothschild & Sons Professor of Mathematical Physics at Cambridge in 2006.

[6]Gordon Fraser: *Cosmic Anger: Abdus Salam The First Muslim Nobel Laureate*; Oxford University Press, 2008, p 220.

whatever that means. The actual mathematical expression for the theory was neither simple nor aesthetically appealing. Tom Kibble recalled his first impressions of Weinberg's 1967 paper years later, after the theory had been vindicated, "It was very intriguing that one could do something like this, but it was such an extra ordinarily adhoc and ugly theory that it was clearly nonsense". Even Weinberg used the phrase "repulsive" for his theory in the year 1971!

However the major reason for lack of interest in the theory concerned renormalisability. Both Salam and Weinberg had expressed the belief that the theory was renormalisable i.e. it would yield finite answers to all levels of precision when exactly solved. Coleman has remarked that Salam "even gave the kernel of a correct argument for his belief". This argument was presented in response to a question at the end of the talk in which Salam presented his theory (during the 1968 Nobel Symposium in Gotenburg, Sweden).

It was in 1971 that a 24 year old Dutch student 't Hooft proved that the theory was renormalisable. It is interesting to observe that Weinberg, as he admitted in his Nobel Prize lecture in 1979, had been grappling quietly, but relentlessly, with the problem of renormalisability of the theory. Yet it was not the accomplished Weinberg, but a research student in a different continent, who succeeded in solving the problem. Almost twenty years earlier, Salam, at almost the same age as 't Hooft, had done for meson theories what 't Hooft did for the electro-weak theory! Except that Salam did everything analytically, without any help from computers.

Once the theory was shown to be renormalisable experimentalists pounced upon it. The change in attitude towards the theory is eloquently described by Coleman's phrase "'t Hooft's work turned the Weinberg - Salam frog into an enchanted prince". The first significant test was the discovery of the predicted, and hitherto unobserved, neutral current processes. All processes involving the weak nuclear force known until 1973 were such that when a neutrino or anti - neutrino (these carry only the weak charge) interacted with a proton or neutron it altered their electric charge (a proton would become a neutron or vice versa) getting transformed in the process into an electrically charged particle, the electron or mu meson or their anti particles (the mu meson, also called muon, is a kind of heavy electron). These purely weak interaction processes involving the transformation, upon interaction, of a neutrino into a mu meson were called charged current processes. The question was whether or not a neutrino could interact with a particle through its weak charge without getting altered in the process? These so called neutral current processes were not allowed in Fermi's theory of the weak force. But the Glashow-Salam-Weinberg theory allowed these because of the existence of Z_0. If one refers back to part (B) above, and subsequent sections, one can see that of the three particles, W^+, W^- and Z_0, the first two cause charged current processes while the last one is responsible for neutral current processes. These processes are very difficult to observe experimentally because experimental techniques can only observe electrically charged particles conveniently.

Experiments carried at the giant accelerator laboratory at the European Centre for Nuclear Research (CERN) confirmed the existence of neutral current processes in 1973. In his Nobel Prize lecture Salam narrates:

> I still remember Paul Matthews and I getting off the train at Aix-en-Provence for the 1973 European Conference and foolishly deciding to walk with our rather heavy luggage to the student hostel where we were billeted. A car drove from behind us, stopped, and the man at the wheel leaned out. This was Musset whom I did not know personally well then. He peered out of the window and said 'Are you Salam?' I said 'Yes'. He said 'Get in to the car. I have news for you. We have found neutral currents'.

Once neutral currents were discovered experiments to test other implications of the theory were carried out. In every case there was complete agreement between theory and experiment, a situation which persists even today after more and more stringent tests have been carried out. Certain delicate and precise measurements at the Stanford Linear Accelerator Centre (SLAC) in 1978 confirmed the theory to an extent that it became possible to award the 1979 Nobel Prize in Physics to Glashow, Salam and Weinberg for their contributions to electro-weak unification.

The most important prediction of the theory was the existence of the three electro-weak force messengers, W^+, W^-, and Z_0 whose masses were predicted by the theory. Since these were very heavy particles their discovery had to await the construction of powerful accelerator machines where colliding particles would have enough spare energy which could congeal into these massive particles. This decisive discovery was made in 1983 by a team of experimentalists at CERN. The Italian physicist Carlo Rubbia and the Dutch Van der Meer were awarded the 1984 Nobel Prize for this discovery. The discovery was similar to the historic discovery, in 1888, by Hertz, of electromagnetic waves, which were predicted by Maxwell as a consequence of his unification of the electric and magnetic forces. By analogy one talks of electro-weak waves whose energy is transmitted by the three messengers mentioned above.

The electro-weak unification carried out in the period 1960-70 was applicable only to leptons - particles like the electron, neutrino, the mu meson, and their anti-particles. Leptons do not feel the strong nuclear force. The bulk of visible matter in the universe however is made out of hadrons, particles like the neutron, proton and many others which feel the strong nuclear force. Hadrons, it must be borne in mind, respond to the weak nuclear force as well.

The incorporation of hadrons into the scheme of electro-weak unification had to wait until the work of Glashow, Iliopolous and Maiani (GIM) in 1970. This work in turn could not have been done without a knowledge of the inner structure of hadrons (leptons do not, as far as we know, appear to possess inner structure - they are 'point' particles which under the gaze of the most powerful microscopes do not reveal any substructure or spatial extension. In this sense leptons are truly 'elementary' particles). Let us therefore briefly sum up the situation concerning the substructure of hadrons.

As a result of the construction of accelerators (giant machines known popularly as atom smashers - these are in fact the 'microscopes' of particle hunters) many new hadrons were observed in the 1950s in particular. Their number steadily proliferated and during the 1960s over a hundred hadrons were known. A feeling therefore developed among physicists that hadrons might be made out of other particles is intuitively unacceptable. Salam once summed up this intuitive feeling in an Orwellian phrase adapted to particle physics - "All particles are elementary but some are more elementary than others".

In 1964 Gell-Mann, and independently Zweig, proposed the idea that all hadrons were built out of only three types (flavors) of more elementary entities called up, down and strange[7] quarks. With these one could account for the properties of all known hadrons. Not only that one could predict the existence of new ones with definite values of charge, spin, etc. During the 1960s it appeared certain that three flavors of quarks were enough to explain the properties of all known hadrons.

In a remarkably prescient paper, published in 1964, Glashow and Bjorken speculated on the existence of a fourth quark. Their motivation was aesthetic - if quarks and leptons are the fundamental entities of nature, then there should be a parallelism between them. If the number of leptons is four (4 leptons were known then - the electron, muon and two types of neutrinos) then the number of quarks should also be four. Bjorken and Glashow named the fourth quark charmed or c quark.

It turned out later that the idea of equality of the number of quarks and leptons is highly important (it does not matter whether they are 4 or 6, etc) when one tries to adapt the electro-weak theory for leptons to quarks. Us-

[7]The quarks are denoted by symbols, using the first letters of their names. The up, down, strange and charmed quarks are denoted as u, d, s and c respectively.

ing this idea Glashow, Iliopolous and Maiani (GIM) were able to get rid of certain inconsistencies in the electro-weak model proposed for leptons and quarks. The model predicted the existence of a certain class of processes (called SCNC - strangeness changing neutral currents) that were known not to exist. The fourth quark got rid of these bringing agreement between theory and experiment regarding the non existence of SCNC process. In November 1974 new hadrons containing the charmed quark were observed in experiments partly carried out as a result of the prodding of Glashow who persuaded the experimentalists to look for these hadrons (the discovery of charm is known as the November Revolution in Particle Physics!).

With the discovery of the fourth quark the electro-weak theory attained a logical consistency. The scenario, at that time (1974), was as follows: there are 4 leptons (electron, muon, two neutrinos) and 4 quarks (up, down, strange, charmed). All these are point particles. All quarks and leptons can interact 'electro-weakly' and their electro-weak interactions obey the gauge symmetry $SU_(2)_L \times U(1)$. This essentially means that quarks as well as leptons come in pairs of two each and that the W^+, W^- and Z_0 and the photon are the electro-weak messengers. Further the number of lepton pairs must equal the number of quarks. In its present day version we have three lepton pairs (two leptons called the tau and tau neutrino have been added to the list) and three quark pairs (two more quarks known as the top and the bottom have been added). The top quark was observed in the mid 1990s.

The single missing piece of the theory was the Higgs particle. The discovery of the Higgs particle was announced at CERN on July 4th 2012. The search for the Higgs spanned almost three decades during which physicists at Fermilab USA and at CERN literally combed a wide energy range systematically to pin down the Higgs. It would be fair to say that the amount of effort and money spent in searching for the Higgs has not been spent on any other particle in the history of physics. It is important to note that the three messengers the$W^{\pm}$ and the Z_0 were discovered in 1983. Almost three decades were to elapse before the Higgs could be nailed down. The difficulty had to do with the fact that the mass of the Higgs was unknown a-priori.

Salam was jointly awarded the 1979 physics Nobel Prize with Glashow and Weinberg. At the time they had carried out the unification work both, Glashow and Weinberg, worked at Harvard. Salam's community had been declared non-muslim by an act of the Parliament under Z.A. Bhutto. Hence the Zia-ul-Haq regime was very cautious in its response to this unprecedented honor won by a Pakistani citizen, partly out of fear of annoying the religious orthodoxy. The reaction of the Pakistani authorities has been summed up by Salam's friend K.K.

Aziz in his book:[8]

> Immediately after the news of his Nobel Prize was published in October the Government of India invited him to tour the country. There was no reaction from Pakistan until the Pakistan High Commissioner in London informed his government of India's invitation. Only then did the Government of Pakistan ask him to visit his home country. Salam decided to visit Pakistan first and India a year later.
> In December 1979, on his arrival in Lahore, Peshawar and Islamabad he was received by junior army officers who were military secretaries to the provincial governors and the President. The convocation of the Quaid-i-Azam University in Islamabad summoned to bestow on him the honorary Doctorate of Science was canceled because of the warning from the students belonging to the right-wing Jam'at-i-Islami to disrupt the function, and the venue was shifted to the hall of the National Assembly.[9] In Lahore his lecture ar-

[8]K.K. Aziz: *The Coffee House of Lahore - A Memoir 1942-57*; Sang e Meel Publishers, 2008, p 207, 208.

[9]General Zia-ul-Haq, being President of the country, was, at that time, the Chancellor of the Qauid-i-Azam University and the degree could not have been awarded without his consent.

> ranged to be held at the campus of the Punjab University had to be moved to the Senate Hall in the city because certain groups had demonstrated a day earlier and threatened to murder Salam. The University of the Punjab refused to honor him with a degree.[10] The Government College did not invite him even to visit its precinct.

He met Zia-ul-Haq on this visit and, as Professor Salam once said to me, Zia expressed his pride and happiness at the award. He also told me that during the meeting he had requested Zia-ul-Haq not to ban the magazine *Al-Fazal* published by his community. Salam told me that Zia-ul-Haq said that the magazine would not be banned and he, as Professor Salam told me, "kept his word." In the 1980s and 1990s he received honorary degrees from four Indian universities among others. Indira Gandhi invited Salam to her residence, made coffee for him with her own hands, and sat on the carpet saying that it was her way of honoring him.[11]

In one sense the reaction to Salam's Nobel Prize in Pakistan was not dissimilar to the reaction in Germany,

[10]The Univeristy of the Punjab (spelt as Panjab at that time) had already awarded Salam an honorary doctorate in 1957, the first ever honorary degree to be bestowed on him.

[11]K.K. Aziz: *The Coffee House of Lahore - A Memoir 1942-57*; Sang e Meel Publishers, 2008, p 208.

to the award of the Nobel Prize to the Jewish Albert Einstein in 1923[12] - the bigoted element attacked Einstein in Germany just as Salam was attacked in Pakistan. There was another similarity - both, the German press, and the Pakistani press played a positive role in covering Einstein and Salam respectively. The press coverage and the comments in both cases were overwhelmingly positive except an occasional comment by some bigot.

While the highest civilian award, the Order of Nishan-i-Imtiaz, was conferred on Salam in 1979, the overall attitude of the administration of the country was unbecoming of any self respecting administration. The failure of the administration to hold the ceremonies and functions where they should have been held was shameful. It simply backed off before the noise of intolerance when it should have persuaded the noise-makers with firmness and clarity. The administration should have realized that the Quran has clearly enjoined that there shall be no compulsion in matters of religion. This point should have been raised with those who were unhappy with Salam's community. Regardless of the religious factor, Salam was a Pakistani, who had earned respect for the country, and who, despite repeated rejections by the authorities, refused to give up his nationality.

[12]See e.g. Mujahid Kamran: *Einstein and Germany*, Sang e Meel Publishers, 2009, 2012 and references cited therein.

Chapter 11

Other Contributions

As soon as electro-weak unification was carried out leading physicists began attempts at unifying the strong nuclear force with the electro-weak force; electro-nuclear force as Salam called it. As Tom Kibble, one of the foremost physicists of his generation, put it in a talk in 1993:

> His real goal was always to find the ultimate theory that would describe the weak, electromagnetic and strong interactions, and even gravity - what we would now call a theory of everything. ⋯
>
> And, of course Salam went on to even greater unification, for example in his work with Pati on lepton-hadron unification and with Strathdee on supersymmetry and su-

perfields and on Kaluza-Klien theory; I could mention many others.

Foremost among those who led the movement for a broader unification of the fundamental forces of nature were Salam and Pati, and Georgi and Glashow. In attempting the electro-nuclear synthesis Salam and Pati introduced a very bold idea. Instead of regarding quarks and leptons as fundamentally distinct entities they put them together in a single family, or multiplet as it is technically called. Such a scheme then allows a quark to convert into a lepton once in a while because transitions between members of a multiplet are allowed. Since a proton is made out of quarks this led to the thrilling possibility that a proton could decay into something else giving rise to leptons in the process - in other words it could decay with leptons in the decay products. This was a sensational idea as a proton is considered to be the most stable of hadrons and its decay would destroy the feeling of permanence associated with it.

The proton lifetime predicted by Grand Unified Theories (GUTS) is about ten billion billion billion, or equivalently, ten thousand trillion trillion (10^{28}) years. Experiments conducted thus far have failed to detect proton decay with such a lifetime - if the proton decays it does so with a lifetime much longer than that predicted by current versions of GUTS. But proton decay is a fascinating possibility which we owe to Pati and Salam who first conceived it.

Pati has described the essence of this work in the following words[1]:

> Together, we introduced the idea of an underlying unity of quarks and leptons and simultaneously, of their weak, electromagnetic and strong gauge forces. Believing in SU(4) color symmetry for quark-lepton unification and seeking a compelling reason for quantization of electric charge, we introduced the concept of left-right symmetry. This in turn led us to predict the existence of right handed neutrinos accompanying the left-handed ones - a prediction that now plays a part in proposed solutions to the solar neutrino puzzle and in theories of dark matter.

Jogesh Pati has described the human side of his collaboration with Salam in an interesting paragraph. Writing for *Physics Today* (August 1977 issue) Pati states:

> During our collaboration Salam always reacted to our occasional disagreements with a good-natured spirit. If he were greatly excited about an idea I did not like, he would impatiently

[1]Pati, J.C. Obituaries Abdus Salam, *Physics Today*, August 1997.

> ask, "My dear Sir, what do you want? Blood?" I would reply, "No Professor Salam, I would like something better." Whether I was right or wrong, he never took it ill.

Salam has also made important contributions to supersymmetry (SUSY) and to String Theory in his search for the ultimate synthesis of electro-weak, strong nuclear and gravitational forces. As remarked by N.S. Craigie, Salam and Strathdee's formulation of supersymmetry in terms of superalgebra is the most elegant. Supersymmetry is essentially a symmetry which enables physicists to connect particles that carry integer units of spin (i.e. 0, 1, 2, units) with those carrying half odd integer (i.e. 1/2, 3/2, 5/2, etc) units of spin. The two categories have always been considered as being distinct in some profound way.

Peter West has described his interaction with Salam as a Ph.D. student working on supersymmetry. He states:[2]

> I carried out my doctorate studies at Imperial College and had the good fortune to have Abdus Salam as my supervisor. When I began research, the paper of Wess and Zumino had induced many of Europe' leading physicists to work on supersymmetry and Abdus Salam

[2]Reproduced in *Science for Peace and Progress: Life and Work of Abdus Salam* compiled by Anwar Dil, publishers Intercultural Forum, San Diego and Islamabad (iforum@aol.com), 2008, p 499.

and John Strathdee had written their classic paper discovering superspace and super-Feymman rules. With such rapid progress being made it was not easy for a graduate student to achieve anything of significance, but despite many commitments Abdus Salam was always ready to give helpful advice and encouragement. It was impossible not to be infected by his great enthusiasm for new ideas and the enjoyment he derived from doing physics. One came away from his office feeling that all was possible and that failure was only a temporary phenomenon.

Although it had been understood how to break supersymmetry using the classical potential, it was though more desirable if it could be broken using radiative corrections. Abdus Salam characteristically encouraged Bob Delbourgo and myself to systematically examine every possibility. He also, however, advocated that if all else failed one could always tell the truth. In this case, as I eventually found the truth was that if supersymmetry was preserved classically then the effective potential vanished. It was this theorem which allowed others to observe that supersymmetry solved the technical hierarchy problem.

Salam also contributed to String Theory which envisions one dimensional objects of incredibly small size (strings) as the basic objects in nature instead of point particles. String theory is believed to be the most likely way of bringing Einstein's stubbornly recalcitrant theory of Gravitation within the fold of Quantum Theory.

Mike Duff was a student of Salam at Imperial. He wrote "It was inevitable that Salam would not rest until the fourth and most enigmatic force of gravity was unified with the other three." In a very interesting tribute to Salam at Puri, India in December 1996, Duff stated that Salam had aroused his interest in the Quantum Theory of Gravity at a time when the subject was pursued "only by mad dogs and Englishmen". Duff's Ph.D. work resulted from a bet between Herman Bondi and Salam as to whether one could generate the Schwarzchild radius using Feynman diagrams. Salam won the bet as Duff was able to prove that indeed one could.

In the last phase of his productive life Salam developed an interest in the application of physics, rather particle physics, to the problem of origin of life. It was Schrodinger, one of the founders of quantum mechanics, a mechanics that deals successfully with atoms and molecules, who wrote a seminal book with the title *What is Life* in 1944. It was this book that led to researches into the molecular basis of life. Salam wrote two papers, one in 1991 and the other in 1992, with the respective titles

The Role of Chirality in the Origin of Life and *Chirality, Phase Transitions and Their Induction in Amino Acids*. The first of these appeared in the Journal of Molecular Evolution and the latter in Physics Letters B. He felt that this work could become important - he told me so himself. In his lecture titled *Physics and Life*, the noted writer Paul C. Davies states:[3]

> All this is well and good, but is physics relevant to life's specific and peculiar properties? One person who was convinced that physics plays a direct role in life, at least in its genesis, was Abdus Salam, in whose honor this paper is delivered. His work on molecular chirality was a bold attempt to trace the well-known handedness of biological molecules to parity violation in electroweak interactions, a subject he himself founded. If this link is correct, it provides a key biological role for one of the most fundamental aspects of particle physics.

How did Salam drift in this direction? It is difficult to say. His illustrious friend and contemporary Freeman J. Dyson also had some interest in the relation of physics and life. It is however not unlikely that his interest in

[3]Paul C. Davies: *Physics and Life*; in *The First Steps of Life in the Universe* Proceedings of the Sixth Trieste Conference on Chemical Evolution. Trieste, Italy, 18-22 September.

the relation between life and physics could have been triggered because his English wife Louise Johnson was a biophysicist. She eventually rose to the position of a Professor of biophysics at Oxford.

Salam remained productive as long as his body supported him. Only when his illness incapacitated him physically, did he stop creating.

Abdus Salam

عبدالسلام

At his office in Trieste

The 26 years old Salam and Sir G. P. Thomson at the University of the Punjab, 1952

With Nobel Laureate Francis Crick, 1968

ICTP's first scientific Council, IAEA, Vienna, 1964, chaired by R. Oppenheimer (right)

Left to right; Glashow, Salam and Weimberg at 1979 Nobel Prize Ceremony

With the Queen at the Nobel Prize Ceremony

With Chinese Premier Chou En-Lai, 1972

Standing left to right, Shaukat Ali, Zakariya Butt, Pervez Akhtar, MSK Razmi, Mujahid Kamran

With Prof. Riazuddin

With his children in the Miramare Park, 1987

Celebrating Award of Nobel Prize at ICTP

With Nobel Laureate Sheldon L. Glashow, 1986

With Paolo Budinich and Nobel Laureate Carlo Rubbia, 1984

With Javier Perez de Cuellar, Secretary-General of the United Nations, 1985

With A. Zichichi and Ed Witten

Budinich and Salam at the 1960 Trieste Conference

Salam with Fred Hoyle, 1985

With Rexhep Meidani, ICTP Associate and later President of Albania, 1987

With Philosopher Karl R. Popper, 1983

Salam, Bhutto and Munir

With Football Team in Lahore

Chapter 12

Science and Religion

Abdus Salam had a deep interest in the relationship between Science and Religion. He was always an avid reader but while at Cambridge he delved more deeply into religion, science and history, utilizing the excellent library facilities. Once he had established himself as a scientist of the highest calibre he began expressing himself more frequently on the relationship between science and religion. He was also deeply concerned with the question of as to whether the Muslims had contributed significantly to science. This question was of great importance for him, and for the contemporary Islamic world.

12.1 Science versus Religion

The fundamental question is as to whether science and religion are on a collision course? Is the entire Universe with all its laws and its spiritual aspects, a subject only for science? Can science cover all these areas? Or are there areas that remain and are likely to remain beyond the ken of science? Will science supplant religion? Or is it possible for science and religion to complement each other? Speaking at a conference organized by the Giovanni Agnelli Foundation at Turin, Italy in 1988 he stated:[1]

> I have divided my talk into three parts. First, I wish to consider an issue raised by my esteemed colleagues - some of whom are Nobel Laureates - who have opined that "Science is the creation of the Western, democratic, Judeo-Christian religion." I disagree with them and I will explain why. Secondly, I would like to reflect - in the context of the three Abrahamic religions (Judaism, Christianity, Islam) - on the topic we have been

[1] M. Abdus Salam: *Renaissance of Science in Islamic Countries*; Editors: H. R. Dalafi and M. H. A. Hassan; World Scientific Publishers 1994. The talk from which we have quoted is reproduced in this book and is titled *Scientific Thinking - Between the Secularisation and the Transcendent An Islamic Viewpoint*, p 133-162.

> asked to speak on, i.e., Scientific Thinking (as a bridge) between Secularisation and the Transcendent. (I shall not speak about the high traditions of the three non-Abrahamic world-creeds - Hinduism, Buddhism, Confucianism. This is simply because of ignorance.) Thirdly I shall speak on the question - why am I a believer?

Salam then addressed the broad question as to whether Science is anti-religion and vice versa? "Is this correct?" he asks. He then states:

> Now if there is one hallmark of true science, if there is one perception that scientific knowledge heightens, it is the spirit of wonder; the deeper one goes, the more profound one's insight, the more is one's sense of wonder increased. This sentiment was expressed in eloquent verse by Faiz Ahmad Faiz: "Moved by the mystery it evokes, many a time have I dissected the heart of the smallest particle. But this eye of wonder; its wonder-sense is never assuaged!"
>
> In this context Einstein, the most famous scientist of our century has written: "The most beautiful experience we can have is of the mysterious. Whoever does not know it and

> can no longer wonder, no longer marvel, is as good as dead, and his eyes are dimmed. It was the experience of mystery - even if mixed with fear - that engendered religion. A knowledge of the existence of something we cannot penetrate, our perceptions of the profoundest reason and the most radiant beauty, which in only in their most primitive forms are accessible to our minds - it is this knowledge and this emotion that constitute true religiosity; in this sense, and in this alone, I am a religious man."

Einstein was Jewish by birth and considered himself religious in his outlook about the mystery of existence in a bewildering universe of unimaginable immensity, as may be inferred from the above quote cited by Salam. Taking a broad view of the stance of the Abrahamic religions about the question of meaning of the universe and human life, i.e. the "transcendent" aspects, Salam states:

> These religions speak of a Lord who not only created (1) Natural Law and the Universe in His Glory, His own Holiness and His Majesty; but also created *us*, the human beings, in His own image, endowing us not only with speech, but also with spiritual life and spiritual longings. This is one aspect of transcendence. (2)

> The second aspect of the Lord is who answers prayers when one turns to Him in distress. (3) The third is of the Lord who, in the eyes of the Mystic and the Sufi, personifies eternal beauty and is to be adored for this. These transcendent aspects of religion as a rule lead to a heightening of one's obligation towards living beings. (4) The fourth is the Lord who endows some humans - the prophets and His chosen saints - with divinely inspired knowledge through revelation.

Having summed up the viewpoint about man, life and the universe as propounded by the Abrahamic religions Salam then goes on to what he calls the "societal" or "secularist" aspects of these religions. These he lists as:

> (1) The Lord who is also the Guardian of the Moral Law - the precept which states that "Like one does, one shall be done by"; (2) The Lord who gives a meaning to the history of mankind - the rise and fall of nations for disobedience to His commandments; (3) the Lord who specifies what should be human belief as well as ideal conduct of human affairs; (4) and finally the Lord who rewards one's good deeds and punishes wrong-doing (like a Father), in this world or in a life hereafter.

Having outlined the transcendental and secularist (or "societal") viewpoint of the Abrahamic religions Salam then comments:

> While many scientists in varying degrees do subscribe to the first three aspects of transcendentalism, not many subscribe to the "societal" aspects of religiosity.

Salam then proceeds to sum up what he calls "The Three Viewpoints of Science". These he calls the "religious and transcendental" attitude such as that of Einstein, the "anthropic" and the "self-consistent" viewpoint in which there is no room for God. He states:

> Let us start with Natural law which governs the Universe. There are scientists who will take issue with Einstein's view that there is a sublime beauty about the laws of nature and that the deepest (religious) feelings of man spring from the sense of wonder evoked by this beauty. These scientists would instead like to deduce the laws of nature from a self-consistency and "naturalness" principle, which made the universe come into being spontaneously. This should need something like the doctrine of spontaneous creation of life and its Darwinian evolution - only now carried to the realm of all laws of nature and

> the whole Universe. If successful, this, in their view, would lead to the irrelevance of a deity. Man's spiritual dimension, so called, would be nothing but a manifestation of physiological processes inside the human brain (not fully understood at present), but their hope would be that a molecular basis would one day be discovered for this. Contrasting with this is the view of the anthropic scientist who believes the Universe was created purposefully with such attributes and in such a manner that sentient beings could arise.

Salam emphasizes the limitations of science. He states that there are "*questions which are beyond the ken of present (or even future) sciences.*" Science owes its success to having limited itself to certain types of inquiry. Regarding questions beyond the scope of present day science he states:

> We may speculate about them, but there would be no way to verify empirically our metaphysical speculations. And it is empirical verification that is the essence of modern science ⋯ The scientist of today knows when and where he is speculating; he would claim no finality for associated modes of thought. And about accepted facts, we recognize that newer facts

> may be discovered which, without falsifying the earlier discoveries, may lead to generalizations; in turn, necessitating, revolutionary changes in our "concepts" and "world-view".

Salam makes an interesting comment on modern scientific ideas about cosmo-genesis which postulate that the universe was created out of nothing and about the possibility that the universe may not be four dimensional as believed by established physics, but ten dimensional. He writes:

> Creation from nothing, extra and hidden dimensions - strange topics for late twentieth century physics - which appear no different from metaphysical preoccupations of earlier times; however they are all driven by a self-consistency principle. So far as Physics is concerned, mark the insistence of physical verification at each stage.
>
> For the agnostic, self-consistency (if successful) may connote irrelevance for a deity; for the believer it provides no more than an unraveling of a small part of the Lord's design - its profundity - in the areas it illuminates, it only enhances his reverence for the beauty of the design itself.

He also emphasizes that "One of the most difficult questions which the self-consistent scientist has to to answer is - 'Why this decree?'"

Salam quotes the following lines from Heinz Pagels about a fascinating experience of the physics Nobel Laureate Richard P. Feynman, one of the most important physicists of the twentieth century:

> He was in a sensory-deprivation tank and had an exosomatic experience - he felt that he "came out of his body" lying before him. To test the reality of his experience, he tried moving his arm, and indeed he saw his arm on his body move. As he described this, he said he then became concerned that he might remain out of his body and decided to return to it. After he concluded his story, I asked him what he made of his unusual experience. Feynman replied with the observational precision of a true scientist: "I didn't see no laws of physics being violated."

Salam then adds:

> I have myself never seen any dichotomy between my faith and my science - since faith was predicated for me by the timeless spiritual message of Islam, on matters on which

> *Physics is silent and will remain so.*[2] It was given meaning to me by the very first verse of the Quran after the opening
> "*This is the Book*
> *Wherein there is no doubt,*
> *A guidance for the God-fearing,*
> *Who believe in the Unseen.*"
> "The Unseen", "Beyond the reach of human ken"; "The Unknowable; ···

12.2 Science: Whose Legacy?

Salam was deeply concerned with the question as to whether Science is the sole creation of the Western world, as emphasized by many writers, or have other civilizations contributed to science significantly. He was also interested in the question of the contribution of the Islamic Civilization to science. As he writes:[3]

> Science and Technology are cyclical. They are the shared heritage of all mankind. East and West, South and North have all equally participated in their creation in the past, as, we

[2]Italics in original.

[3]Abdus Salam: *Science, Technology and Science Education in the Development of the South; prepared for the South Commission*, 1991; The Third World Academy of Sciences.

> hope, they will in the future - the joint endeavor in Sciences becoming one of the unifying forces among the diverse peoples on this globe.

In the same piece he also states:

> The first thing to realize about the Science and Technology gap between the South and the North is that it is of relatively recent origin. In respect of Sciences, George Sarton, in his monumental History of Science, chose to divide his story of achievement into Ages, each age lasting half a century. With each half-century he associated one central figure. Thus 450-400 B.C. Sarton calls the Age of Plato; this is followed by half century of Aristotle, of Euclid, of Archimedes and so on. These were scientists from the Greek Commonwealth consisting (in addition to the Greeks) of Egyptians, Southern Italians and ancestors of modern Syrians and Turks.
> From 600 AD to 650 AD in Sarton's recount is the Chinese half-century of Hsiian Tsang. From 650 to 700 AD is the age of I-Ching and the Indian mathematician, Brahmagupta, followed by the ages of Jabir, Khwarizmi, Razi, Masudi, Wafa, Biruni, and then Omar Khayam - Chinese, Hindus, Arabs, Persians, Turks

> and Afghans - an unbroken Third World succession for 500 years. After 1100 the first Western names begin to appear; Gerard of Cremona, Roger Bacon and others - but the honors are shared for another 250 years with the Third World men of science like Ibn-Rushd, Naseer-ud-din Tusi, Musa bin Maimoun and Sultan Ulugh Beg.

He then cites a similar situation in regard to the history of Technology. He refers to technology transfer from the East to West:

> Charles Singer, in the Epilogue to the second volume of *A History of Technology*, discussed some of these points ··· Referring to the Eurocentrism of Western historians, Singer wrote: "Europe however, is but a small peninsula extending from the great land masses of Afrasia. This is indeed its geographical status and this, until at least the thirteenth century, was generally also its technological status." In skill and inventiveness during most of the period 500 to 1500 AD, Singer continues, "The Near East was superior to the West ··· For nearly all branches of Technology the best products available to the West were those of the Near East ··· Technologically, the West had little

> to bring to the East. The technological movement was in the other direction."

He points out that it is only around 1450 does the Third World begin to lose out, except for the occasional flash of brilliance. The crucial thing to note in regard to the subject of this chapter is that from 750-1100 AD there are seven unbroken ages named after Muslim scientists, followed by several others. In his Agnelli Foundation lecture cited earlier in this chapter, as well as in several other writings, Salam emphasized that this outburst of scientific brilliance in the Islamic world that lasted for several centuries was the direct result of Quranic injunctions. In the Giovanni Agnelli Foundation lecture Salam comments:

> How seriously did the Muslims take these injunctions in the Holy Quran and of the Holy Prophet?
>
> Barely a hundred years after the Prophet's death, the Muslims had made it their task to master the then-known sciences. Founding institutes of advanced study (*Bait-ul-Hikmas*), they acquired an ascendancy in the sciences and technology that lasted up to around 1450 AD when Constantinople fell to the technologically superior Turkish cannonade.

In an earlier contribution prepared for the United Nations University Symposium at Kuwait in 1981, Salam had stated:

> The reason why Muslims searched for and developed sciences in their Golden Age in the eight, ninth, tenth and eleventh centuries is not hard to seek. They were following the repeated injunctions of the Holy Book and the Holy Prophet. According to Dr. Muhammad Aijaz ul Khatib of Damascus University, nothing can emphasize the science more than the remark "in contrast to 250 verses which are legislative, some 750 verses of the Holy Quran - almost one eighth of it - exhort the believers to study Nature, to reflect, to make the best use of reason and to make the scientific enterprise an integral part of the Community's life."

He then goes on to quote Robert Briffault:[4]

[4]Salam cites from Iqbal who quotes Briffault. However in this book, which in my days as a Ph.D. student a Edinburgh in the second half of the 1970s, had to obtained on inter-library loan (I was at Edinburgh University, Scotland, UK), was published in the earlier part of the twentieth century. Robert Briffault: *The Making of Humanity*; The book has been translated into Urdu by Abdul Majeed Salik as *Tashkeel e Insanyat.*

> The Greeks systematized, generalized and theorized, but the patient ways of detailed and prolonged observation and experimental inquiry were altogether alien to the Greek temperament ··· What we call science arose as a result of new methods of experiment, observation, and measurement, which were introduced into Europe by the Arabs ··· (Modern) Science is the most momentous contribution of the Islamic Civilization ···

In fact Briffault also emphasizes that a systematic and deep attempt has been made to destroy the sources which reveal the profound influence of the Islamic Civilization on the West. He then adds that despite this, the surviving sources reveal the great impact of the Islamic Civilization on the West. It is generally seen that in most histories of scientific knowledge many historians jump from the Greek and Roman ages to the Renaissance. The intervening period is left in complete dark. The dark ages is the period that Sarton and Briffault and Salam and some others (in the West) point out as a glorious period of the contribution of the Islamic Civilization to Science. As Salam states:

> The Golden Age of Science in Islam was doubtless the Age around 1000 AD, the age of Ibn-i-Sina (Avicenna), the last of the medievalists, and of his contemporaries, the first of

the moderns, Ibn-al-Haitham and Al Biruni.
Ibn-al-Haitham (Alhazen, 965-1039 AD) was one of the greatest physicists of all time. He made experimental contributions of the highest order in optics. He "enunciated that a ray of light, in passing though a medium, takes a path which is the easier and the 'quickest'". In this, he was anticipating Fermat's Principle of Least Time by many centuries. He enunciated the law of inertia - later, and independently - to become part of Galileo's and Newton's laws of motion. He was the first man to conceive of the Aswan Dam though he was unable to build it because the technology of the time could not keep up with his ideas (he had to feign madness in order to escape the wrath of the Fatmid Caliph, Al Hakim of Egypt, for having proposed the idea of the dam and NOT actually building it.).
Al Biruni (973-1048 AD), Ibn-i-Sina's second illustrious contemporary worked in today's Afghanistan. He was an empirical scientist like Ibn-al-Haitham; as modern and unmedieval in outlook as Galileo six centuries later.[5]

[5]In his Dirac Memorial Lecture delivered at Cambridge in 1988 Salam specifically mentioned Al Biruni in the context the Galilean Principle. He stated:"The first name I would like to mention in

One of the misleading arguments put forward by many authors, who probably wish to belittle the achievements and contributions of the Islamic Civilization to Science, is that the Muslim contribution was a "derived" science, borrowed from the Greeks, or obtained by following the Greek theoretical tradition blindly. While the work of men like George Sarton, Robert Briffault and many other Western historians is enough to rebut such a claim, one may also cite Salam on the subject. About such an argument or statement he writes:

> This statement is false. Listen to the assessment of Aristotle by Al Biruni: "The trouble with most people is their extravagance in respect of Aristotle's opinions; they believe that there is no possibility of mistakes in his views, though they know that he was theorizing to the best of his capacity." Or Al Biruni on medieval superstition. "People say that on the 6th (of January) there is an hour during which all salt water of the earth gets sweet. Since all these qualities occurring in water depend

this context is that of Al Biruni who flourished in Afghanistan as a likely place where high class physics could be done. Al Biruni however, to my knowledge, was the first physicist to say explicitly that physical phenomena on the Sun, Earth and the Moon obey the same laws. Abdus Salam: *Unification of Fundamental Forces*; Cambridge University Press, 1990; p 7,8. The lecture notes were compiled by Jonathan Evans and Gerard Watts.

> exclusively on the nature of the soil ⋯ these qualities are of a stable nature ⋯ Therefore this statement ⋯ is entirely unfounded. Continual and leisurely experimentation will show to anyone the futility of this assertion."

He then quotes Al Biruni on geology "with his insistence on observation":

> But if you see the soil of India with your own eyes and meditate on its nature, if you consider the rounded stones found near the mountains and in the earth however deeply you dig, stones that are huge near the mountains and where the rivers have a violent current; stones that are of smaller size at a greater distance from the mountains and where the streams flow more slowly; stones that appear pulverized in the shape of sand where the streams begin to stagnate near their mouths and near the sea - if you consider all this you can scarcely help thinking that India was once a sea, which by degrees has been filled up by the alluvium of streams."[6]

[6] Al Biruni was the first one to assert, correctly, that a part of the Indo Pakistan subcontinent was under the sea at one time. He also measured the diameter of the earth to a very high degree of accuracy from a point (Fort Nandana) in the Salt Range moun-

Without a deep understanding of the Quran, knowledge of history and without wide reading habits Salam would not have been able to stand up to those who, through ignorance, prejudice, or for other reasons, fail to acknowledge the contributions of the Islamic Civilization to Science and also fail to see the relationship between the Quranic injunctions and the profound contributions of this civilization to the advancement of human Knowledge. Not only did he have to contend with those in the West but also with petty writers in Muslim countries who blindly followed the prejudice of some of the Western historians. Some of them appear to display a greater contempt for their heritage as compared to some Western writers.

In his essay *Renaissance of Sciences in the Arab and Islamic Lands*, a contribution for the United Nations Uni-

tains located in the province of Punjab, Pakistan. see N.A. Baloch: *Beruni and his Experiment at Nandana, District Jhelum*, p154 - 214, in his book *Lands of Pakistan Perspectives: historical and cultural*; El Mashriqi Foundation, Islamabad, 1995. Baloch points out that the difference in the measurement of earth's radius as carried out by Al Biruni and modern measurements is approximately 12 miles! This region also has the second largest salt mine in the world at Khewra, not far from where he measured the diameter of the earth. The salt mine was "discovered" by a horse belonging to Alexander the Great's army that started licking the ground as it appeared to contain salt. He spent time in this region and also wrote a book on the habits of the people of India. His book on the subject is a major sociological study.

versity Symposium at Kuwait in 1981, Salam stated:

> When I joined Cambridge as an undergraduate in 1946, I was older than my contemporary British students. I knew more science than they did. But they possessed an arrogance from belonging to a nation of Newton, Maxwell, Darwin and Dirac. Recall that in your past, too, there are men like Ibn-al-Haitham, Ibn-i-Sina, Al Biruni. Assume that you will be given all the facilities and all the resources you want for Pure and Applied Science. Assume that you will have self-governance within your communities and involvement in your society's plans of development. For those outside, assume that you will be called upon to play your designate roles in bringing the renaissance of Sciences about.

The one thing Salam emphasized throughout his writings was that scientific creativity and advancement depends on freedom within a substantially sized scientific community, regardless of the political system prevalent in a society. As he put it in the above mentioned talk:

> I am sure it is painful for some of you to hear, and painful for me to say, that excellence in sciences is dependent on the freedom and openness within the scientific community

> in any society (assuming that such a community is large enough) and NOT necessarily on the openness or democracy within the society at large.

This observation is relevant to all times, not just the modern period. In fact he attributes one of the reasons for the success of the scientific enterprise in the Islamic Civilization in the middle ages to the spirit of tolerance that resulted from Quranic injunctions and the example and sayings of the Holy Prophet. In his essay *Liberty of Scientific Belief in Islam*,[7] Salam begins by citing six verses from the Holy Quran, each emphasizing freedom of religious belief. He also quotes from speeches of the Holy Prophet and cites important incidents from history establishing that religious tolerance is one of the basic tenets of Islam. He quotes from T.W. Arnold, who in turn quotes a lament of a native Muslim driven out of Spain:

> Did our ancestors ever once attempt to extirpate Christianity out of Spain, when it was in their power? Did they not suffer your forefathers to enjoy the free use of their rites? ··· Is it not the absolute injunction of our Prophet, that whatever nation is conquered

[7]Reproduced in M. Abdus Salam: *Renaissance of Science in Islamic Countries*; Editors: H. R. Dalafi and M. H. A. Hassan; World Scientific Publishers 1994.

> by Muslims should be permitted to preserve in its own pristine persuasion ··· You can never produce among us any blood thirsty formal tribunal, on account of of different persuasions in points of faith ···"

Salam touches on persecution of non-Muslims as well as Muslims by Muslims and the decline of sciences in the Islamic civilization. He writes:

> Was there no persecution, ever of non-Muslims in Islamic lands? Regretfully there was, and particularly from the period I have reported on. This was either activated for reasons of political domination or came as a result of the fanaticism from the learned theologians concerned with what they thought of the purity of Islamic religious traditions. It is a tragedy in most religions that whatever the teachings of the their founders, these usually get perverted by later generations.
>
> However in the case of Islam there is no official clergy and any suggested repressive measures cannot always be taken as a criterion of actual practice. As Arnold remarks, it is the failure to realize this fact that accounts for the highly-colored pictures of sufferings of the non-Muslims under Islamic rule, drawn

> by writers who have assumed that the prescriptions of certain Muslim theologians represented an invariable practice.

Salam cites counter examples from the reign of Caliph Umar bin-al-Khattab to the reign of the much maligned Aurangzeb Alamgir, the last of the great Mughal emperors of India. He then goes on to the case of persecution of Muslims by fellow Muslims and sums it up in the following words (italics in original):

> I would not say that this practice of ex-communicating fellow Muslims has disappeared, even today. *Thus, in a sense, the actual practice in Islam regarding religious liberty has been harsher on those inside the community than on those outside.* Within Islam there have always coexisted two major traditions: the mystical traditions of the Sufis[8] - stressing more the spiritual values of Islam (as a

[8]Soon after the award of the Nobel Prize, Salam visited Lahore. While in Lahore he visited the shrine of a famous sufi known informally as Data Ganj Bukhsh. This shrine is located very close to Government College, Lahore where he studied and taught. Sir Zafarulla Chaudhri, who belonged to Salam's community, was unhappy with Salam for having visited a sufi shrine. Despite the fact that Salam held Sir Chaudhri Zafrulla in high esteem, he did not like Sir Chaudhri Zafrulla's reaction. Salam mentioned the incident to the then Vice Chancellor of the University of the Punjab and said that he went there because, as he put it, "my heart

> whole this has been a tolerant tradition) - and the tradition of jurisprudence (the unofficial clergy) who have been concerned more with doctrinal and ritual matters, political theory and state-craft in Islam. At the present epoch of history, it is the second tradition which is ascendant in most Islamic countries, as a reaction against the West's cultural and political domination.

Regarding the decline of the scientific tradition in Islamic civilization Salam writes:

> But the scientific tradition started declining around the year 1100, dying out completely two hundred and fifty years later. Why did creative science die out in Islam?
> In my view, the demise of living science within the Islamic commonwealth was due firstly to the inward-turning and isolation of our scientific enterprise and secondly to the discour-

wanted it." Salam was different from Sir Zafarulla Chaudhri. Sir Chaudhri Zafrulla was the Foreign Minister of Pakistan when the founder of the nation M.A. Jinnah (Quaid-e-Azam) died. He was present at the funeral but did not participate in the funeral prayer. When asked about his behavior he responded by saying: "I may be conisdered a kafir (i.e. non-Muslim) Foreign Minister of a Muslim country or a Muslim Foreign Minister of a kafir state." Some members of his community dispute this statement.

> agement of innovation (*taqlid*). The later parts of the eleventh and early twelfth centuries in Islam were intense politically-motivated, sectarian and religious strife. This was the period when there came to prevail in Islam a rigid orthodoxy with a lack of tolerance (*taqlid*) for innovation (*ijtihad*) in all fields of learning, including the sciences.

Salam quotes from one of the greatest social historians of all time, Ibn Khaldun (italics in original):

> *We have heard of late, that in the land of Franks, and on the northern shores of the Mediterranean, there is a great cultivation of philosophical sciences. They are said to be studied there again, and to be taught in numerous classes. Existing systematic expositions of them are said to be comprehensive, the people who know them numerous, and the students of them very many ⋯ Allah knows better what exists there ⋯ But it is clear that the problems of physics are of no importance for us in our religious affairs. Therefore we must leave them alone.*

Salam then makes a most pertinent observation:

> Ibn Khaldun displays little curiosity, no wistfulness. The apathy towards acquiring new

> knowledge which the words appear to convey was symbolic of the drawing inwards of the scientific enterprise. As everyone knows, isolation in sciences and the veneration for authority it engenders spells intellectual death. In our great days in the ninth and tenth centuries, the Muslims had founded, in Baghdad and Cairo, international institutes of advanced study (*Bait-ul-Hikmas*), and assembled international concourses of scholars there. But from 1300 C.E. this no longer occurred.

Salam concluded that classical science is a Graeco-Islamic legacy. He also believed that there are questions that will always remain beyond the ken of science. He expresses his belief in the "efficacy of prayer in times of distress". He states that he is also a believer because of what his Holy Book teaches "about doing good for mankind." He states:

> I believe in the Moral Lord; and there is a metaphorical balance; on the one side are placed one's good deeds, on the other one's transgressions against humanity. One is rewarded - already here on earth - if one outweighs the other.

He specifically states: "I have myself never seen any dichotomy between my faith and my science."

Chapter 13

Pakistani Science and Education

When Salam went back to England in 1954 he had spent almost three years in the wilderness of Pakistani academic life. He was well aware of its shortcomings and had an understanding of what needed to be done. He was also very keen to do something for his country so that it could occupy a respectable place in the world of science. He was also concerned about problems that required scientific expertise for their solution. He was well aware that without scientific knowledge his country would remain poor and weak. He had a deep comprehension of international politics and of the exploitation that was taking place in third world countries. He understood very well that the real difference between the North and the South, between the developed and undeveloped world lay in the fact that the developed countries had realized that Knowledge of Nature, in the widest and deepest sense, was the key to power and prosperity and were far ahead in this realm. Everything else followed from this difference. Pakistan was no exception.

In his address at the University of Stockholm in 1975 he described how economic manipulation and exploitation was being carried out and how ignorance on the part of underdeveloped countries enabled this exploitation. The lack of specialized intellectual manpower was at the root of the problem that the undeveloped societies faced. They could be misled and exploited any way on account of their deep ignorance. This continues to date. Talking of the period soon after Pakistan's independence in 1947, he stated:

> We imported highly talented planners from Harvard University. They told us we need not to put up a steel industry. We could in any case buy any amount from Pittsburgh. We leased out our oil imports and even the distribution of petroleum within the country to multinationals who conducted - in an age of oil surpluses - a half-hearted search for it. Pakistan was thus a classic case of a post-colonial economy; political tutelage was inter-

changed for economic tutelage. In the scheme of things, we were to provide cheap commodities - principally jute, tea, cotton, raw unprocessed leather. It was in 1956 that I remember hearing for the first time the scandal of commodity prices - of a continuous downward trend in the prices of what we produced, with violent fluctuations superposed, while industrial prices of goods we imported went equally inexorably up as a consequence of the welfare and security policies the developed countries had instituted within our own societies. All this was called Market Economics. And when we did build up manufacturing industries with expensively imported machinery - for example, cotton cloth - stiff tariff barriers were raised against these imports from us. With our cheaper labor we were accused of unfair practice.[1]

[1]To some extent similar objections are now raised against China - the Chinese are accused by US authorities of unfair practices of a similar nature. The media does not ask as to who allowed outsourcing of US jobs to China? The richest families on the planet, who own all major banks and business, including oil and defense industry, also own the media and appear to control the US government as well as the Congress and the Senate. These families outsource jobs to China and then deceive their public through the media that they own. Maintenance of perpetual tension, war, "revolutions" and as-

Salam further elaborates this by pointing out that if Pakistan were to export raw materials, e.g. cotton seeds, the tariffs would be low. As soon as the seeds were processed into oil the tariffs would go up say from US $ 100 per ton on seed to US $ 600 per ton on oil. Pakistan was forced to buy expensive technology but could not export products manufactured through such technology! And there were other restrictions. Pakistan, in 1955, was not allowed to buy the technology of manufacturing something like say Penicillin. As he puts it:

> We were to be markets for steel, for machinery, for armaments. We must not export anything resembling manufacture. No wonder we have been bankrupted.

It was against this background that Salam had to think of his life as a physicist and as a self-respecting Pakistani. To quote him

> In the early 1950s I looked upon my future as contributing to Pakistan's advance to technology and advancement as non-existent. I could help my country in only one way - as a good teacher - and that was to produce more

sassinations are the main components of their strategy to control and own global resources. The so called "Market Economics" is probably manipulated by these families in many cases.

> physicists who, for lack of any industry, would in their turn, become teachers themselves, or leave the country.

Salam then wrote that it was not possible for him to survive even as a good teacher in an environment in which he was totally isolated from the international research stream. He had to get back into the international stream and from there he would have some hope, through his high level scientific contacts, made possible by his stature as an outstanding physicist, to contribute to Pakistani science and education.

In this conclusion Salam was correct. Had he stayed in Pakistan, subordinated to the subordinates of a narrow minded, arrogant and vision-less bureaucracy that manipulated the shallow and bankrupt politician at will, he would have died as a physicist and as a man who could make a difference. The fact that he became a teacher at Cambridge and then a very young Professor at Imperial had an impact on the minds of the bureaucrats, politicians and the military generals, most of whom are overawed by the West because very few of them have excelled in creativity. They are mostly mere vision-less managers, imprisoned in their "legal" and "administrative" trappings, with limited and negative mindsets, unaware of and untouched by the sweep of real Knowledge.

Salam's first opportunity to get into a working relation with international organizations, which were to later enable him to play his role for Pakistan as well, came in 1955 while he was still a 29 year old lecturer at Cambridge. This was the occasion of the First Atoms for Peace Conference which introduced him to the UN. He writes:

> For me personally, this conference was important, for this was my first introduction to the United Nations. I remember entering the Holy Edifice in New York in June 1955 and falling in love with all that the organization represented - the Family of Man, in all its hues, its diversity, brought together for Peace and Betterment. I did not then realize how weak an organization it was, how fragile and how frustrating in its inaction, but I shall speak of this later. *It seemed to me then that any ideas I may have of helping Pakistan physics - and developing countries' physics - must be implemented through United Nations actions.*[2]

During this Conference Salam's introduction to the UN was most valuable. In the second *Atoms for Peace Conference* held in 1958 Salam was to act as Secretary under the then Director General IAEA, Dr. Sigvard Ekulnd

[2]Italics added.

whom he referred to as "one of the greatest Swedes in international affairs." This year became important for two reasons. Firstly, as Salam puts it:

> One consequence of the 1958 Conference was that the Pakistan Government became interested in Atomic Energy. Pakistan had no oil, little gas, some hydro-potential. Pakistan needed atomic energy. In 1958 President Ayub Khan assumed power; I was recalled to Pakistan and asked to help with the creation of the Atomic Energy Commission.

Ayub Khan was a serious minded and solid administrator. I once asked Salam what kind of a relation existed between him and President Ayub Khan. He said that Ayub Khan respected him and that Ayub Khan was very impressed by the fact that he was a Professor at a leading British institution. This is also confirmed by the remarks of President Ayub at a Conference in 1959:

> In the end I must say how happy I am to see Professor Abdus Salam in our midst. His attainments in the field of science at such a young age, are a source of pride and inspiration for us and I am sure his association with the Commission will help to impart weight and prestige to the recommendations of the Commission.

In fact the 1957 story in the daily *Pakistan Times*, alluded to in a previous chapter, had introduced Salam as a scientist of stature in the eyes of the Pakistanis. In his book, Salam's brother mentioned that Salam used to say that as a result of the 1957 story Pakistan had "rediscovered" him. This was probably the reason that in 1957 the University of the Punjab, Lahore bestowed a D.Sc. Honoris Cause on Salam, his first honorary degree.

Salam met President Ayub Khan for the first time in 1958 at a conference in Karachi. The President asked him to advise the government on matters of science and technology. In 1958 he was made a member of the Atomic Energy Commission, in 1959 Salam was formally appointed as Adviser to the Education Commission and in 1961 he was appointed Chief Scientific Advisor to the President of Pakistan. Dr. Ishfaq Ahmad, who was the Chairman of the Pakistan Atomic Energy Commission (PAEC) at the time of the nuclear tests conducted by Pakistan (1998), had a long association with PAEC as well as Salam. He writes:[3]

> During the same period the Government of Pakistan established a Department of Atomic Energy in Pakistan with Dr. Nazir Ahmad as its first Chairman. A vital contribution of Salam was the induction of Dr. I.H. Usmani

[3]Ishfaq Ahmad: *The Nucleus*, Vol 33, No 1-2, p 1-3, 1996; this journal is a publication of the PAEC.

> as Member of the Atomic Energy Commission and later its Chairman.

I.H. Usmani was the real architect of the PAEC but in this he had continuous advice, input and help from Salam.

> One of the first actions of Usmani as Chairman was to plan for sending out about five hundred physicists, mathematicians, health scientists and biologists abroad. Salam helped Usmani not only in the formulation of this plan but also in its execution by helping in the placement of these scientists and engineers at the best academic institutions in the US and UK.

I have in my possession an obituary note written by Professor Salam on July 13, 1992 on the death of I.H. Usmani (19 June 1992). He had sent it to me and I had passed it on to some papers. None, except the monthly *The Concept*, appearing from Islamabad published this note. Excerpts from this note are very informative and revealing. Talking of a meal they had together Salam writes:

> I still remember the enjoyment with which we talked to each other and discovered that we were both indebted to the Nobel Laureate, G.P. Thomson, who had been his supervisor

at Imperial College. I was Professor at the same college and also indebted to G.P. Thomson for many courtesies. Dr. Usmani had just been shifted from his position as the Chief of Imports and Exports of Pakistan. He had been given a job as Joint Secretary to the Government of Pakistan, in charge of mineral development and the Geological Survey of Pakistan. The shifting of people like this irrespective of a consideration of their previous training was a standard ploy of the administration for getting someone cut to size. I sensed his great desire to get back into nuclear physics for which he had been trained by G.P. Thomson.

During the next few days, I met the President of Pakistan, General Ayub Khan and the Finance Minister, Mr. Mohammad Shoaib. They both asked me who, in my opinion, would be the best person for taking over as Chief of the Pakistan Atomic Energy Commission. I naturally suggested Dr. Usmani. I still possess the letter which was written in reply by General Ayub Khan to me from Karachi. The President had ordered Dr. Usmani and he was taking over as member of the Atomic Energy Commission immediately and as Chief in a

> year's time.

In the same note Salam reveals how he attempted to have the ICTP set up in Pakistan. He writes:

> In 1960 we had the occasion of speaking about the Atomic Energy Commission of Pakistan as being the host of a possible future International Center for Theoretical Physics which is now housed in Trieste. This Institute was a glean in one's eyes in the beginning but as time went on became more and more serious and occupied more and more of our thoughts. In 1965, on the invitation of Prime Minister Chou En Lai, I also visited China for the first time in my life together with President Ayub Khan and Mr. Bhutto.

Regarding the matter of of ICTP being set up in Pakistan, Ishfaq Ahmad has stated in his article:

> Using the tremendous influence he enjoyed, Salam convinced President Ayub Khan about the usefulness of the of the proposed Center. The proposal was formally approved by the Government of Pakistan who also issued instructions for allocation of the necessary funds for this purpose. However, Pakistan lost its bid for the Center to Italy which offered better conditions for hosting the Center.

It is said that it was Mohammad Shoaib, the Finance Minister of Field Marshal Ayub Khan, who killed the chances of setting up ICTP in Pakistan. He was probably also assisted in this by by M.M. Ahmed, Chairman Planning Commission.

In his obituary note Salam listed five great achievements of Usmani. These were:

1. Sending 500 scientists and engineers abroad for training and higher education;
2. Arrangements that these men and women would get better positions compared to their peers in the Civil Services;
3. Setting up the Pakistan Institute of Nuclear Science and Technology (PINSTECH);
4. Commissioning of what was, at the time, Pakistan's only nuclear reactor KANUPP;
5. The establishment of the Space and Upper Atmosphere Research Commission (SUPARCO).

In giving Usmani credit for these Salam was very generous. However, the fact is that Salam had a hand in all five achievements - all of them carry the imprint of his thinking. In his article published in the *Nucleus* in 1996 Ishfaq Ahmad, former Chairman PAEC, has pointed out that the proposal for SUPARCO was jointly authored by Salam and Usmani. The proposal was approved by the Government of Pakistan in 1961. Ishfaq Ahmad further writes:

> Professor Salam also actively worked with Dr. Usmani in establishing PINSTECH and installing the first nuclear power plant of Pakistan, KANUPP. He was personally involved in selecting the present site for PINSTECH. The respect he enjoyed in the Pakistan Atomic Energy Commission is obvious from the fact that Dr. Usmani invariably requested Prof. Salam to preside over the meetings of the Commission which are normally chaired by its Chairman ⋯
>
> The Nathiagali Summer Colleges which have been held regularly since 1976, was also Salam's idea.

Professor Salam's involvement with building the PAEC and SUPARCO is also evident from the fact that he, despite his commitments at Imperial College, devoted time to building the base of Pakistani Science and Technology. Not only did he give time he also protected Dr. Usmani because Dr. Usmani was a most valuable and a strong administrator who had the ability to take a stand. This Dr. Usmani could not have done without Salam's support. In the obituary note on Dr. Usmani, Salam mentions two things:

> I paid Dr. Usmani a visit regularly every

> six months for three weeks each time. Sir Patrick Linstead, the Rector of Imperial College, where I had been appointed, took pride in the fact that I was so much in demand by the Commission. We were thus making up for the time lost in not having a Science policy for Pakistan ···
>
> Since Usmani was not an easy person to deal with and not much of a diplomat so far as his own interests were concerned, he was getting into trouble all the time with Ministries. My major task and my humble service to him was to rescue him from the wrath of the President and his Ministers.

Dr. Usmani was succeeded by Mr. Munir Ahmad Khan, a non-Ph.D., who was appointed when Mr. Bhutto assumed power. Munir Ahmad Khan lacked the stature and qualities of Dr. Usmani. He was a small man placed atop excellent academicians. Salam subtly alludes to this in his obituary note. Salam was present on the occasion of the inauguration of the KANUPP reactor which became functional after Usmani's departure. He writes: "I think I was the only one who, in his speech, referred to Dr. Usmani's contribution in getting this reactor installed."

Apart from the nuclear aspect Salam also paid attention to other problems. In his Stockholm address (1975) he had noted that in Pakistan the British had opened 31 liberal High Schools and Arts colleges and only one college each for agriculture and engineering for a population approaching 40 million. As he noted:

> The results of these policies could have been foreseen. The chemical revolution of fertilizers and pesticides touched us not. The manufacturing crafts went into complete oblivion. Even a steel plough had to be imported from England.

Pakistan had inherited about 10,000 miles of canal network to irrigate about 23 million acres of land. The network had been built by the British. The slope, width and depth of these canals had been so adjusted that the flow of water would neither erode the land nor choke itself through excessive deposition of sediments. However a serious problem arose. The problem was known as waterlogging and salinity. Apparently the water table rose and with it salts also came to the surface making the land uncultivable. In the period 1950-60 almost a million acres per annum became useless for cultivation. As Salam wrote:

> In 1961, the values of high level scientific and technological contacts were rather strikingly brought home to us in Pakistan ··· In 1961 Professor J. Weisner, President Kennedy's Science Adviser, assembled a team of university

> scientists, hydrologists, agriculturists and engineers, led by Roger Revelle to advise on the problem of water-logging and salinity. This team suggested continuous pumping out of saline water to lower the water table, but with the important caveat that the pumping operation must be simultaneous over a contiguous area as large as one million acres - otherwise the the quantity of water seeping in from the periphery would exceed the quantities pumped out.

The above simple solution worked.[4]

In his diaries published 33 years after his death, Field

[4]Salam gradually became very influential in international circles. When he was campaigning for the setting up of the ICTP he addressed the Board of Governors of the IAEA at Vienna. Munir Ahmad Khan writes:

> He was very eloquent before the Board. At the end of the debate Prof. Smythe of Princeton University, who was on the Governing Board, remarked: "A large number of member states support ICTP. So does Prof. Salam - and he is equal to several member states."

Quoted in *Science for Peace and Progress: Life and Work of Abdus Salam* compiled by Anwar Dil, publishers Intercultural Forum, San Diego and Islamabad (iforum@aol.com), 2008, pp 601-602.

Marshal Ayub Khan notes on August 13, 1967:[5]

> Dr. Salam, my scientific advisor, came to see me. He pleaded that now we are setting up a nuclear power plant we must also invest in a plutonium separation plant. It will help us produce our own nuclear fuel and also give us a nuclear option. Secondly, he brought a proposal from Dr. Revelle of USA on how India and Pakistan could benefit from planned utilization of waters of the eastern rivers and then, if agreeable, he could contact India too and then come out here to discuss details. I personally see no harm in this. ⋯
>
> Dr. Salam said something which is profound and true. There are no moral values left in international relations and the law of jungle prevails. Look at what is happening in Vietnam, the Middle East and other places. A nation that is not capable of looking after itself has no future. So we must be prepared to meet all eventualities. I assured him that I am doing my best to see that the country is well prepared to meet such a situation.

[5] *Diaries of Field Marshal Mohammad Ayub Khan 1966-1972*; Edited and annotated by Craig Baxter, Oxford University Press, 2007, p 132.

In an address before the Planning Commission in Islamabad in 1986 (the author was present on the occasion) he raised the question:[6] "What is wrong with Pakistan's Science and Technology?" His assessment was as under:

> i) There is no national commitment to acquiring and enhancing scientific knowledge among us - and no realization that science can be applied to national problems · · ·
>
> A consequence of this lack of commitment is that the number of active scientists in Pakistan is *sub-critical* and *dwindling* as the years go on; likewise for the outlay of Sciences.
>
> ii) The enterprise of Science in our countries is not run by young, vigorous, working scientists as is the tradition elsewhere. Barring a few exceptions, our universities do not create Science.[7] Pakistan is a veritable paradise of

[6]Abdus Salam: *On Pakistan Science 1986* in the book *Science and Education in Pakistan*; Third World Academy of Sciences, Trieste, 1988.

[7]This situation has changed significantly on account of HEC policies after 2002. Salam would have been happy with this development. However the current government (in 2012) is seriously undermining HEC out of petty personalized considerations, and if unchallenged it could set back the research effort currently underway in universities.

> paper research organizations, with no mechanism of amalgamating or closing them, if they are not viable.
>
> iii) In technology, none of our governments has made it a national goal to acquire self reliance - even for defense technology.[8]

On July 26, 1968, Field Marshal Ayub Khan wrote in his diary:

> Professor Dr. Salam, one of our famous mathematicians, came to see me and brought several good books and reading material. He was worried that Islamabd University[9] had not included biology as one of the subjects. This he considered essential for developing

[8]The situation has improved somewhat. He did not live to see Pakistan's successful nuclear tests and the development of indigenous missile technology. Before his community was declared non-Muslim in 1974, Salam had a peripheral association with the nuclear program as Adviser to the Government of Pakistan on Science and Technology. I believe Dr. Masud Ahmed, who, at one time, probably headed the bomb design group at the PAEC, was persuaded by Salam to give up theoretical elementary particle physics and join the nuclear project. This program was initiated by Mr. Z.A. Bhutto in response to Indian's nuclear explosion. This author knows that Salam was aware of the fact that the Government of Pakistan had initiated a nuclear weapons program.

[9]Present name Quaid-i-Azam University.

> the art of plant genetics for agriculture. He also thought that duplication of certain subjects that are taught in Pakistan Institute of Nuclear Sciences was not necessary. In fact, this institute should be a part of the university. I told him to come over to Pakistan and discuss things with us. But his suggestion makes me think that perhaps all institutions imparting higher education research organizations should come under this university. It would then be possible to obtain further co-ordination amongst them. Perhaps we might even go further and establish a ministry of science and technology.[10]

Salam was also deeply concerned with the education sector. From time to time he would write detailed notes on Pakistan's educational system and science in academic institutions. These had little effect. He once asked me if there was any point in his writing such notes. I responded by saying that he had put down the basic thinking and suggestions for reform of education and science in the country and anybody who wished to improve this sector would have to proceed on the lines he had suggested. The opportunity for such a reform in the Higher Education

[10] *Diaries of Field Marshal Mohammad Ayub Khan 1966-1972*; Edited and annotated by Craig Baxter, Oxford University Press, 2007, p 244.

sector came in 2002 when Atta-ur-Rahman FRS was appointed Chairman of the Higher Education Commission. Professor Atta-ur-Rahman, Pakistan's foremost chemist, had known Salam and was familiar with his thinking. The time period when Atta-ur-Rahman was the Chairman of the Higher Education Commission was the time of greatest expansion and enhancement of research output in Pakistani universities.

The Third World Academy of Sciences at Trieste published a book by Abdus Salam with the title *Science and Education in Pakistan* in 1988. This book contains various essays, reports and speeches on the topic written by Salam during the period 1967-1988.

A report authored by Salam in summer 1969 carries the title: *A Note On Structural Changes in Pakistan's Educational System.* He notes that structural changes are required in the Pakistani system of education. He notes:

> These structural changes are basic to reform. These have been identified and recommended by countless commissions; their implementation, however, has been impeded by bureaucratic resistance, especially departmental jurisdictional disputes - an impediment which Martial law can dispose of.

He emphasizes that the educational system must have two main objectives:

> a) the conscious creation of a feeling of Pakistani nationhood through the educational process;
> b) the creation of skilled employable manpower, capable of building a modern nation.

Salam emphasizes that "after a period of compulsory education, all modern societies provide two educational systems." These are (italics in original):

> (a) *The System of Professional Further Education*, comprising technical, vocational, agricultural and commercial courses.
> (b) *The System of Higher Education*, comprising university level courses in the arts, sciences, higher engineering and mathematics

He then remarks (italics in original): "*The major structural failing of Pakistan's educational system is that no credible professional education system was ever erected.*" Salam argues for the creation of a single Technical Vocational Educational Authority with the object of bringing order into the chaos of a "half-hearted system of polytechnics, industrial training and vocational schools" that existed. He argues that first task of such an authority should be to bring (italics in original) "*a measure of prestige to this second system of education.*" He writes:

> What I have in mind is this. Parallel with the present liberal system of education we create

> a second - the professional. Each award, the middle school, the matriculation, the intermediate, B.A. (or B.Sc) - may be obtained either after the present "liberal" courses in arts or sciences, as now, or after technical, agricultural or a commercial school. So far as job opportunities in administrative services are concerned all B.A.s (general, technical, commercial), *all* intermediates (general, technical, commercial), *all* matriculates of whatever variety would count as equivalent. Only thus will the exclusive hold on the public mind of the present prestigious "liberal" system of education be broken.

This dream of Salam remains unfulfilled four decades later. Leading Pakistani politicians are generally bankrupt intellectually and the bureaucracy is controlled by the "liberal" graduates who have an interest in maintaining the status quo.

Salam also wrote about the role of teachers. Here, as usual, his thinking was radical but right. He wrote:

> The quality of education depends, in the last analysis, on one thing alone - the quality of teacher, his involvement in the creation of the subject, with creative teaching and with his pupils.

> In the past the tendency has been to belittle the Pakistani teacher, to decry his attainments, to deny him influence in running the institution, to accord him a low social standing. This must change. Since the teacher is the pivot of the system, he is the one who must always be right.
>
> Not till our secondary schools and junior colleges get staffed - as in Japan - by the (unemployed) M.A.s, M.Sc.s and Ph.D.s, will the quality of education improve. For this to happen it is essential to raise salaries. I would give a Ph.D. in a high school more salary than the one working in a research council.

With regard to universities Salam repeatedly lamented, over the years, the small size of the teaching community, the accumulated "dead wood" among them, the woefully inadequate research facilities, isolation of university teachers from the international research stream,[11] lack of emphasis on research and lack of say of teachers in running universities.

[11]He wrote: "The creation of his subject was never considered part of the duties of a university teacher. Even on a more elementary level, university teachers were denied the opportunity of keeping in touch with developments in their subjects; attendance at international seminars has been treated as an unnecessary luxury - to be frowned upon or at best sanctioned as a privilege rather than as a right."

Salam emphasized that the autonomy of universities was of paramount importance. He stated that the way to achieve this was through "Building up the University Grants Commission receiving funds from the Treasury and disbursing university finance. (The higher education sector finance will have to be increased at least five times before we get a viable system.)" Z.A. Bhutto set up the University Grants Commission and then in 2002 it was transformed into a powerful Higher Education Commission (HEC). The funding situation for HEC remained good, as Salam would have wanted, during 2002-2008 with remarkable results.[12]

[12]The elected government that succeeded the Musharraf regime has now (i.e. 2012-13) begun to strangulate HEC with the connivance of sections of the bureaucracy and a great battle is being fought between the academia and the government. Mr. Rohail Asghar MNA, Chairman of the Standing Committee on Education and Training, told this author that both, the politicians of the ruling party, as well as the bureaucrats were persistently trying to kill HEC. He told me that some leading members of the ruling party, including Ministers, had asked him repeatedly to sign the legislation which he, thankfully, refused to. One Federal Secretary had called him several times asking him to allow the piece of legislation, intended to kill HEC, through his Standing Committee to the National Assembly. The real reason for this assault had to do with the fact that not only had the Minister of Education, a bogus educational certificate (he has now been convicted in a court of law), some leaders very high up in the ruling Pakistan People's Party have fake degrees and were behind this move. The courts have begun sending fake degree holders to jail. (This note was added at

When one looks at Salam's commitments at Imperial College as well as ICTP, it is remarkable that he was able to contribute deeply and thoroughly in institution building in the country and to continue to write and speak on educational policies, despite the indifference of authorities, except in the case of Ayub Khan, with regard to the PAEC. His writings till the last decade of his life, clearly show his commitment to the country. Salam resigned as Chief Scientific Adviser to the Government of Pakistan after his community was declared non-Muslim by an Act of Parliament under the Bhutto regime in 1974. Salam had served in the position for 13 years (1961-74). His influence, but not his commitment, waned after that.

Sometime in the late 1980s, or early 1990s, it was observed that Salam had changed his named from Abdus Salam to Muhammad Abdus Salam. This name appeared on at least two of his books. Both of these were first published in the early 1990s. Since people speculated about this change of name, this author decided to ask him. In the early 1990s I aksed him as to why had he changed his name. His answer was as follows: "The Arabs say that the word Abdus Salam, on its own, is meaningless - it should be Muhammad Abdus Salam. So I changed it accordingly." The Morroccan Royal Academy called him Abu Ahmad Abdus Salam whereas the Kuwaitis named him Abdus Salam bin Hussain.

proof-reading stage.)

Chapter 14

ICTP

Salam had a powerful and profound world view. He was fond of quoting the great philosopher-mathematician Alfred North Whitehead:[1]

> In the conditions of modern life the rule is absolute, the race which does not value trained intelligence is doomed. Not all your heroism, not all your social charm, not all your wit, not all your victories on land or at sea, can move back the finger of fate. Today we maintain ourselves. To-morrow science will have moved forward yet one more step, and there

[1] A.N. Whitehead: *The Aims of Education and Other Essays*; Williams and Norgate, London; third impression 1955, pp 22-23.

> will be no appeal from the judgement which will then be pronounced on the uneducated.

There was a constant anguish that dominated his being - he wanted the '*Les Miserables*' of the developing countries, as he once called them, to take charge of their destiny through cultivation of scientific knowledge. He identified with them and the chasm between the North and the South troubled his soul, and his self respect, deeply. Addressing the people of developing countries he once wrote:[2]

> Why am I so passionately advocating our engaging this enterprise of creating scientific knowledge? This is not just because Allah has endowed us with the urge to know, this is not just because in the conditions of today this knowledge is power and science in application the major instrument of material progress - it is also that as members of the international community, one feels that lash of contempt for us - unspoken but still there - of those who create this knowledge.

Salam had a deep sense of self respect and also understood that in order to stand on their own feet, and in

[2]Muhammad Abdus Salam: *The Future of Science in Islam* in *Renaissance of Sciences in Islamic Countries*; Edited by H.R. Daladi and Hassan, M.H.A; World Scientific 1994; p 68.

order to do justice to themselves, the undeveloped world must cultivate knowledge. However the social, political, cultural and educational environment of the vast majority of such countries does not allow the survival of even the most brilliant potential or actual scientists. The phenomenon of brain-drain takes place precisely for this reason. In order for science to develop in such countries it was important to stem brain-drain. Individual scientists in these countries had to be salvaged without having to migrate to the advanced world. Salam's own experience was irrefutable proof of the fact even the most brilliant of scientists of the developing countries could not survive the inhospitable environments of their countries, and could not last more than a few years. This experience led him to the creation, (through admirable help of men like Bethe, Budinich, Kemmer, Marshak, Serber, Van Hove and others) of that unique institution, the International Center for Theoretical Physics (ICTP) at Trieste in Northern Italy.[3]

When, after doing world class work as a Ph.D. student, Salam returned to Pakistan he felt isolated. As he once told Nigel Calder "You have to know what other physicists are thinking and you have to talk to them. I feared that if I stayed in Lahore my work would deteriorate. Then what use would I be to my country?" Out of

[3]After Salam's death the ICTP has been renamed Abdus Salam ICTP.

this dilemma was conceived the idea of ICTP, perhaps the most effective instrument of checking brain-drain among physicists of the under developed world. ICTP allows deserving physicists from poor countries to benefit from contact with the leaders in their field, as well as from excellent library facilities, by spending some time at the Center. This obviates the necessity of migration for survival as scientists.

The story of how things began to take shape can be pieced together from the talks and writings, not just of Salam, but also of those who were involved in the process from the beginning. As Paolo Budinich narrated in his talk at the Abdus Salam Commemoration Meeting held at Trieste from November 19-21, 1997:[4]

> The establishment of the International Center for Theoretical Physics (ICTP) at Trieste in 1964 and of several international institutions thereafter is due to a series of accidental but well correlated events. The first was Abdus Salam's participation, in June 1960, in one of the international symposia on elementary particle physics and field theory which we organized at Castelletto of Miramare, where

[4]P. Budinich: *Fulfilled and Not Yet Realized Dreams*; reproduced in *Science for Peace and Progress: Life and Work of Abdus Salam* compiled by Anwar Dil, publishers Intercultural Forum, San Diego and Islamabad (iforum@aol.com), 2008, p 552.

> we discussed $SU(3)$ symmetry and renormalisation. The second was his proposal, in the September of the same year, at the General Conference of the International Atomic Energy Agency in Vienna, for the creation of an international center for physics under the flag of the United Nations. I accidentally learned about it a few days later from Edoardo Amaldi in Rome. This early notice gave us the possibility of convincing our Government to immediately submit the Italian candidature of Trieste for such an institution. As a result of these happenings, after three years of difficult diplomatic battles which we, Italians, fought in Vienna together with Abdus Salam, the ICTP was inaugurated in Trieste in 1964 under his direction. Without that timing of events the ICTP would have been established elsewhere in Italy - in Florence or Naples - or otherwise in Copenhagen or in Vienna.

At the same meeting, Luciano Bertocchi pointed out that the meeting at Castelletto of Miramare organized by Budinich in 1960,[5] "probably has been the most important one of the scientific future of Trieste as the City of Science." In view of Budinich's role in setting up the Center,

[5] L. Bertocchi: *My Association with Abdus Salam*; *Ibid*, p 554.

it was befitting that he became the first Deputy Director of ICTP.

In order to set up the ICTP Salam had to address the IAEA Annual Conference to convince the delegates that such a Center was needed, and was indeed within the scope of activities of IAEA. Addressing the 1962 IAEA Annual Conference Salam raised the following questions:[6]

> In considering the question whether the Agency should set up a Center, there are three questions we should ask ourselves:-
> (1) Does research in theoretical physics fall within the scope of the Agency's activities?
> (2) Do physicists from emerging countries really need and desire such a Centre
> (3) If the Center is desirable, can it be created and can the Agency afford it?

His answers to the questions ran as follows:

> Even if we ignore the fact that Einstein was the first scientist to dream of equivalence of mass and energy and to create the whole basis of our science, even if we forget that two of the world's leading theoretical physicists,

[6]Abdus Salam: *Need For An International Center for Theoretical Physics*; reproduced in *Ideals and Realities: Selected Essays of Abdus Salam*; Editor C.H. Lai, World Scientific, 1987, pp 113-117.

> Fermi and Wigner, actually built the world's first atomic reactor, we should not forget that there are still uncharted areas in theoretical plasma physics which are vital to the tapping of fusion power. We must not forget that in spite of all our advances in nuclear physics, we still do not know the theoretical expression for the law of force between two nucleons. These indeed are areas in theoretical physics of direct and immediate concern to the Agency; with research in them its major responsibility ...
>
> Finally do the physicists from the underdeveloped countries want such a Center? We have before us a document signed by 53 of the participants who attended the Seminar at Trieste. Let me read from this document:
> "While important cross-fertilization of ideas has taken place during the six weeks of the Seminar has served to underline the need for a Center - in order for important joint work to be done, contact for more than six weeks of a summer seminar is necessary –"

Regarding the possibility of setting up such a Center, he pointed out that if one were to find three or four prominent physicists of stature who could join the Center as permanent staff they would be able to make an important contribution. Others could be requested to come as visiting Professors. As he put it:[7]

> We humbly submit that the answer to these questions cannot be given at a meeting of the Board of Governors. The answer depends on whether the world community of physicists is enthusiastic about such a Center. I know for fact that men like Neils Bohr, Hideki Yukawa, Hans Bethe, Robert Oppenheimer, Victor Weisskopf, Robert Marshak, Julian Schwinger, Abraham Pais, Leopold Infeld, to name but a few, are strongly in favor of an International Center. No such Center exists now; once it is created there are scores of activities it can engage in, like arrangement of seminars in developing countries. Inevitably the Center will become the clearing house for new ideas. With it is associated at present the idealism of the world community of theoretical physicists.

The above quotes not only elaborate what was in his mind, they also, incidentally, reveal his extensive contacts with the most important theoreticians on the world stage. He must have discussed the idea with them to able to state that they supported it.

[7] *Ibid*, p 116.

The ICTP, established in 1964, is funded by the Italian Government, International Atomic Energy Agency and UNESCO. Over the decades, the Italian Government has provided the lion's share of funding for the Center, testifying to the idealism that permeates Italian culture.[8] Abdus Salam was appointed its first Director, a position to which he was repeatedly reappointed, until, almost three decades later, in 1993, ill health forced him to retire. Starting from humble beginnings in a rented building in downtown Trieste, the ICTP is now housed in a set of four buildings, set against the backdrop of green hills with the Adriatic Sea in the foreground.

In 1992 Salam wrote the following about the ICTP:[9]

> I believe that one of the best anti-brain-drain devices is that pioneered by the IAEA-UNESCO-run ICTP in Trieste, the Associateship

[8] A table on p 188 of the book *Science and Technology: Challenge for the South*, by Abdus Salam (issued by Third World Academy of Sciences and the Third World Network of Scientific Organizations, November 1992) gives a table of the grants from the three institutions, IAEA, UNESCO and the Italian Government, during the period 1964-1991. In 1964 the Italian Government provided $278,000/-, the IAEA $ 55000, and UNESCO $ 22,000. The respective amounts in 1991 were $6,870,229, $1,320,000 and $288,200. Interestingly there was an enhanced grant from the Italian Government during 1987-1990, the grant in these four years being, respectively, $12.775 m, $11.65 m, $13.485 m and $14.342 m.

[9] *Ibid*, pp 81-82.

> scheme, whereby distinguished scientists working and living in DC's have a guarantee of spending 6 -12 weeks at the Center at times of their own choosing, three times during a period of six years. Their fares and living expenses are met by ICTP. No salaries are paid. Over 400 physicists working in the Third World are at present ICTP Associates. After more than 25,000 visits made over the last 28 years by research physicists from the Third World, there has not been a single case of brain-drain from among the Associates and Fellows who have come to work at this prestigious Center ...
>
> It is important to state clearly and emphatically, that scientists (unlike medical men, for example) do not leave their own countries for monetary reasons. They almost always do so because of (i) isolation, (ii) lack of similar individuals, (iii) paucity of scientific literature and similar infrastructure.

Salam was right in his above assessment. As a beneficiary of the ICTP Associateship and Senior Associateship schemes, this author would testify to the fact ICTP allowed many physicists in DC's to survive as physicists and enabled them to continue living in their own countries. It also furthered their careers by enabling them to research of a quality much higher than what they could achieve in their countries, by bringing them into contact with counterparts in the advanced world, and keeping them active, energizing them and feeding their enthusiasm about their work.

The well known theoretician GianCarlo Ghirardi gave the following assessment of the thinking behind the Associateship and Federation Arrangement Programs:[10]

> The two programs that he had launched had two purposes for him: on the one hand the primary purpose of fighting the isolation of promising young scientists in the developing world; and on the other hand, to make the existence and relevance of the Center adequately known in all countries in order to attract young scientists from the Third World. Consistently with these objectives, he also wanted to make the industrialized countries aware of the high scientific level and relevant aims of this institution, in order to obtain the collaboration of prestigious scientists for the activities of the Center, and to convince the

[10]GianCarlo Ghirardi: *Abdus Salam and the Department of Theoretical Physics*; reproduced in *Science for Peace and Progress: Life and Work of Abdus Salam* compiled by Anwar Dil, publishers Intercultural Forum, San Diego and Islamabad (iforum@aol.com), 2008, p 559.

> governments of such countries to imitate the generosity of Italy in supporting this wonderful institution.

The idea of bringing promising young physicists to ICTP for a period of 6-12 weeks in a year (the Associateship scheme) emerged out of his own experience as the following quote shows:[11]

> Looking back at my own period of work in Lahore, as I said, I felt terribly isolated. If at that time someone had said to me, we shall give you the opportunity every year to travel to an active Center to Europe or the United States for three months of your vacation to work with your peers; would you then be happy to stay the remaining nine months at Lahore. I would have said yes. No one made the offer. I felt then and I feel now that this is one way of halting brain-drain, of keeping active men happy and contented within their own countries. They must be kept there to build for the future, but their scientific integrity must be preserved. By providing them

[11] A. Salam: *The Isolation of the Scientist in Developing Countries*: in *Ideals and Realities: Selected Essays of Abdus Salam*; World Scientific 1987, pp 29-30; the article first appeared in *Physics Today* of November 1978.

> with this guaranteed opportunity for remaining in contact with their peers, we believe we are making a contribution to solving the problem of isolation.

The benevolent Italian Government provided additional funds for the creation of two more centers on the pattern of ICTP. One of these is the ICS (International Center for Science and High Technology) while the other Center deals with genetic engineering and biotechnology. "The International Centre for Science and High Technology (ICS-UNIDO) operates within the legal framework of the United Nations Industrial Development Organization, in Trieste (Italy) and is financially supported by the Italian Ministry of Foreign Affairs."[12] In 1987 an International Center for Genetic Engineering and Biotechnology (ICGEB) was established at Trieste. The ICGEB was obviously inspired by ICTP and celebrated its 25 years in 2012.

So deep was his commitment to this cause that he told this author that he wanted to create twenty such centers! He told me in 1990 that the Italian Government had expressed its desire to reward him and wanted to know what he desired in this regard. "I said if they could give me more funds for the Center that would be my reward".

It is an interesting diplomatic consequence of the set-

[12]http://www.linkedin.com/company/ics-unido—international-centre-for-science-and-high-technology

ting up of ICTP at Trieste, that Trieste has been catapulted to global fame in academic and diplomatic circles and has become known worldwide as an Italian city. It was, from 1382-1918, a part of the Austro-Hungarian empire, and was united with Italy only after WW I. Also Salam's presence helped make Trieste a City of Science.

Salam devoted a great deal of thought to the causes of the scientific slumber of developing countries. He listed several causes for this state of backwardness. These include lack of meaningful commitment to science, no serious urge for self reliance, the wrong manner in which the enterprise of science is run,[13] and the uncaring attitude, towards technology transfer, of those in the North who matter. Salam also cites political instability as a major factor affecting the development of science in the South. As he puts it "Creativity in science had depended, in the last analysis, on stability and leisure in all civilization".

Salam remained the most powerful spokes-man crusading for the cause of science everywhere. As he wrote in his book "*Science Technology and Science Education in the Development of the South*":[14]

---

[13]As he once put it - "Science depends for its advance on towering individuals. An active enterprise of science must be run by scientists themselves and not by professional administrators."

[14]This 381 page document, issued by the Third World Academy of Sciences in May 1991, was prepared for the last meeting of the South Commission and for the meeting of the UN Economic and Social Council (ECOSOC) held in Geneva in July 1991. This book

> Today, the Third World is only slowly waking up to the realization that in the final analysis, creation, mastery and utilization of modern Science and Technology is basically what distinguishes the South from the North The widening gap in Economics and Influence between the nations of the South and the North is essentially the Science and Technology gap. Nothing else - neither differing cultural mores, nor differing perceptions of thought, - can explain why the North (to the exclusion of the South) can master this globe of ours and beyond.

Urging leaders of developing countries to patronize science whole-heartedly and generously he talks of Merlin a court magician in the court of legendary King Arthur. Merlin was responsible for providing magic medicinal potions and for using magic to forge steel swords. "The scientists are Merlins of today. They can perform feats of magic undreamt of by Merlins of yesteryears. They can, indeed, transform society".

As Director ICTP Salam operated with great ease and skill in the world of science and diplomacy. He had his 'men' all over the world - his admirers and followers who shared his vision. He was extremely well informed about

---

makes a most interesting reading - almost half of it contains most useful appendices.

world affairs and had first hand information about the politics of Asian, African and Latin American countries, apart from having direct access to many Heads of States and ministers all over the world.

While Salam was Director ICTP, one of the great treats for visiting scientists from developing countries was the opportunity to see the great names in 20th century physics. These great physicists arrived at ICTP only because Salam was there. While they were alive Dirac and Heisenberg came to ICTP. There is a staircase at ICTP known as Scala Dirac. Actually the walk down from Salam's residence as well as the wonderful park in its vicinity, to the ICTP building, involves a rather steep descent in some parts. Apparently Salam, from the window of his office, saw Professor Dirac facing some difficulty at that portion of the descent. He had stairs built there and named it Scala Dirac! This author saw David Gross (Nobel Prize 2004), Y. Nambu (Nobel Prize 2008), Edward Witten, Cooper (of the BCS theory, Nobel Prize 1972), Miani, Burton Richter (Nobel Prize 1974), Leon Lederman (Nobel Prize 1988), Altarelli, John Ellis and others at ICTP. One had the opportunity to attend their inspiring talks.

The discoverer of the neutrino, the Nobel Laureate Frederick Reines visited Trieste in 1989 and penned down a poem for Salam. The poem carries the date November 3, 1989. It goes as follows:

From out of the East there came a man
Who thought to divine the cosmic plan
To unify the hearts of man
And make whole, concepts deep and grand.

From out of the West came Nobility
To grace the deep insight, the unity
Arising from diversity.

From out of the East there came such a man
Whose heart and mind did nobly span
Man's highest hopes and dreams and plans
Transcendent with love and humility.

From out of the depths of the human soul
Came this man so well crafted for this role
Came this man who would make
That which is fragmented whole.

Apart from physicists other important personalities visited Trieste. Two Secretary Generals of the U.N. visited ICTP, U Thant in 1971 and Javier Perez de Cuellar in 1985. The Italian President Guilio Andreotti also came to ICTP. When Pope John Paul II visited Trieste University in 1994, Salam was seated on his right. With his departure that glamor was gone. ICTP is still alive 16 years after his death and that would please him the most. In the last decade of his life whenever this author met him alone, Salam would invariably ask the question as to who should succeed him. The succession question was on his mind because he knew that without capable successors ICTP would die out. That was his nightmare.

ICTP had a great role in keeping many physicists of developing countries alive as physicists and helping them build their careers.[15] Many of those associated with ICTP came to occupy important positions in the educational and scientific establishment of their countries. Interestingly, many a time, physicists of the same country got to know each other at Trieste. ICTP thus created a network of physicists from developing countries who were able to link up with each other as well as with physicists of the developed world.

In his contribution to the 1997 Salam Commemoration Meeting, Rexhep Meidani, the President of Albania, who was an Associate of the ICTP, gave his assessment of the Center, in the following words:[16]

> During the course of a decade it was always a real pleasure to work and stay at ICTP. It is no exaggeration if I define this Center as a goodness of Salam. Invented by this spe-

[15]This author is one of numerous such beneficiaries.

[16]Rexhep Meidani: A Lighthouse for Young Scientists; reproduced in *Science for Peace and Progress: Life and Work of Abdus Salam* compiled by Anwar Dil, publishers Intercultural Forum, San Diego and Islamabad (iforum@aol.com), 2008, p 583.

> cial scientific, political and diplomatic brain it has served as a modern concentrated model of spiritual freedom, intellectual independence and real humanity, of scientific salvation and encouragement for poor countries, and a symbol of sociability for all physicists around the world.
>
> Salam's target was not only to create a scientific center, but also to capture, through his human and spiritual imagination, the most advancded model of a community and a new building of collaboration, independent from race, religion, nationality or political affiliation, and moreover to light the path of an integrated peaceful world of free people with an open heart and original mind.

At the same Commemoration Meeting of Abdus Salam held at ICTP from November 19-21, 1997, Mr. Nawaz Sharif, the then Prime Minister of Pakistan, and himself a former student of Government College, Lahore and the University of the Punjab, sent a message to the Director ICTP and to the Center. This message was a welcome change from the petty attitude of almost all previous Pakistani Governments after the Ayub Khan regime. Mr. Sharif's letter was read out by the then Director ICTP

Miguel A. Virasaro. It stated:[17]

> I am delighted to learn that the Steering Committee of the International Center for Theoretical Physics, together with its major sponsors, namely the Government of Italy, the International Atomic Energy Agency, and the United Nations Educational, Scientific and Cultural Organization, have decided to rename this Center as the Abdus Salam International Center for Theoretical Physics.
>
> Renaming this highly prestigious Center is not only an honor for the memory of Professor Abdus Salam. He was a scientist of world stature and built up this Center over a period of three decades. We are proud of him as the only Nobel Laureate of Pakistan. As the Scientific Advisor to the President of Pakistan for eleven years he rendered invaluable services to his country. As Director of the ICTP, he served a cause, not only of the international physics community but also of scientists of the Third World. He made outstanding contribution toward expanding the frontiers of human knowledge and promoting

[17]Reproduced in *Science for Peace and Progress: Life and Work of Abdus Salam* compiled by Anwar Dil, publishers Intercultural Forum, San Diego and Islamabad (iforum@aol.com), 2008, p 549.

> science and technology throughout the world. I am sure that the renaming of the Center will be a source of great inspiration to the younger scientists everywhere.

The same Nawaz Sharif had, in 1987, invited Professor Abdus Salam officially, when he was the Chief Minister of the Punjab province. The then President of Pakistan, the late Mr. Farooq Leghari, called a meeting of physicists at the Presidency in Islamabad, at which the author happened to be present. A Salam Chair was instituted, on his orders, at Salam's alma-mater, the Government College, Lahore. The meeting had apparently been called at the instance of Dr. Ishfaq Ahmad, former Chairman Pakistan Atomic Energy Commission and at that time the Adviser to the President. To date one center named after him[18] has been set up in his home country. This is all the country did to honor his memory. No road or street is named after him. The combination of bigotry and political expediency that has allowed the bigoted element to intimidate the sane elements is deeply disturbing. This has been accentuated because of Zia-ul-Haq cum CIA training of mullahs for the Afghan Jihad.[19]

---

[18]The Abdus Salam School for Mathematical Sciences was set up at G.C. University, Lahore, presumably on the advice of Professor Asghar Qadir, who, incidentally, did his Ph.D. with Roger Penrose.

[19]In his book *Education, Inequalities and Freedom*, (publishers: Narratives, 2012, p142) Shahid Siddiqui writes about textbooks

There is perhaps a deeper reason - there may be a profound flaw in the national psyche, a deep lack of integrity in the sense of standing up for what is right.

At Salam's Commemoration Meeting in Trieste, Pervez Hoodbhoy stated:

> Right here we have the biggest, by far, theoretical physics institution in the world named

---

that were designed at Nebraska University, under a USD 50 million USAID grant from 1986-1994. He states:

> A third grade mathematics textbook asked: "One group of *mujahideen* attacked 50 Russian soldiers. In the attack 20 Russian soldiers were killed. How many Russians fled?" The scariest fact is that children who were reading such primers should now be in their 30s and 40s. They were exposed to this kind of literature in their formative years. So the violence we see around us today was implanted, encouraged, popularized and rewarded in those times for the sole reason that it was being used for the lofty aim of defeating communism.

Now that the objective has been achieved and the US occupation forces have replaced Soviet occupation forces, agencies like the USAID (which is connected to the CIA according to informed writers) and various British organizations (presumably connected to MI 6) are pumping money into Pakistan for school education "reform". They are revising school curricula and clamoring for removal of "hate material", the very same material that these, and similar, agencies got inserted in the first place. The new insertions will have other objectives.

> after Salam. But in the country of his birth and citizenship, no scientific or other institution, building, or even a street, bears his name. School textbooks do not mention him, nor are children told about him by their teachers. Fake heroes are splattered all over the place but Salam is never to be found. ···
> It is a fact that Salam had easy access to most world leaders, UN high officials, the Pope, but found it very difficult to be heard by the leaders of his own country. In 1988 I was in Salam's hotel room in Islamabad where he had been patiently waiting for two days to meet with the Prime Minister Benazir Bhutto ··· It was not right, I thought to myself, for a person of this stature to be kept waiting in this manner. Suddenly the phone rang and his face momentarily lit up. Then I saw his face fall as BB's secretary told him that the meeting had been called off.

After the novel and successful experiment of ICTP, Salam should have become the Director General of UNESCO. There was no one in the world more suited to the assignment than Salam. But the government of his own country, out of sheer expediency, opposed his candidature. That was the unkindest cut of all delivered by the Zia regime. As his longtime Secretary at ICTP, Anne

Gatti, told two young interviewers making a documentary on Salam:[20]

> That is when his illness really started I think. I think a lot of it had to do with his disapppointment at Pakistan - they had put up another candidate which really blocked his chances. ··· He was loyal to Pakistan to his end.

[20]http://vimeo.com/58447727; the documentary is being made by two young men Zakir Thaver and Omar Vandal.

Chapter 15

Abdus Salam - the Physicist and the Man

Abdus Salam was a man with a vision. Two passions dominated his life - a hunger for creating and acquiring knowledge at the highest level, and a burning desire to see the developing world stand up on its feet through cultivation of knowledge. He was hemmed between two worlds - on the one hand he wanted to fire the dormant South, the disease ridden world of the poor, the ignorant, and the sluggish with a thirst for knowledge; on the other hand, he kept prodding the conscience of the relevant sections of the North, the world of great scientists and narrow minded politicians, of idealists and giant vested interests, of plenty and power. He once conveyed his torment to Robert Walgate by bursting out with these lines of Omar Khayyam.

Ah love! could thou and I with fate conspire
To grasp this sorry scheme of things entire
Would we not shatter it to bits - and then
Remould it nearer to the heart's desire

15.1 Salam as a Physicist

Given Salam's brilliance, his first passion enabled him to join the ranks of the greatest physicists of the twentieth century. Salam's distinguishing feature as a physicist was his uncanny knack for scenting out, from the plethora of confusing possibilities, the one idea that turns out to matter and leads to the deepest insight into the problem. It was a combination of this gift with his burning commitment that enabled him to stay, for four decades, in the forefront of research in High Energy Physics, an area in which even the most brilliant minds usually fade out after shinning for a few years.

In 1964, the journal *Nature* wrote of him:

> There are very few physicists in the world who have maintained such a constant and fertile flow of brilliant ideas as Abdus Salam has achieved during the past thirteen years.

This sentence remained true for another three decades. In almost every significant development in High Energy Physics in the period 1950-1992 (he was forced by illness to give up working in 1993), be it renormalisation, elucidation of the behavior of the weak nuclear force, unitary symmetry, electro-weak unification, supersymmetry, string theory or grand unification, Salam played a significant role.

It has been said of Salam's scientific acumen that "His nose always points in the right direction". (The late Professor M.S.K. Razmi, to whom I owe this sentence could not recall whether it had been uttered by Glashow or someone else). In summer 1990 I asked Salam what his "nose" told him about current ideas in his field. He said there was "definitely something" in supersymmetry. "It will always be there but may be at very high energies" he told me.

Mike Duff narrates that in the period 1969-72, when he was a graduate student at Imperial the Veneziano model was a hot topic. This model was used for strong nuclear interactions. He writes:[1]

> I distinctly remember Salam remarking on the apparent similarity between the mass and angular momentum of a Regge trajectory and that of an extreme black hole. Nowadays, of

[1] M.J. Duff: in *SalamfestSchrift*, World Scientific, Editors: A. Ali, J. Ellis, Randjbar-Daemi, 1994, p 568.

> course, string theorists would juxtapose black holes and Regge slopes without batting an eyelid but to suggest that black holes could behave as elementary particles in the late sixties was considered preposterous by minds lesser than Salam.

Salam's student Delbourgo has made an interesting observation about Salam's ability to guess what would be right without having worked out the mathematics at all. He writes:[2]

> When standing up to argue with him on one of the finer points of the problem you had to be pretty darn sure of what you said because he had a wonderful intuition about the answer and was much more often right than wrong. When out of desperation you would confront him and ask him how he could be so certain, he would break into one of his wicked smiles, twiddle his thumbs, lean back in his chair, raise his finger and point upwards. Mind you if you stood your ground and (on the odd occasion) turned out to be correct, he did respect you for it.

[2] R. Delbourgo: *Teacher, Colleague and Friend*; in *Science for Peace and Progress: Life and Work of Abdus Salam* compiled by Anwar Dil, publishers Intercultural Forum, San Diego and Islamabad (iforum@aol.com), 2008, p 569.

Luciano Bertocchi, who worked as Deputy Director ICTP, has made interesting comments. He had, in Fall 1956, received a copy of hand written lecture notes on dispersion relations delivered by Salam at Rochester. He states that the lecture notes were "very typical of Salam's style." He then adds:[3]

> Even for the formulae, although the beginning as well as the final result were correct, the intermediate passages were full of mistakes; but the final result was right. This was typical of Salam: to be able to pick up, in physics as well as in other domains, the most important points, and to look at them very carefully, neglecting the less important details, provided the final result was correct.

The observations of Professor Gordon Feldman of John Hopkins University, regarding Salam's passion about physics are quite interesting. He had studied at Imperial College. He states:[4]

[3]L. Bertocchi: *My Association with Abdus Salam*; in *Science for Peace and Progress: Life and Work of Abdus Salam* compiled by Anwar Dil, publishers Intercultural Forum, San Diego and Islamabad (iforum@aol.com), 2008, p 554.

[4]Gordon Feldman: *Fun with Abdus Salam*; in *Science for Peace and Progress: Life and Work of Abdus Salam* compiled by Anwar Dil, publishers Intercultural Forum, San Diego and Islamabad (iforum@aol.com), 2008, p 573.

> Abdus was not only excited about his own ideas but also excited when he read about something but he had not known before and thought was simply beautiful. I remember his bursting into the office once and on the blackboard he drew a short line segment with two little circles attached to the end and with his eyes glowing with excitement he said "that's SU(3)". Needless to say neither Paul (Matthews) nor I had a clue to what he was talking about. Abdus had just started reading the works of Dynkin and although he couldn't answer any of our halting questions he knew the work was very significant and his joy was very infectious. I could go on with many more such episodes which filled the days with joy, happiness and laughter.

Incidentally in the same talk Gordon Feldman mentioned how he had received from Salam, a copy of a cutting from a Swedish newspaper, that appeared one day before the award of the 1975 Nobel Prize. Feldman had the article translated with the help of a Danish colleague. The article speculated that Abdus Salam and Steven Weinberg were possible candidates for the 1975 Nobel Prize.[5] The said article contained the following sentence in the very

[5]The 1975 Nobel Prize was awarded to Aage Bohr, B. Mottleson and J. Rainwater.

first paragraph: "Salam who is fifty, and Weinberg, forty two, are both theoretical physicists, the former (Salam) is considered the modern day Einstein."

The well known theoretician GianCarlo Ghirardi was interested in the foundations of quantum theory, an area in which Salam, surprisingly, had little interest. He states that Salam had told him several times: "Do figures not come out all right when you use the theory - quantum mechanics - in its standard formulations, to calculate the outcomes of any actual experiment? Then what are you worried about?" However when Sir Karl Popper was to deliver a lecture at ICTP Salam called Ghirardi and asked him to make "a long, incisive comment on the speech of Popper, so that it will be clear to everybody that at the Center we have adequate competencies in all fields related to Science." When Ghirardi told him that he was very critical of Popper's views and that he could prove Popper wrong, Salam gave him the go ahead and Ghirardi duly went to the blackboard after Popper's talk and proved that Popper's gedanken experiment would imply a falsification of quantum mechanics or relativity. Salam called Ghirardi on the following day to thank him for clarifying some interesting problems that had hitherto not caught his attention. He also told Akhtar Said, former Minister of Education, Government of the Punjab in a video recorded interview that he had no interest in the work on foundations of quantum theory.

Bertocchi has remarked that for Salam, "learning was as important as creating." Referring to a discussion regarding physics that he had with him, when Salam's illness was advanced, Bertocchi states:[6]

> He was asking me whether I knew a paper in which corrections to the semiclassical Wentzel-Kramers-Brillouin (WKB) approximation were discussed, since he felt he would need higher order corrections to semiclassical calculations in what he was doing at the moment in biophysics. Since we - Fubini, Furlan and myself - had written a paper on the subject thirty years ago, I gave him a copy of that. The day after he called me again, to discuss details in our paper. One day for him was more than enough, and by that time he already knew more about the subject than I did.

In a video interview given to Akhtar Said at the end of 1987, Salam confirmed what Bertocchi has stated. He told the interviewer that he was studying a new type of mathematics[7] which has not been used in physics before, that of Riemann surfaces. With a lovely smile full of

[6] *Ibid*, p 556.

[7] He qualified this by saying that the mathematics was about 50 years old or 100 years old or 20 years old depending on which part of the book you look at.

pleasure he said:[8]

> We are studying it Sir, we are studying it, and it is very hard because we are in competition at this time with 24 year olds. You see you are competing with boys who are 24 and have nothing else to do. They are young, their bodies are supple, and apart from this they have nothing else to do - this is very important. We have to do all kinds of things.

When the interviewer asked him whether he had not yet stopped his theoretical work he replied: "How can you finish? How can you stop? Stopping is like death. It is like writing poetry. Do poets die? Perhaps they do." When Akhter Said asked him if he had "any disappointments in creative work?" he replied:

> The biggest disappointment is that I do not get enough time to do work in physics. That is the biggest disappointment. Like all physicists from the Third World our biggest responsibility is to do something for our nation. That's the biggest disappointment and that affects your work. You can't be as fully discharging your duties to physics as a man from

[8]Akhtar Said has very kindly provided me with a CD of the interview.

> the rich countries is. This is a great disappointment.

In the days when Salam was busy setting up and consolidating ICTP, he was in transit frequently. As Delbourgo put it: "The rumor that he did much of his research in transit or upon an aircraft is not far fetched." Salam remained creative as long as his body supported him. He was stating his philosophy, by which he lived, when he said that to stop was to die. He never wanted to stop working, learning and creating.

Salam's scientific stature and his pioneering contributions towards the spread of science in developing countries were recognized the world over. But Salam was not just a spokesman for science for developing countries. He played a leadership role in advancing the cause of physics research in the advanced world too. When he felt that the British Goverment was thinking of cutting Britain's participation in CERN he spoke out. In an article titled *Particle Physics: Will Britain Kill Its Own Creation?*, that appeared in the *New Scientist* of 3 January 1985, he wrote:

> I must say it comes as a great surprise to me that the British Government should have assembled a committee under the chairmanship of Sir John Kendrew to review British participation in high energy particle physics in

> general, and in the CERN enterprise in particular. The unkindest cut is the committee's second term of reference, which asks it to reflect on re-allocation of the resources released, in whole or in part, to other areas of science. I am reminded of the Galahad story in P.G. Wodehouse where, at a convivial party, one of the Wodehouse characters biffs another with a round of beef. The latter falls unconscious, and all the "undertakers present" start bidding for the body ···
> Thus to find Britain, of all the countries, should contemplate withdrawing from the international pursuit of a subject that constitutes one of the frontier areas of science, appears to me incredibly destructive for the morale of the scientific enterprise worldwide.

While addressing a colloquium at CERN in Salam's memory, the Nobel Laureate Carlo Rubbia pointed out:[9]

> Abdus had an important role in advising on the CERN programs in particular as a member of the SPC. In 1987, when LEP was not

[9]Carlo Rubbia: *The Standard Model, Abdus Salam and CERN*; paper presented at the Special Colloquium in Memory of Abdus Salam at the European Organisation for Nuclear Research (CERN), Switzerland, September 23, 1997.

> yet operational, CERN Council and then DG, Herwig Schopper, created the so-called "Long Range Planning Committee" to define the further steps for CERN, Abdus, together with Giorgio Brianti, Pierre Darriulat, Kjell Johnson, Sam Ting, and Simon Van der Meer, helped us in laying the foundation of what is today the present and future of CERN. It was in this small circle of seven people that the names LHC and CLIC were coined and the relative merits and potentialities of the hadron and linear colliders were elaborated and evaluated in depth. I still recall the vivid enthusiasm and clarity of Abdus' vision on the future of CERN: he used to insist on the relevance of concentrating primarily on key, strategic choices related to fundamental questions. I believe that he has contributed in a major way in defining the next twenty years of CERN strategy in its essentials $\cdots$
> I have no doubt that Abdus' influence has significantly motivated also the emergence of the modern field of non-accelerator, underground experiments.

Salam was elected honorary fellow of many prestigious scientific bodies from the (former) *USSR Academy of Science* to the *American Academy of Arts and Sciences.* He was a recipient of numerous prestigious prizes, including the highest prize to which a scientist may aspire, the Nobel Prize. Salam was awarded D.Sc. Honoris Cause by forty six institutions world wide. With the exception of Australia and Antarctica, he was awarded honorary doctorates from institutions in five continents viz. Asia, Africa, Europe, North America and South America. This may well be a world record of some sort. He was an author or co-author of about 275 research papers and several books.[10]

15.2 Human Aspects

Salam was a very fascinating man who could relate with the highest and the lowest with the greatest of ease. The following introductory remarks by Salam before the lecture by Werner Heisenberg, the discoverer of Quantum Mechanics, give an idea of Salam's great subtlety and sense of nuance:[11]

> In 1748 the Shahinshah of Persia, invaded India and he marched on to Delhi. He inflicted

[10]See appendix A for details of his biodata.

[11]*From a Life of Physics: Evening Lectures at the International Center for Theoretical Physics*; A special supplement of the IAEA Bulletin, printed 1969; p 31.

> a severe defeat on the great Mogul of India. Delhi submitted and the two kings met to negotiate peace. At the conclusion of these negotiations, which included the transfer of the famous Peacock Throne to Iran from Delhi, the Grand Vizier of the defeated Indian King, Asifijah, was summoned to present to the two monarchs some wine to pledge the peace. The Vizier was faced with a real dilemma of protocol. The dilemma was this; to whom should he present his first cup of wine? If he presented if first to his own master, the insulted Persian might draw his sword and slice the Vizier's head off. If he presented it to the Persian invader first, his own master might resent it. After a moment of reflection, the Grand Vizier hit on a brilliant solution. He presented a golden tray with two cups on it to his own master and retired saying 'Sire, it is not my station to present wine today. Only a King may serve a King.' In this spirit I request one Grand Master of our subject, Professor Dirac, to introduce another Grand Master, Professor Werner Heisenberg.

Salam was remarkably free of complexes. He was pleasant to talk to and was easily accessible. Salam was an avid reader.[12] Even as a young student he used to read widely. Science, history, literature, philosophy and religion were his main interests. As a child he learnt Arabic and read the Quran which deeply influenced his thinking. The flow of his writings resulted from a combination of factors - his vision, wide reading, mastery over language and deep conviction.

Ram Prakash Bambah knew him from his student days at Government College. He has narrated an incident that throws light on Salam's character even at that early age. He mentions that Salam became a member of an informal group of students who had topped in various examinations. Bambah writes:[13]

> Soon after Salam joined us, one of us, Prem Luther, got an attack of appendicitis and had to be rushed to the hospital. Salam looked up everything about appendicitis in the Encyclopedia Britannica and went to Prem's bedside to help nurse him. In the system, then and now, the hospital did rely on attention from friends and relatives to see people through

[12]One of his close relatives told me that even the wash room in his London home would be stacked with reading material!

[13]Ram Prakash Bambah: *Together In Lahore and Cambridge* in *Science for Peace and Progress: Life and Work of Abdus Salam* compiled by Anwar Dil, publishers Intercultural Forum, San Diego and Islamabad (iforum@aol.com), 2008, p 576.

> their illness there. Salam spent forty eight sleepless hours attending to Prem after his surgery. This endeared him to all of us and made him a very close member of the group. Also his laughter, such vigorous laughter in such a small body, made sure that wherever Salam was, there was a lot of friendship.

Salam remained helpful to people, regardless of race, color or religion, throughout his life. He always helped people in a quiet way. He knew how to make and retain friends. This author met him in 1979 but before that Professor Kemmer had mentioned to him the hearty laughter of Abdus Salam. All these traits were present in him as early as sixteen, as is obvious from Bambah's description.

Salam had exceptional perseverance. The indifference of the world did not deter him from his goal. He pursued his goal with single minded determination - his staff would testify to this. Qaiser Shafi, a physicist, once asked Salam to forget about science in Pakistan because of the lack of interest on the part of the authorities. He instantly replied: "Oh, but we cannot give up."

Salam had the remarkable ability to switch instantly from scientific research to administrative work and back again. As Bertocchi stated:[14]

[14]L. Bertocchi: *My Association with Abdus Salam*; in *Science for Peace and Progress: Life and Work of Abdus Salam* compiled by

> What impressed me about Salam were two aspects.
> 1) The capacity of switching very rapidly, almost instantly, from scientific to managerial aspects, and especially vice versa, from managerial to scientific, always immediately identifying the key points.
> 2) His great enthusiasm: his will to try, to explore new avenues, to launch new projects, even when he was not sure of success.
> In physics, as well as in managing and creating new things, he always preferred to do one hundred things, ten of which were wrong, eighty right but normal, and ten excellent, rather than carefully analyzing a new idea before trying, and in this way avoiding failures by doing only ten things, nine of which were right and normal, and only one excellent.

In an interview for a documentary film Bertocchi stated:[15]

> I think he had two halves of his brain that were coexisting and one half was working in parallel with the other. He was able to switch

Anwar Dil, publishers Intercultural Forum, San Diego and Islamabad (iforum@aol.com), 2008, p 556.

[15]http://vimeo.com/58447727; the documentary is being made by two young men Zakir Thaver and Omar Vandal.

> from scientific administration, or administration, to science in a microsecond.

In his last years Salam was severely handicapped by an unidentified ailment that finally confined him to the wheel chair for all practical purposes. He resisted the onslaught of the disease with phenomenal strength. He would insist on walking on his own with the result that he fell many times hurting himself badly on several occasions. He suffered a fracture on at least one occasion but continued to work and to come to his office. He was a fighter and this was probably connected with his Rajput background as well as his religious spirit.

Referring to his illness, he once told me, "They don't understand it" - perhaps he did not want to accept the diagnosis, whatever it was. In a jointly written article his daughters Aziza Rahman and Bushra Salam Bajwa have pointed out that Salam suffered from PSP - para supranuclear palsy.[16] It was a measure of his enormous prestige (and a reflection upon the character of the Chinese) that upon learning of his illness the Chinese embassy in Rome directed two Chinese experts in acupuncture to treat him. I learned about this from Salam in summer in 1990. In view of his illness he decided to relinquish charge as Director ICTP at the end of 1993, two years before the

[16]Aziza Rahman and Bushra Salam Bajwa: *My Father, Abdus Salam*; in Quarterly *Al-Nahl*, Special issue on Abdus Salam, Vol 8, Issue, Fall 1997, p 54.

expiry of his term. He remained honorary President of ICTP until his last day.

One of Salam's most outstanding virtues was his fondness for the younger generation. He encouraged younger people and if he saw any spark in them he encouraged and projected them immediately and whole-heartedly. This he did without asking for, or expecting anything in return. Salam instituted prizes to encourage younger scientists. From his share of the Nobel Prize money he instituted the Salam Prize (US $1000 plus certificate) to be awarded every year to outstanding Pakistani scientists under 35 years of age.

In the words of Sir John Ziman (FRS) "Abdus Salam is a man whose heart is as great as his mind." He was very generous and magnanimous in praising and appreciating the work of others. He made it a point to reward those eminent scientists who have not been sufficiently rewarded despite the importance of their contribution. The prestigious Dirac Prize, instituted by the ICTP, is an example. It has been used to honor younger as well as senior physicists. Its recipients include young men like Witten and David Gross as well as people like Nambu (who, as Salam said at an award ceremony of the Dirac Prize, had been in the "wilderness for too long" - this author was present on the occasion) to whom we owe many deep ideas in physics.

What did Salam look like? His photographs of his

younger days reveal him as a handsome young man. Even in old age, when he cared to dress up he sparkled. Glashow visited Salam around 1960. In 1988 he wrote of his impressions of Salam:[17]

> In the early spring I was invited to speak about my work at Imperial College, the London haunt of Abdus Salam, with whom I was to share the Nobel Prize twenty years later. Then, as now, Salam had the presence of an oriental potentate with a Cambridge education and a gift for speaking perfect English.

However as noted by Delbourgo he did not, like Dirac, bother about material things.

Salam's eyes had a special shine which could be noticed even in his old age. Professor G.Murtaza, who was his student at Imperial has specifically mentioned this in an essay.[18] He writes:

> Salam's awe inspiring personality, his dominance and his august temperament, and on

[17]Sheldon L. Glashow with Ben Bova: *Interactions: A Journey Through the Mind of a Particle Physicist and the Matter of This World*; Warner Books, 1988.

[18]I have translated this from an Urdu article of his, a copy of which he kindly gave me. The article is titled: *Professor Abdus Salam - Ehad Saaz Shakhsiat aur Azeem Ustad*; (Epoch-making Personality and Great Teacher).

> top of it the shine in his eyes - nobody could dare to look into his eyes and talk to him ··· There is an interesting incident regarding the dazzling brilliance of his eyes. Salam's secretary, who on account of her mannerism, could have belonged to the world of theater, complained to P.T. Matthews about Salam. With tears in her eyes she complained: "What kind of a person is Salam? He calls me in office, and without either saying hello or looking at me, starts dictating! P.T. Matthews (who was a very kind person to whom everybody would air their grievances) consoled her and said: "You should be thankful that he did not look at you for you would have trembled out of fear!"

The stream of visitors in Salam's Trieste office always gave one the feeling that Salam was a "People's Emperor" loved and revered by his "people", the scientific community of developing countries. They looked to him for guidance and sought his benevolence in sorting out their difficulties. They acknowledged him as their true leader on account of his deep contributions to physics and his deep understanding of their difficulties. He was always a "people's" man. Delbourgo describes this side of his personality in the following words referring to the time when Salam was at Imperial College:[19]

> Many of you will remember that Salam was a totally unpretentious person. Curiously he quite enjoyed English refectory food (can you imagine that?) and was at his happiest when mixing with the "plebeians" (as he called the student body) in contrast to the "patricians" (or staff). On one occasion when Bruno Zumino was visiting us from CERN and Salam insisted on taking him for lunch to the student cafeteria rather than the Staff Common Room, as he preferred to rub shoulders with the "common man". I think this tells us something about his personality.

In his heart Salam was a man who cared for the common people. His nephew Nasir Iqbal, who was employed at ICTP for some time, mentioned to this author that the well known physicist Luciano Fonda had told the Salam memorial meeting at Trieste in 1997 that Salam used to support, from his own pocket, students of Trieste University who faced financial difficulties. He never really cared for money for his own person. When he won

[19] R. Delbourgo: *Teacher, Colleague and Friend*; in *Science for Peace and Progress: Life and Work of Abdus Salam* compiled by Anwar Dil, publishers Intercultural Forum, San Diego and Islamabad (iforum@aol.com), 2008, p 569.

the Catalunya Prize, he, subsequently, received a cheque worth U.S. $200,000. Salam gave the cheque to his Secretary Anne Gatti and asked her to deposit the check, not in his personal account, but in an account to be utilized for others.

Professor Luciano Fonda writes:[20]

> And then I became aware of his great humanity, of his donations to the poor without making himself conspicuous. As a matter of fact, only a few people know that with the money he received from prizes conferred upon him, he constituted a fund for donations of instrumentation to the physics departments of developing countries. Together with Strathdee, I was incharge of endorsing his checks. These were extremely generous actions, which he carried out without showing off.

This author was told by a senior colleague that when he was doing his Ph.D. in London in the early 1970s, he, at some point, ran into financial difficulties and went to Salam for help. He told this author that Salam gave him

[20]Luciano Fonda: *From the Advanced School in Physics to the Synchrotron* in *Science for Peace and Progress: Life and Work of Abdus Salam* compiled by Anwar Dil, publishers Intercultural Forum, San Diego and Islamabad (iforum@aol.com), 2008, p 558.

some money that alleviated his difficulty.

Professor Bertocchi, a former Deputy Director of ICTP, narrates:[21]

> To give you one example of his humanity, I will mention the following. A few years ago, a thief entered the villa where he was living and most of his medals were stolen. At the same time, he also entered the home of the caretaker, stealing his money. Salam's immediate preoccupation was to reimburse the caretaker what he had lost; and we had indeed to find a way within the rules to do exactly that.

There used to be a very interesting and revealing photograph of Salam in the ICTP corridors. It is probably still there but this author has not been to ICTP since 1995. In this photograph Salam is shaking hands with the French President (probably Mitterand). Everyone in the picture, including Salam, is dressed in the most elegant suits. But funnily enough, in the city which is the very heart of elegance, and while shaking hands with the Head of State of a country which prides itself on elegance and sophistication, Salam is holding a plastic bag in his

[21] L. Bertocchi: *My Association with Abdus Salam*; in *Science for Peace and Progress: Life and Work of Abdus Salam* compiled by Anwar Dil, publishers Intercultural Forum, San Diego and Islamabad (iforum@aol.com), 2008, p 556.

left hand! Why would he do that? Did he not care? But he was a man of great sense of nuance. Christiana Winter, one of the Secretaries at ICTP, burst out in laughter when she discussed it with this author, and laughingly commented: "I think he does it deliberately." May be he did! As Professor Bertocchi stated:[22] "He always dealt in the same way with heads of states and with the poorest and youngest scientists." One is reminded of Lord Rutherford who had no deference for authority.

Salam relished speaking in Punjabi, his mother tongue. The Secretary General of the Pakistan People's Party, Jahangir Bader, told this author that on a visit to Pakistan in 1989, Professor Salam conveyed to him his desire to see Bader in his office as he was, at that time, a Federal Minister of Science and Technology (as well as Oil and Gas). Jahangir Bader told this author that instead of fixing a meeting in his office he decided to call on Professor Salam in his hotel room in Islamabad. After Bader had introduced himslef in English and had uttered a few sentences, Salam interrupted him and asked him to speak in Punjabi instead of English. This author and many visitors to ICTP who spoke Punjabi, know that Salam always talked to them in Punjabi.

Salam was lonely in a deep way. The rejection by his government and the establishment, as well as by the orthodoxy, an orthodoxy that gained ground and momen-

[22] *Ibid*, p 556.

tum during the era of Gen. Zia-ul-Haq and the Afghan war, pained him.[23] A Pakistani physicist, Professor Abdul Waheed, once told me that when he informed Salam that he had prayed for him at the Holy Kaabah[24] Salam's eyes turned wet. This author saw Salam's eyes turn wet on several occasions when it was pointed out to him that the ordinary people of Pakistan respected him.

K.K. Aziz has described an incident involving Salam that reflects the conflict between the orthodox and sane elements in Muslim countries. Aziz was in Khartoum, Sudan for fifteen years and happened to be there when the incident took place in January 1983. Khartoum University had invited Salam to bestow upon him an honorary Ph.D. degree and the ceremony was to be held on January 9th. At the time General Ja'fer Nameri was the

[23]Salam once told Zia-ul-Haq that members of his community, working for the Pakistan Atomic Energy Commission, were being discriminated against. Zia-ul-Haq asked Salam that if he were to be provided with the list of their names he would ensure that they would not be discriminated against. When this list of all such members of Salam's community was provided to Zia-ul-Haq, all of them were removed from work on the nuclear bomb project! When Zia-ul-Haq's plane crashed an Italian Secretary Mariam (Italian name Loisa) Durrani informed him in his office. Apparently Salam's reaction indicated his sense of satisfaction at the death of Zia-ul-Haq. He had cause to be bitter about Zia-ul-Haq.

[24]Salam's community had been declared non-Muslim by an act of the Parliament during Z.A. Bhutto's regime and therefore he was not allowed to visit the Holy Kaabah.

ruler of Sudan. Aziz narrates:[25]

> On 7 January the Saudi ambassador met Nameri and asked him to cancel the university's special convocation where Salam was to be given an honorary degree. Nameri called the Vice Chancellor the same day and told him of the Saudi objection. The Vice Chancellor decided to take a stand and said he would consult the academic staff to find out their reaction on the crisis. An emergency meeting was held the same evening and after a short debate the entire Sudanese staff decided to confront the Chancellor and declared that it would resign if the convocation was canceled. Next morning the Vice Chancellor and all the deans and heads of departments and institutes met Nameri and conveyed to him the local staff's to flout the Saudi "orders", adding that the expatriate staff, though not involved in the crisis, had been informally consulted and they stood behind the decision to tender *en mass* resignations. It was an act of great courage to face the Saudi pressure and of a military ruler who enjoyed untrammeled authority. All the credit goes to Nameri for

[25]K.K. Aziz: *The Coffee House of Lahore - A Memoir 1942-57*; Sang e Meel Publishers, 2008, pp 215-216.

> acceptance of the staff's decision, his respect for the autonomy of the university and his promise to attend the convocation and award the degree to Salam.

His illness added much more to his loneliness as he increasingly became physically incapacitated. This author owes much of his information on Salam's last days to Nasir Iqbal, son of the late Col. G.M. Iqbal, (Salam's first wife Amtul Hafeez was the real sister of Col. Iqbal.). Nasir Iqbal worked at ICTP for several years and since he was Salam's nephew he had access to Salam after office hours. Nasir has told this author many incidents which have probably not been penned down before. These incidents shed light on Salam's lonely life in its last phase and also on the wonderful attitude of the Italians, the Triestinos in particular, towards Salam.

Nasir Iqbal stated that Salam was much loved and admired by the people of Trieste as he had transformed Trieste into a science city. Nasir Iqbal narrated that he needed to buy some flowers on a particular St. Valentine's day. The florist, an old lady, asked Nasir where he came from. When Nasir mentioned that he was from Pakistan she said that there was a Pakistani Nobel Prize winner in Trieste. When Nasir pointed out he was Salam's nephew she refused to take any money for the flowers from him and said that it was an honor for her that he was Salam's nephew. She then gave him a flower for

Salam and asked him to tell Salam that "We love him." Salam was so touched by this incident when he came to know of it that his "eyes became wet and tears rolled down his eyes." He was ill at that time and lay in bed.

Nasir told this author that one night Salam fell down in his Trieste residence where he resided all alone. He was hurt and bled and lay on the floor all night as he could not get up. He also was unable to call anyone or raise any kind of alarm. Pierre Agbedjro, who used to drive his official car, went inside his residence around 7.00 AM the next morning and saw him lying where he had fallen.

Apparently his Pakistani wife never wanted to live in Trieste as she felt lonely there. Salam had four children from her, three daughters (in order of their ages) named Aziza, Asifah and Bushra, and a son, the youngest of the four, named Ahmad Salam.[26] Ahmad Salam stated in an interview for a documentary being made on Salam that he saw so little of his father that when he was six or seven years old he would ask his mother if he could bring his bedding into Salam's bedroom and put it on the floor just to be close to him. "I wanted to be with him as much as possible."[27] Two of his daughters have given us valuable glimpses of his family life and his work

[26] Aziza has a PhD in biochemistry, while Ahmad has a degree in Finance and works for a Kuwaiti company from London. All three daughters are housewives.

[27] http://vimeo.com/58447727

habits. They write:[28]

> His travels took him all over the world ⋯ Thus, his work left him little time for the family life. ⋯ He was quite strict at home, especially where our studies were concerned. He would bring us each workbooks and before going to his college he would set us certain pages that we had to do. Whenever he returned from an overseas trip, he would call us into his room and check on our grades and progress. He encouraged us and gave us confidence by constantly reminding us of one of his favorite sayings, "Do your best and leave the rest to Allah." ⋯
> He himself never stopped working. ⋯ My father maintained his meticulous work habits in an unflagging routine punctuated by "catnaps" and endless supplies of sweets and hot tea ⋯ He would go to bed around eight or nine o' clock in the evening, and arise a very few hours later to work in the silent hours before dawn when his level of concentration and creativity would perhaps reach its peak, sustained by a thermos of hot, sweet tea and

[28]Aziza Rahman and Bushra Salam Bajwa: *My Father, Abdus Salam*; in Quarterly *Al-Nahl*, Special issue on Abdus Salam, Vol 8, Issue, Fall 1997, p 51-52.

> some snacks that we would place by his bedside before sleeping.

Nasir sometimes cooked Pakistani food for Salam, food which Salam relished.[29] He used to wait for Nasir sometimes so that Nasir could cook something that he missed because he had lived in the West, mostly on his own. As a student his favorite dish was mutton-potato curry. One day Nasir cooked mincemeat-potato curry for him. Salam enjoyed the dish so much that he held Nasir's hand and prayed for him. Nasir told me that one day Salam held his hand and would not let go - there were tears in his eyes. Nasir said that he could not bear to see that - the plight of such a great man made him very emotional. But Salam was to stay alone. He had devoted his life to physics and to ICTP and maybe his son felt neglected. In the absence of his eldest son Nasir had become a surrogate son. Thus even when he was ill he had no companion, no one to be with him at his home in Trieste. But, as Nasir Iqbal said: "Salam never wanted to surrender - he kept struggling to the very end, trying to stand up and walk."

Nasir told me that Salam had a sweet tooth. He said: "He always used to have sweets and fruit by his bedside

[29] When, in 1987, Salam was an official guest of the Government of the Punjab, he told this author in Lahore: "People here don't even realize what one misses when abroad. They invited me to dinner in a Chinese resturant. I have refused."

on the left and a lot of books on the right. He would take short naps. Between the naps he would get up and start reading." This description of his last years is consistent with what his daughters have described about his habits during the Imperial College years before ICTP was set up. Because of his love of reading he never allowed a TV in his house during the Imperial College years despite the protestation of his kids. However his daughters wrote after his death that they were grateful that they had no TV since they "spent more time reading." Salam almost never vacationed. He worked continuously throughout his life, as long as his body supported him. His son Umar Salam told interviewers for a documentary film:[30]

> He had three full time jobs at least. He was Professor of Physics at Imperial, he was setting up ICTP, and he was also Chief Scientific Adviser to the Government of Pakistan. And how he managed to combine these things I cannot even begin to imagine. It is superhuman and yet I think that he was all the time subject to very human fears. He was always worried he wasn't doing enough.

A day or two before Salam died I began receiving calls from his cousin Col. G.M. Iqbal who said that Salam

[30] http://vimeo.com/58447727; the documentary is being made by two young men Zakir Thaver and Omar Vandal.

was not well and asked me to pray for him. Col. Iqbal called me as soon as Salam passed away to inform me of the sad event. He told me that although Salam had been almost unconscious for a while the doctors felt that he had a very stout heart. I was reminded of what one of the secretaries at ICTP, Mrs Ondina Turra once said to me - Salam had then been fairly confined - she said that it was very sad as, in the days when his health was good, "He was like a lion". He died in the early hours of November 21, 1996 at the residence of his English wife Professor Dame Louise Johnson.[31] I think he preferred staying with Louise. There is no other apparent reason as to why he chose to spend his last days with her. This impression is confirmed by an obituary in the daily *The Telegraph*:[32]

[31]Louise Johnson was an FRS and a Professor of Molecular Biophysics in Oxford. They had two children, a son and a daughter. The son is named Umar Salam and the daughter Saeeda Hajira. I am told that Umar has completed his Ph.D. in mathematics from Cambridge. I remember that it was during a summer of the mid 1980s, that Salam asked me to teach Urdu to Umar. I did so for a few days. When I asked Umar if he was really interested in learning Urdu, Umar said that he was doing it only because his father wanted him to learn Urdu. Interestingly, one day Salam checked the words I had taught him and their transliteration.

[32]Daily Telegraph 8 October 2012; *Professor Dame Louise Johnson*:
http://www.telegraph.co.uk/news/obituaries/9594182/Professor-Dame-Louise-Johnson.html

> Iftikhar Ahmed, a physicist who worked very closely with Salam, recalled them as being "madly in love - it was always 'my darling' this, and 'my darling' that ... I never saw him happier than when he was with Louise".

Salam and Louise Johnson were married in 1968.

When I first met Salam in 1979 he had come to Edinburgh to attend the retirement ceremony of his supervisor Professor Kemmer. He told me that when he checked into the hotel, the man at the counter discreetly asked how long had he been in Britain. When Salam said twenty five years, the receptionist said that he must then be a British citizen. When Salam replied in the negative the receptionist was very surprised and said that he would then have to ask for his passport. This says something about Salam's loyalty and sense of identification with Pakistan. His body was brought to Pakistan and placed at the main center of his community in Lahore before being taken to what was once called Rabwah,[33] at one time the home of his community in Pakistan, where his parents lay buried. Everyone who knew him in his healthy days and saw the body was shocked at the transformation.[34] The news of

[33]The city has been renamed Chenabnagar under pressure of some local religious leaders.

[34]Salam used to weigh around 85 kg but by December 1995, almost a year before his death, he had lost so much weight that, according to Nasir Iqbal, who last saw him on December 5, 1995,

his death hit headlines immediately. The President and the Prime Minister of Pakistan issued the usual statements but the news of the arrival of his dead body was practically blacked out by the official media. However people had lined the road to see the body being carried in a vehicle, the body of a man whose greatness appears to increase with time.

His son Ahmad Salam, who had accompanied the dead body,[35] said that the kind of huge reception they got on arrival of the dead body in Lahore was "absolutely unexpected". It was dark and, he said, that the people who had lined the road were not just the people of his community. He said that: "The line of the people went so far back because they had been told that the body of Abdus Salam was coming through. These were ordinary people." He was buried in former Rabwah (Chenabnagar) and his funeral was attended by about 35,000 people.

Those who knew Salam as a student remember that he was very obedient to his father. His daughters have also confirmed this in their article.[36] It was his will that he be buried near his parents in what was formerly called Rabwah (Chenabnagar). His daughters mention that among

he had become a "skeleton" weighing about 40-45 kg.

[35]Dame Professor Louise Johnson also accompanied the body with their two children.

[36]Aziza Rahman and Bushra Salam Bajwa: *My Father, Abdus Salam*; in Quarterly *Al-Nahl*, Special issue on Abdus Salam, Vol 8, Issue, Fall 1997, p 53.

his papers, the following note was found:[37]

> If for any reason it is not possible to take me to Rabwah, then let my tombstone read: "He wished to lie at his mother's feet."

For many years Salam had a pet overcoat and a pet hat.[38] These would hang in the lobby outside his office if he were around. He carried them with him wherever he went, regardless of the season. Sometimes, when I used to see him from behind, trudging along in his hat and overcoat, he looked like a homeless tramp! Perhaps in a profound way he had no home, like Einstein. He reminded one of his counterpart in politics, Mao tse Tung, who once said that he felt like a lonely monk walking through a rainy world with a leaky umbrella. Thus Salam has passed into history along side the great unifiers of twentieth century physics - Einstein, Bohr, Heisenberg, Dirac, Schrodinger, Glashow, Weinberg and others - and as a crusader consumed by the quest for a great ideal.

[37] *Ibid*, p 53.

[38] It has been pointed out by Munir Ahmad Khan that Salam developed the habit of overdressing because during his studies at Cambridge there was no heating in classrooms and he would wear heavy coats during lectures.

Appendix A

Salam's Biodata

Appointments

Head of the Mathematics Department, University of the Punjab, Lahore (1951-1954)

Professor, Government College, Lahore (1951-1954)

Lecturer, Cambridge University, Cambridge (1954-1956)

Professor of Theoretical Physics, London University, Imperial College (1957-1993)

Founder and Director International Center for Theoretical Physics, Trieste (1964-1993)

President, International Center for Theoretical Physics, Trieste (1994-1996)

Elected Fellow, St. John's College, Cambridge (1951-1956)

Member, Institute of Advanced Study, Princeton (1951)

Elected, Honorary Life Fellow, St. John's College, Cambridge (1971)

Awarded Honorary Professorship, Peking University, Peking

Emeritus Scientist of CentroBrasileiro de Pesquuisas Fisicas - CBPF, Rio de Janiero

Senior Research Fellow, Department of Physics, Imperial College, London (1994)

UN ASSIGNMENTS

Scientific Secretary, Geneva Conferences on Peaceful Uses of Atomic Energy (1955, 1958)

Elected Member of the Board of Governors IAEA, Vienna (1962-1963)

Member, United Nations Advisory Committee on Science and Technology (1964-1975)

Elected President, United Nations Advisory Committee on Science and Technology (1971-1972)

Member, United Nations Panel and Foundation Committee for United Nations University (1970-1973)

Member, United Nations University Advisory Committee (1981-1983)

Member, Council, University for Peace, Costa Rica (1981-1986)

Elected Chairman, UNESCO Advisory panel on Science, Technoogy and Society (1981)

OTHER ASSIGNMENTS

Member, Scientific Council SIPRI[1] (1970)

Elected Vice President, IUPAP[2] (1972-1978)

[1]Stockholm International Peace Research Institute.
[2]International Union of Pure and Applied Physics.

First President, TWAS[3] (1983-1994)

Member of the CERN Scientific Policy Committee (1983-1986)

Member of the Board of Directors of the Beijir Insttute of the Royal Swedish Academy of Sciences (1986-1989)

Member of the South Commission (1987-1990)

First President of TWNSO[4] (1988-1994)

Honorary President for Life, TWAS (1995-1996)

Honorary President, TWNSO (1995-1996)

Academies and Societies

1. Fellow, Pakistan Academy of Sciences (Islamabad) (1954)
2. Fellow, The Royal Society, London (1959)
3. Fellow, Royal Swedish Academy of Science (Stockholm) (1970)

[3]Third World Academy of Sciences.
[4]Third World Network of Scientific Organizations.

4. Foreign Member of the American Academy of Arts and Sciences (Boston) (1971)
5. Foreign Member of the USSR Academy of Sciences (Moscow) (1971)
6. Member, Club of Rome (1976)
7. Honorary Fellow, Tata Institute of Fundamental Research (Bombay) (1978)
8. Foreign Associate, USA National Academy of Sciences (Washington) (1979)
9. Foreign Member, Accademia Nazionale dei Lincei (Rome) (1979)
10. Foreign Member, Accademia Tiberina (Rome) (1979)
11. Iraqi Academy (Baghdad) (1979)
12. Honorary Member, Korean Physics Society (Seoul) (1979)
13. Member, Academy of the Kingdom of Morocco (Rabat) (1980)
14. Foreign Member, Accademia Nazionale delle Scienze (dei XL) (Rome) (1980)
15. Member, European Academy of Sciences, Arts and Humanities (Paris) (1980)
16. Associate Member, Josef Stefan Institute (Ljublijana) (1980)
17. Foreign Fellow, Indian National Sciences Academy (New Delhi) (1980)
18. Fellow, Bangladesh Academy of Sciences (Dhaka) (1980)
19. Member, Pontifical Academy of Sciences (Vatican

City) (1981)
20. Honorary Fellow, National Academy of Sciences, Allahabad, India (1981)
21. Corresponding Member, Portuguese Academy of Sciences (Lisbon) (1981)
22. Founding Member, Third World Academy of Sciences Trieste (1983)
23. Corresponding Member, Yugoslav Academy of Sciences and Arts (Zagreb) (1983)
24. Honorary Fellow, Ghana Academy of Arts and Sciences (1984)
25. Honorary Member, Polish Academy of Sciences (1985)
26. Corresponding Member, Academia de Ciencias Medicas, Fisicas y Naturales de Guatemala (1986)
27. Honorary Life Fellow, London Physical Society (1986)
28. Fellow, World Academy of Art and Science (Stockholm) (1986)
29. Corresponding Member, Academia de Ciencias Fisicas, Mathematicas y Naturales de Venezuela (1987)
30. Fellow, Pakistan Academy of Medical Sciences (1987)
31. Honorary Fellow, Indian Academy of Sciences, Bangalore (1988)
32. Distinguished International Fellow of Sigma Xi (1988)
33. Foreign Fellow African Academy of Sciences (1988)
34. Honorary Member, Brazilian Mathematical Society (1989)
35. Honorary Member, National Academy of Exact, Phys-

ical and Natural Sciences, Argentina (1989)
36. Honorary Member, Nepal Physical Society (1989)
37. Member "Creation" International Association of Scientists and Intelligentsia, USSR (1989)
38. Member Academia Europaea (1989)
39. Elected, Honorary Member, Hungarian Academy of Sciences (1990)
40. Honorary Member, Societa Dante Alighieri di Tucuman, Argentina (1990)
41. Honorary Member, Centro Internacional de Fisica, Bogota (1991)
42. Member, Russian Academy of Creative Endeavors (1992)
43. Foreign Member, American Philosophical Society (1992)
44. Foreign Member, Russian Academy of Sciences (1992)
45. Fellow, American Physical Society (1993)
46. Honorary Member, Academia Nacional de Ciencia y Tecnologia, Peru (1993)

D.Sc. HONORIS CAUSE

1. University of the Punjab,[5] Lahore, Pakistan (1957)

[5] At that time the word Punjab was spelt as Panjab. I have not been able to dig out from the records as to how and when the spellings were changed, but it appears that the change from Panjab to Punjab took place sometime in 1957 or 1958.

2. University of Edinburgh, Edinburgh, UK (1971)
3. University of Trieste, Trieste, Italy (1979)
4. University of Islamabad, Islamabad, Pakistan (1979)
5. Universidad Nacional de Ingenieria, Lima, Peru (1980)
6. University of San Marcos, Lima, Peru (1980)
7. National University of San Antonio Abad, Cuzco, Peru (1980)
8. Universidad Simon Bolivar, Caracas, Venezuela (1980)
9. University of Wroclow, Wroclow, Poland (1980)
10. Yarmouk University, Yarmouk, Jordan (1980)
11. University of Istanbul, Istanbul, Turkey (1980)
12. Guru Nanak Dev University, Amritsar, India (1981)
13. Muslim University, Aligarh, India (1981)
14. Hindu University, Banaras, India (1981)
15. University of Chittagong, Bangladesh (1981)
16. University of Bristol, Bristol, UK (1981)
17. University of Maiduguri, Maiduguri, Nigeria (1981)
18. University of Philippines, Quezon City, Philippines (1982)
19. University of Khartoum, Khartoum, Sudan (1983)
20. Universidad Complutense de Madrid, Spain (1983)
21. The City College, The City University of New York, USA (1984)
22. University of Nairobi, Nairobi, Kenya (1984)
23. Universidad Nacional de Cuyo, Cuyo, Argentina (1985)
24. Universidad Nacional de la Plata, La Plata, Argentina (1985)

25. University of Cambridge, Cambridge, UK (1985)
26. University of Goteborg, Goteborg, Sweden (1985)
27. Kliment Ohridski University of Sofia, Sofia, Bulgaria (1986)
28. University of Glasgow, Glasgow, Scotland (1986)
29. University of Science and Technology, Heifei, China (1986)
30. The City University, London, UK (1986)
31. Panjab University, Chandigarh, India (1987)
32. Medicina Alternativa, Colombo, Sri Lanka (1987)
33. National University of Benin, Contonou, Benin (1987)
34. University of Exeter, UK (1987)
35. University of Gent, Belgium (1988)
36. Bendel State University, Ekpoma, Nigeria (1990)
37. University of Ghana, Ghana (1990)
38. University of Tucuman, Argentina (1990)
39. University of Warwick, UK (1991)
40. University of Dakar, Senegal (1991)
41. University of Lagos, Nigeria (1992)
42. University of South Carolina, USA (1992)
43. University of the West Indies, Jamaica (1992)
44. St. Petersburgh University, Russia (1992)
45. Gulbarga University, India (1993)
46. Dhaka University, Bangladesh (1993)

PHYSICS AWARDS

Hopkins Prize (Cambridge University) for the most outstanding contribution to Physics during 1957-1958 (1958)

Adams Prize (Cambridge University) (1958)

First recipient of Maxwell Medal and Award (Physical Society, London) (1958)

Hughes Medal (Royal Society, London) (1964)

J. Robert Oppenheimer Memorial Medal and Prize (University of Miami) (1971)

Guthrie Medal and Prize (Institute of Physics, London) (1978)

Sir Devaprasad Sarvadhikary Gold Medal (Culcutta University) (1977)

Matteuci Medal (Academia Nazionale di XL, Rome)(1978)

John Torrence Tate Medal (American Institute of Physics) (1978)

Royal Medal (Royal Society, London) (1978)

Nobel Prize for Physics (Nobel Foundation) (1979)

Einstein Medal (UNESCO, Paris) (1979)

Josef Stefan Medal (Josef Stefan Institute, Ljublijana)(1980)

Shri R.D. Birla Award (Indian Physics Association)(1981)

Gold Medal for Outstanding Contributions to Physics (Czechoslovak Academy of Sciences, Prague) (1981)

Lomonosov Gold Medal (USSR Academy of Sciences)(1983)

Copley Medal (Royal Society, London) (1990)

Gold Medal (Slovak Academy of Sciences) (1992)

J.C. Maxwell Prize and Medal (Academy of Creative Endeavors, Moscow) (1995)

OTHER AWARDS

Atoms for Peace Medal and Award (AToms for Peace Foundation, New York) (1968)

International Prize for Peace and International Understanding, UNESCO Center, Florence, Italy (1978)

Peace Medal (Charles University, Prague) (1981)

Diploma of Highest Merit and Honor, Club of Turkish Intellectuals of Istanbul (1981)

The Medal of the City of Paris (Echelon Vermeil) (1983)

Premio Europa Umberto Biancamano (Italy) (1985)

Dayemi International Peace Award (Bangladesh) (1986)

Genoa International Development of Peoples Prize (Italy) (1988)

First Edinburgh Medal and Prize (Scotland) (1989)

"Ettore Majorana" - Erice - Science for Peace Prize (Italy) (1989)

Catalunya International Prize (Spain) (1990)

Medal of the 260th Anniversary of the University of Havana (Cuba) (1991)

Mazhar Ali Applied Science Medal (Pakistan League of America) (1992)

International Leoncino d'Oro Prize (Italy) (1993)

PAKISTANI AWARDS

Sitara-i-Pakistan (S.Pk.) (1959)

Pride of Perforamnce Medal and Award (1959)

The Order of Nishan-i-Imtiaz (the Highest Civilian Award) (1979)

PAKISTANI ASSIGNMENTS

Member, Pakistan Atomic Energy Commission (1958-1974)

Elected President, Pakistan Association for Advancement of Science (1961-1962)

Advisor, Education Commission (1959)

Member Scientific Commission (1959)

Chief Scientific Advisor to President of Pakistan (1961-1974)

Founder Chairman, Pakistan Space and Upper Atmosphere Committee (1961-1964)

Governor from Pakistan to the International Atomic Energy Agency (1962-1963)

Member National Science Council (1963-1975)

Member, Board of Pakistan Science Foundation (1973-1977)

ORDERS AND OTHER DISTINCTIONS

Order of Nishan-i-Imtiaz (Pakistan) (1979)

Honorary Citizen of Trieste, Italy (1979)

Order of Andres Bello (Venezuela) (1980)

Order of Istiqlal (Jordan) (1980)

Cavaliere di Gran Croce dell'Ordine al Merito della Repubblica Italiana (1980)

Honorary Knight Commander of the Order of the British Empire[6] (1989)

Brazilian Order of Scientific Merit in the Grade of Great Cross (1994)

BOOKS

Symmetry Concepts in Modern Physics: Iqbal Memorial Lectures by Abdus Salam (Atomic Energy Center, Lahore) 1966.

Aspects of Quantum Mechanics: Edited by Abdus Salam and E.P. Wigner, Cambridge University Press, 1972

Ideals and Realities: Selected Essays of Abdus Salam: First Edition edited by Z. Hassan and C.H. Lai. Second Edition edited by C.H. Lai 1987. Third Edition edited

[6]Since Professor Abdus Salam did not possess British citizenship he could not be addressed as Sir Abdus Salam.

by C.H. Lai and Azim Kidwai 1989. Also translated and published in Arabic, Bengali, Chinese, French, Italian, Persian, Punjabi, Romanian, Turkish and Urdu.

Science and Education in Pakistan by Abdus Salam; Third World Academy of Sciences, Trieste 1987.

Science, Education and Development: A Collection of Essay by and About Abdus Salam; Research Center for Cooperation with Developing Countries, Ljubljana, Yuoslavia, 1987. Also published in French, Italian, Persian and Spanish.

Supergravity in Diverse Dimensions; Volumes I and II by Abdus Salam and Ergin Sezgin; World Scientific Publishing Co, Singapore; 1988

From a Life of Physics: Edited by Abdus Salam; World Scientific Publishing Co, Singapore; 1989

Unification of Fundamental Forces: The First of Dirac Memorial Lectures by Abdus Salam; Cambridge University Press, 1990. Also published in French, Greek, Italian, Japanese, Portuguese and Spanish.
World Scientific Publishing Co, Singapore; 1989

Notes on Science, Technology and Science Education in

the Developnment of the South; (Red Book) by Abdus Salam; Thirteen editions of this book were published by Third World Acdemy of Sciences, Trieste; the last one in May 1991; also published in Arabic, Chinese, French, Italian, Persian amd Spanish.

Science and Technology: Challenge for the South; by Muhammad Abdus Salam, Third World Academy of Sciences, November 1992

Selected Papers by Abdus Salam (With Commentary); Edited by A. Ali, C. Isham, T. Kibble and Riazuddin; World Scientific Publishing Co 1994

Renaissance of Sciences in Islamic Countries; Edited by H.R. Dalafi and M.H.A. Hassan; World Scientific Publishing Co, Singapore 1994

BIOGRAPHIES OF SALAM

Abdus Salam by Dr. Abdul Ghani; Ma'aref Printers Limited, Defence Housing Society, Karachi, 1982.

The Greats in Science from the Third World: Abdus Salam by Azim Kidwai; Third World Academy of Sciences, Trieste, 1989.

Abdus Salam un Physicien Entretein avec Jacques Vauthier, Beauchesne Editeur, Paris 1990.

Abdus Salam: A Biography by Jagjit Singh, Penguin Books, India, 1992.

Abdus Salam: by Mary Joseph, Great Scientists Series, Learners Press, India, 1994.

Alami Shohrat Yafta Sciencedaan Abdus Salam (World Renowned Scientist Abdus Salam) by Abdul Hameed Chaudhari; published by Ahmad Salam, 8 Campion Road, SW 15, 6 NW, London; 1998; this book is written in Urdu.

Cosmic Anger: Abdus Salam The First Muslim Nobel Laureate; by Gordon Fraser, Oxford University Press, 2008.

Appendix B

Results and Detailed Marks of Abdus Salam (Matric to Masters)

Scanned copies of the results of Abdus Salam from his Matriculation (Matric School Leaving Certificate) Exams held in 1940, his Intermediate Exams held in 1942, his B.A. Exams held in 1944, and his M.A. (Mathematics) Exams held in 1946, are shown here and are being made public for the first time. These are available in the records of the office of the Controller of Examinations of the University of the Punjab, Lahore, Pakistan. The spellings of Panjab were changed to Punjab sometime during 1957 or 1958. Salam topped in each of these examinations.

Results & Detailed Marks of

Abdus Salam

(Matric to Masters)

UNIVERSITY OF THE PANJAB

ABBREVIATIONS USED:

RELIGION.		SUBJECT.	
		Science	.. Sc.
Muhammadan	.. M.	Physiology and Hygiene	.. P. & Hg.
Gaur Brahman Agriculturist	.. G.B.A.		
Non-Brahman Hindu	.. H.	Agriculture ..	.. Ag.
" Jat Agriculturist	.. H.J.A.	Civics and Hygiene ..	.. C. & H.
" Rajput "	.. H.R.A.	Bengali ..	.. Bg.
" Saini "	.. H.S.A.	Panjabi ..	.. Pb.
" Ahir "	.. H.A.A.	Pashto ..	.. Pa.
		Domestic Economy ..	.. De.
		Mathematics (for girls) ..	.. M.
Sikh Jat Agriculturist	.. S.J.A.	Arithmetic and Domestic Arithmetic and Household Accounts in place of Mathematics (for girls only)	.. A. & H.
Sikh Rajput "	.. S.R.A.		
" Saini "	.. S.S.A.		
" Ahir "	.. S.A.A.	Drawing ..	.. D.
Christian	.. C.	Sanskrit ..	.. S.
Depressed (or Special) Class	.. S.C.	Arabic ..	.. A.
		Persian ..	.. P.
		Urdu ..	.. U.
Parsi	.. P.	Hindi ..	.. H.
		Shorthand and Typewriting	.. Pho.
		Book-keeping, etc. ..	.. Com.

Total number of candidates appeared for Matriculation	.. 28,534
Total number of candidates passed	.. 20,112
Maximum number of marks	.. 850

Roll No. 14888, Abdus Salam, of Govt. Intermediate College, Jhang, obtained the highest number of marks (765).

S. P. SINGHA,
CONTROLLER OF EXAMINATIONS,
UNIVERSITY OF THE PANJAB.

SENATE HALL, LAHORE:
The 18th May 1940.

MATRICULATION EXAMINATION, 1940—*continued.*

Islamia High School, Chiniot.—(14810—14823).

Roll No.	Name of Candidate.	Elective Subjects.	Marks obtained.	Date of Birth.	Religion.
14810	Ghulam Murtaza	Sc., D., H. G.	511	18-12-25	M.
14811	Mohammed Anwar I	Sc., A., H. G.	538	22-12-24	M.
14812	Mohd Aslam	Sc., A., H. G.	391	7-11-23	M.
14813	Mohd Rafiq	Sc., A., H. G.	541	9-6-24	M.
14814	Mohd Umar I	D., U., H. G.	418	7-2-23	M.
14815	Ahmad Bux II	D., U., H. G.	469	21-1-21	M.
14817	Mohammed Anwer II	A., U., H. G.	588	20-12-22	M.
14818	Mufti Shamas-ud-Din	A., U., H. G.	429	8-7-23	M.
14819	Ahmad Bux I	P., U., H. G.	506	28-6-25	M.

Malik Bhagwan Dass High School, Chiniot.—(14824—14874).

Roll No.	Name of Candidate.	Elective Subjects.	Marks obtained.	Date of Birth.	Religion.
14824	Sardari Lal Malhotra	Sc., S., H. G.	484	9-4-24	H.
14825	Ram Parkash Chopra	Sc., S., H. G.	474	13-4-25	H.
14826	Hakumat Rai	Sc., S., H. G.	337	25-4-23	H.
14827	Shesh Pal	Sc., H. G.	290	6-6-22	H.
14828	Daryai Lall	Sc., S., H. G.	404	4-2-25	H.
14829	Har Sukh Lal	Sc., S., H. G.	372	1-9-24	H,
14831	Jai Chand	Sc., P., H. G.	629	22-6-23	H.
14832	Basheshar Lal Dhawan	Sc., P., H. G.	600	6-7-25	H.
14833	Sardari Lal Datt	Sc., P., H. G.	389	1-2-24	Brahman.
14834	Madan Lal Khanna	Sc., P., H. G.	437	20-8-24	H.
14835	Hans Raj Dhingra	S., U., H. G.	458	20-3-22	H.
14837	Lal Chand	S., U., H. G.	432	1-6-25	Brahman.
14839	Ram Parkash Khanna	S., H., H. G.	311	15-4-25	H.
14841	Amar Nath Wighmal	S., H., H. G.	430	14-3-23	H.
14843	Indarjit	S., H., H. G.	419	4-2-25	H.
14844	Amar Nath Nighawan	S., H., H. G.	366	5-3-23	H.
14846	Om Parkash Dhawan	S., H., H. G.	366	22-12-24	H.
14847	Ravindar Nath Malhotra	S., H., H. G.	322	8-4-25	H.
14848	Ved Parkash Trikha	S., H., H. G.	541	1-2-25	Brahman.
14852	Madan Lal Jhengan	S., H., H. G.	332	18-6-23	Brahman.
14854	Om Prakash Malhotra	S., H., H. G.	386	1-1-24	H.
14857	Har Bagwan Dass	S., H., H. G.	458	4-12-21	H.
14859	Bishambar Lal	S., H., H. G.	434	9-2-25	Brahman.
14860	Sri Ram Malhotra	S., H., H. G.	279	4-11-22	H.
14862	Pushp Kumar	S., H., H. G.	537	24-7-24	Brahman.
14864	Bal Krishan	S., H., H. G.	410	12-2-23	H.
14865	Sunder Lal Dhawan	S., H., H. G.	342	8-2-22	H.
14866	Siri Ram Saighal	P., U., H. G.	337	20-8-23	H.
14873	Hans Raj Kapur II	P., U., H. G.	466	9-10-25	H.
14874	Mohd Nawaz Khan	P., U., H. G.	381	12-12-23	M.

Government Intermediate College, Jhang.—(14875—14938).

Roll No.	Name of Candidate.	Elective Subjects.	Marks obtained.	Date of Birth.	Religion.
14875	Bashir Amad	Sc., D., H. G.	471	1-11-24	M.
14876	Himat Singh	Sc., D.	497	15-10-24	S.-J. A.
14877	Romesh Chander Sethi	Sc., D., H. G.	545	13-9-24	H.
14878	Tara Chand Bali	Sc., D., H. G.	398	20-11-22	Brahman.
14879	Ram Parkash Saigal	Sc., D.	256	13-10-24	H.
14880	Krishan Lal Pambu	Sc., D.	415	4-12-24	Brahman.
14881	Som Datt Nangpal	Sc., H. G.	307	15-10-23	H.
14882	Munshi Lal	Sc., P. & Hg., H. G.	423	9-1-23	H.
14883	Indar Jit Chawla	Sc., P. & Hg., H. G.	529	22-8-24	H.
14884	Krishan Lal Soneja	Sc., P. & Hg., H. G.	520	1-1-24	H.
14885	Nand Lal Girotra	Sc., P. & Hg	448	15-7-23	H.
14886	Prem Chandra Sharma	Sc., S., H. G.	476	9-7-24	Brahman.
14887	Sukh Dyal	Sc., S., H. G.	709	22-3-25	H.
14888	Abdus Salam	Sc., A., H. G.	765	29-1-26	M
14889	Jagan Nath	Sc., P., H. G.	553	1-1-25	H.
14890	Gurbakhsh Singh	Sc., P., H. G.	654	15-4-25	Sikh.
14891	Mulk Raj	Sc., P., H. G.	639	15-2-25	H.
14892	Om Parkash Kharbanda	Sc., P., H. G.	563	15-10-24	H.
14893	Ram Nath Katyal	Sc., P., H. G.	544	20-4-24	H.
14894	Badri Nath	Sc., P., H. G.	440	18-3-25	H.
14895	Hans Raj Bhayana	Sc., P., H. G.	489	2-9-23	H.
14896	Sohan Lal	Sc., P., H. G.	389	11-1-21	Brahman.
14897	Suraj Narain Fialok	Sc., H. G.	396	1-1-25	H.
14898	Om Parkash Sehgel	Sc., P., H. G.	420	14-2-25	H.
14899	Amar Nath	Sc., P., H. G.	367	20-8-24	H.
14900	Wazir Chand Chawla	Sc., P., H. G.	463	1-11-23	H.
14901	Zulfqar Ali Syal	Sc., P., H. G.	500	1-1-25	M.
14904	Maula Bakhsh	D., U., H. G.	457	21-5-24	M.
14907	Sunder Lal	D., U., H. G.	393	8-8-22	H.
14908	Som Nath Katyal	D., U.	403	2-9-20	H.
14909	Hakim Rai Mahandru	D., U., H. G.	468	15-12-20	H.
14910	Raj Kumar Mohla	D., U.	347	23-12-23	Brahman.
14911	Shanti Lal Magoon	D., U., H. G.	384	1-12-24	H.
14913	Hans Raj Girotra	D., U., H. G.	501	23-4-23	H.
14914	Allah Ditta	D., U., H. G.	563	27-10-25	M.

First Division	510 marks or more.
Second Division	382 marks or more.
Third Division	Less than 382 marks.

Result Statement of the Matriculation Examination held in 1940.

First Division—510 marks or more.
Second Division—382 marks or more.
Third Division—Less than 382 marks.

600

NAME OF SCHOOL AND CANDIDATES.		English: Paper A. Part I.	English: Paper A. Part II.	English: Paper B. Part I.	English: Paper B. Part II.	English: Total.	Mathematics (black) or Arithmetic & Domestic Arithmetic & Household Accounts (Green): Mathematics A, Part I or Arithmetic Paper A.	Math. A, Part II or Domestic Arith. and Household Accounts Paper B.	Math. B, Part I.	Math. B, Part II.	Total.	History & Geography: Paper A. Part I.	Paper A. Part II.	Paper B. Part I.	Paper B. Part II.	Total.
Maximum marks ...		50	50	50	50	200	50/100	50/100	50	50	200	45	45	30	30	150
Minimum marks ...						66					66					49
Government Intermediate College, Jhang Contd.																
14876. Himmat Singh Sc., D.	Jhang	28	21	20	31	100	42	30	40	50	162	11	12	15	7	45
14877. Romesh Chander Sethi Sc., D.	"	30	35	21	35	121	41	2	43	43	129	24	28	20	17	89
14878. Tara Chand Bali Sc., D.	"	29	18	14	35	101	14	5	28	30	77	21	23	13	10	67
14879. Ram Parkash Saigal Sc., D.	"	26	25	11	28	90	6	16	22	20	64	2	5	7	4	18
14880. Krishan Lal Pambu Sc., D.	"	30	21	17	32	100	15	41	45	26	127	4	11	17	5	37
14881. Som Datt Nangpal Sc., P&Hg.	"	27	13	19	15	74	35	1	28	25	89	26	20	12	10	68
14882. Munshi Lal Sc., P&Hg.	"	28	19	17	29	93	34	20	26	27	107	29	17	19	20	85
14883. Indar Jit Chawla Sc., P&Hg.	"	35	23	28	35	121	22	24	40	36	122	31	27	18	15	91
14884. Krishan Lal Soneja Sc., P&Hg.	"	36	25	21	35	117	35	24	29	28	116	31	28	19	16	94
14885. Nand Lal Girotra Sc., P&Hg.	"	31	22	17	34	104	43	35	37	42	157	8	16	18	5	47
14886. Prem Chandra Sharma Sc., S.	"	34	37	34	37	142	37	18	23	26	104	19	21	18	10	68
14887. Sukh Dyal Sc., S.	"	40	40	32	39	151	50	48	43	43	184	33	33	25	26	117
14888. Abdus Salam Sc., A.	"	45	46	40	40	171	50	47	49	50	196	32	24	27	28	111
14889. Jagan Nath Sc., P.	"	35	40	24	38	137	45	24	32	29	130	29	30	19	15	93
14890. Gurbakhsh Singh Sc., P.	"	36	38	31	34	139	50	50	44	49	193	21	26	24	17	88
14891. Mukh Raj Sc., P.	"	40	36	31	36	143	42	50	34	42	168	35	32	26	19	112
14892. Om Parkash Kharbanda Sc., P.	"	32	29	29	38	128	50	50	37	37	174	20	20	10	11	61
14893. Ram Nath Katyal Sc., P.	"	32	25	18	37	112	31	42	39	38	150	22	25	21	14	82
14894. Badri Nath Sc., P.	"	33	24	25	32	114	20	18	34	45	117	23	17	19	12	71
14895. Hans Raj Bhayana Sc., P.	"	33	18	17	22	90	39	32	40	36	147	29	27	15	18	89
14896. Soham Lal Sc., P.	"	23	13	13	15	64	50	23	31	6	110	16	23	10	10	59
14897. Suraj Narain Fialok Sc., P.	"	37	12	20	32	101	28	26	23	30	117	32	22	21	20	95
14898. Om Parkash Sehgal Sc., P.	"	30	15	18	19	82	44	43	15	42	144	15	12	17	10	54
14899. Amar Nath Sc., P.	"	32	15	18	22	87	29	0	32	18	79	22	23	19	11	75
14900. Wazir Chand Chawla Sc., P.	"	31	15	20	26	92	48	25	27	20	120	30	24	12	10	76

Roll No.	A Classical Language (Sanskrit (black) or Arabic (red) or Persian (green) or Latin or Hebrew or Greek): Paper A.	Paper B.	Total.	Physics & Chemistry: Paper A.	Paper B.	Total.	Oral and Practical.	Total.	A Modern Indian Language (Urdu (black) or Hindi (red) or Panjabi (green) or Bengali (blue) or Pashto (violet) or French or German): Paper A.	Paper B.	Total.	Physiology & Hygiene: Paper A.	Paper B.	Total.	Oral and Practical.	Total.	Drawing: Paper A.	Paper B.	Total.
Maximum marks	75	75	150	55	55	110	40	150	75	75	150	70	40	110	40	150	75	75	150
Minimum marks			49			36	10	49			49			36	10	49			49
14876				38	39	77	28	105									68	62	130
14877				35	43	78	30	108									54	44	98
14878				19	30	49	13	62									59	32	91
14879				11	25	36	13	49									28	25	53
14880				46	34	80	18	98									45	45	90
14881				24	32	56	20	76				19	15	34	30				
14882				25	23	48	16	64				31	13	44	30	74			
14883				33	48	81	26	107				37	20	57	31	88			
14884				29	43	72	30	102				31	28	59	32	91			
14885				30	40	70	31	101				29	20	49	37	86			
14886	26	51	77	35	29	64	21	85											
14887	72	69	141	43	48	91	25	116											
14888	73	71	144	52	52	104	39	143											
14889	45	46	91	38	47	85	17	102											
14890	59	61	120	45	51	96	18	114											
14891	53	53	106	46	47	93	17	110											
14892	37	49	86	47	40	87	27	114											
14893	52	50	102	42	41	83	15	98											
14894	21	36	57	29	34	63	18	81											
14895	29	57	86	31	32	63	14	77											
14896	25	40	65	40	36	76	15	91											
14897	27	20	47	24	43	67	16	83											
14898	28	42	70	26	32	58	12	70											
14899	36	37	73	14	29	43	10	53											
14900	33	53	86	[illegible]	[illegible]	78	11	89											

Roll No.	Civics & Hygiene: Paper A.	Paper B.	Total.	Oral and Practical.	Total.	Agriculture (black): Paper A.	Paper B.	Total.	Oral and Practical.	Total.	Grand Total.	Passed in additional subject or not.	Roll Number.	Passed or Failed.	REMARKS.
Maximum marks	75	60	135	15	150			100	50	150	850				
Minimum marks			44	3	49			33	12	49	231				
14876											497	×	14876	P	aw
14877											545	one	14877	P	aw
14878											398	one	14878	P	aw
14879											256	×	14879	P	× aw
14880											415	×	14880	P	aw
14881											307	×	14881	P	aw
14882											423	one	14882	P	aw
14883											529	one	14883	P	aw
14884											520	one	14884	P	aw
14885											448	×	14885	P	aw
14886											476	one	14886	P	aw
14887											709	one	14887	P	aw
14888											765	one	14888	P	aw
14889											553	one	14889	P	aw
14890											654	one	14890	P	aw
14891											639	one	14891	P	aw
14892											563	one	14892	P	aw
14893											544	one	14893	P	aw
14894											440	one	14894	P	aw
14895											489	one	14895	P	aw
14896											389	one	14896	P	× aw
14897											396	×	14897	P	aw
14898											420	one	14898	P	aw
14899											367	one	14899	P	aw
14900											463	one	14900	P	aw

P. E. Press, Lahore—13-3-40—1200.

Total of subjects checked by ____________
Rechecked by ____________

Grand Total and Passing and Failing checked by ____________

Roll Nos. (Marks Later cases) ____________
Roll Nos. (Result Later cases) ____________

Total Number of Passes 25 aw
(To be filled in by the scrutineers in ink with initials)

INTERMEDIATE EXAMINATION, 1942—*continued.*

Roll No.	Registered No.	Name of Candidate.	Marks obtained.	Subjects in which passed besides English.	Religion.
		D. A. V. College, Hoshiarpur.			
5331	40 dh. 34	Sant Kumar Likhi	275	S., M., H., Hi.	H.
5333	40 dh. 51	Nand Lal Sharma	341	S., M., Ec., Hi.	Brahman.
5334	40 dh. 16	Chatranjan Dass Vasdev	315	S., M., Ec., Hi.	B. A.
3535	40 dh. 78	Ram Parkash Sharma	339	S., M., Ec., Hi.	Brahman.
5336	40 dh. 15	Sant Ram	406	S., M., Ph., Hi.	Brahman.
5337	40 dh. 20	Randhir Singh	364	S., M., Ph., Hi.	H.-R. A.
5338	40 dh. 27	Bihari Lall Jearth	307	S., H., Ec., Hi.	H.
5339	40 dh. 35	Amrit Lal Ohri	306	S., H., Ec., Hi.	H.
5340	40 dh. 54	Manohar Nath Sharma	303	S., H., Ec., Hi.	Brahman.
5341	40 dh. 82	Rattan Bhaudar Chand Sharma	297	S., H., Ec., Hi.	Brahman.
5342	40 dh. 24	K. Mohar Singh	298	S., H., Ec., Hi.	H. A.
5343	40 dh. 49	Raj Kumar	280	S., H., Ec., Hi.	H. A.
5344	40 dh. 52	K. Kuldip Singh	252	S., H., Ec., Hi.	H. A.
5345	40 dh. 76	Amrit Lal Gupta	365	S., H., Ec., Hi.	H.
5346	40 dh. 81	Kundan Lall Sud	304	S., H., Ec., Hi.	H.
5347	40 dh. 75	K. Satnam Singh	299	S., H., Ec., Hi.	H.-R. A.
5349	40 dh. 25	Bakhshi Ram	250	S., H., Ec., Hi.	S. C.
5351	40 dh. 43	Gian Parkash Puri	313	S., H., Ph., Hi.	H.
5352	40 dh. 48	Bhum Chand	300	S., Ec., Ph., Hi.	H. R.
5353	40 y. 336	Dev Brat	296	S., Ec., Ph., Hi.	H.
5354	40 dh. 32	Avinash Chander Ratan	467	S., Phy., Ch., Hi.	Brahman.
5355	40 dh. 46	Santokh Singh	280	P., M., H., U.	Sikh.
5356	40 dh. 4	Parkash Chand	360	P., M., H., U.	B. A.
5357	40 dh. 64	Kartara Ram	417	P., M., H., U.	S. C.
5359	40 a. 86	Darshan Singh Bains	305	P., M., Ec., U.	S. J.
5360	40 dh. 36	Baldev Ram Agnihotri	441	P., M., Ec., U.	Brahman.
5361	40 dh. 79	Mula Ram Bali	428	P., M., Phy., U.	Brahman.
5363	40 dh. 53	Sansar Chand	310	P., H., Ec., U.	Brahman.
5364	40 dh. 23	Jai Chand	306	P., H., Ec., U.	H. S.
5365	40 dh. 65	Latif Husain Shah	344	P., H., Ec., U.	M.
5366	40 dh. 12	Shadi Lal Bhalla	347	P., H., Ec., U.	H.
5367	40 dh. 21	K. Gurbx Singh	268	P., H., Ec., U.	H. R. A.
5368	40 dh. 80	K. Badan Singh	295	P., H., Ec., U.	H. R. A.
5370	40 dh. 60	Kanwar Raghbir Singh	287	P., H., Ec., U.	H. R. A.
5371	40 dh. 38	Rajindar Singh	325	P., H., Ec., U.	H. R. A.
5372	39 dh. 36	Abdul Salam	262	P., H., Ec., U.	M.
5373	40 dh. 56	Dwarka Dass	315	P., H., Ec., U.	H. A.
5374	39 dh. 35	Rajindar Dev	330	P., H., Ec., U.	H.
5375	39 dh. 11	Brij Mohan	327	P., H., Ec., U.	H. A.
5377	40 s. 120	Tarlochan Singh	286	P., Ec., Ph., U.	S.-J. A.
5379	40 dh. 8	Dewan Chand	244	S., H., Ec., Hi.	B. A.
5385	40 dh. 69	Raghubir Singh	246	P., H., Ec., U.	H.
		Government College, Hoshiarpur.			
5389	40 ih. 82	Romesh Dass Aggarwal	446	S., M., H., Hi.	H.
5390	40 ih. 33	Baldev Mittra	329	S., H., Ph., Hi.	H.
5394	40 ih. 73	Abdul Majid	331	A., H., G., U.	M.
5395	40 ih. 93	Kishen Singh Sehra	262	P., M., H., U.	Sikh.
5396	40 g. 40	Amarjit Singh Ahluwalia	377	P., M., H., U.	Sikh.
5397	40 ih. 48	Ahsan-ul-Haq Khan	285	P., M., H., U.	M.
5398	40 ih. 59	Iftikhar Ahmad	421	P., H., G., U.	M.
5400	40 ih. 50	Madan Mohan	312	P., H., G., U.	H.
5401	39 ih. 63	Baldev Singh Sungha	241	P., H., G., U.	S.-J. A.
5402	40 ih. 18	Pritam Singh	256	P., H., G., Pb.	Sikh.
5403	40 ih. 10	Mumtaz Hussain	264	P., H., Ph., U.	M.
5406	40 ih. 34	Ram Rachhpal Chopra	318	P., H., Ph., U.	H.
5408	40 ih. 91	Daljit Singh	263	P., H., Ph., U.	S.-J. A.
5409	40 ih. 11	Abdul Haq	272	P., H., Ph., U.	M.
5411	40 ih. 36	Salahud Din Ahmed	381	P., H., Ph., U.	M.
		Government College, Jhang.			
5415	40 ij. 41	Harish Chander	282	S., M., H., Hi.	H.
5417	40 ij. 2	Bal Raj	337	S., M., Phy., Hi.	H.
5418	40 ij. 25	Jagdish Mitra	427	S., M., Phy., Hi.	H.
5419	40 ij. 26	Harbans Lal Gugnani	504	S., M., Phy., Hi.	H.
5420	40 ij. 8	Sukh Dyal	462	S., M., Phy., Hi.	H.
5421	40 ij. 5	Abdus Salam	555	A., M., Phy., U.	M.
5422	40 ij. 7	Amir Chand	476	P., M., H., U.	H.
5423	40 ij. 21	Partap Sain	442	P., M., H., U.	H.
5424	40 ij. 59	Harbhagwan Das	444	P., M., H., U.	H.
5425	40 ij. 16	Ahmad Khan Naim	394	P., M., H., U.	M.
5427	40 ij. 30	Ladha Ram Bhatia	310	P., M., H., U.	H.
5428	40 ij. 50	Shanti Lal Sehgal	306	P., M., H., U.	H.
5430	40 ij. 9	Mohd Abdur Rahman	369	P., M., Ph., U.	M.
5431	40 ih. 45	Ram Nath Katyal	344	P., M., Phy., U.	M.
5432	40 ij. 46	Gurbakhsh Singh Kochar	479	P., M., Phy., U.	Sikh.
5433	40 ij. 12	Bodh Raj Ahuja	404	P., M., Phy., U.	H.
5434	40 ij. 56	Mohammad Sharif	330	P., H., Ph., U.	M.

First Division .. 422 marks and above.
Second Division .. 325 marks and above.
Third Division .. Less than 325 marks.

E—472

Result Statement of Intermediate Examination (ARTS / SCIENCE) Faculty of the University of the Panjab held in 1942. 2221

First Division—422 marks or more.
Second Division—not less than 325 marks.
Third Division—less than 325 marks.

NAME OF INSTITUTION AND CANDIDATES. — FIXED AND ELECTIVE SUBJECTS.

(Columns printed on the form but left blank for every candidate on this sheet — A Modern Indian Language, French, Economics, Chemistry, Biology or Physiology or Geology — are not repeated below.)

Name of Institution and Candidates	English Paper A Part I (35)	English Paper A Part II (40)	English Paper B Part I (40)	English Paper B Part II (35)	Total of Paper B (75; min. 24)	Total of Subject (150; min. 49 (37 C.))	Classical Language Paper (a) (75)	Classical Language Paper (b) (75)	Classical Language Total (150; min. 49 (37 C.))	Mathematics Paper (a) (75)	Mathematics Paper (b) (75)	Mathematics Total (150; min. 49 (37 C.))	History Paper (a) (75)	History Paper (b) (75)	History Total (150; min. 49 (37 C.))	Geography Paper (a) (75)	Geography Paper (b) (75)	Geography Total (150; min. 49 (37 C.))	Philosophy Paper (a) (75)	Philosophy Paper (b) (75)	Philosophy Total (150; min. 49 (37 C.))	Physics Paper (a) (50)	Physics Paper (b) (50)	Physics Total (100; min. 33)	Physics Oral & Practical (50; min. 12)	Physics Total of Subject (150; min. 49 (37 C.))	Additional Paper: Urdu, Hindi, Panjabi, Bengali, Pashto, French, German or Military Science (50; min. 16)	Total number of marks obtained (Compartment 280 / 600)	Roll Number	Passed or Failed	Remarks
Government College, Hoshiarpur (Concld.). I. 1942.																															
5401. 39.1h.63. Baldev Singh Sungha P., H., G., U. Hoshiarpur	12	11	18	14	32	55	37	24	61				37	25	62	21	25	46									17	241	5401	P	
5402. 40.1h.18. Pritam Singh P., H., G., Pb. "	13	14	21	11	32	59	35	37	72				32	21	53	22	31	53									19	256	5402	P	
5403. 40.1h.16. Mumtaz Hussain P., H., Ph., U. "	18	13	20	14	34	65	36	43	79				29	20	49				25	25	50						21	264	5403	P	
5404. 40.1h.24. Mohammad Latif P., H., Ph., U. "	12	10	13	11	24	46	40	41	81				22	18	40				25	12	37						21		5404	F	
5405. 40.1h.69. Harbhajan Singh P., H., Ph., U. "	12	14	22	11	33	59	36	25	61				31	21	52				25	16	41						14		5405	F	
5406. 40.1h.34. Ram Rachhpal Chopra P., H., Ph., U. "	22	17	26	16	42	81	37	36	73				32	45	77				38	30	68						19	318	5406	P	
5407. 40.1h.79. Har Mohinder Singh P., H., Ph., U. "	13	10	25	11	36	59	38	37	75				27	34	61				5	26	31						11		5407	F	
5408. 40.1h.91. Daljit Singh P., H., Ph., U. "	13	15	21	12	33	61	35	37	72				30	32	62				25	25	50						18	263	5408	P	
5409. 40.1h.11. Abdul Haq P., H., Ph., U. "	12	15	24	12	36	63	37	[illegible]	78				30	28	58				34	17	51						22	272	5409	P	
5410. 40.1h.35. Nirmal Singh Randhawa P., H., Ph., U. "	13	14	23	15	38	65	33	34	67				31	32	63				20	25	45						14	340	5410	F	Compt. in Philosophy
5411. 40.1h.36. Salahud Din Ahmed P., H., Ph., U. "	23	17	30	27	57	97	53	42	95				34	36	70				44	44	88						31	381	5411	P	
5412. 40.1h.76. Abdul Basit P., H., Ph., U. "	15	17	24	18	42	74	29	43	72				25	26	51				21	17	38						22		5412	F	
5413. 40.1h.5. Man Mohan Singh P., H., Ph., Pb. "	16	7	18	17	35	58	33	33	66				23	29	52				25	19	44						13		5413	F	
5414. 40.1h.41. Kabal Singh P., H., Ph., Pb. "	12	16	17	14	31	59	32	34	66				32	39	71				25	19	44						17	240	5414	F	Compt. in Philosophy
Government College, Jhang.																															
5415. 40.1j.41. Harish Chander S., M., H., Hi. Jhang	12	21	20	17	37	70	32	28	60	32	27	59	27	38	65												28	282	5415	P	
5416. 40.1j.40. Prem Chandra Sharma S., M., Phy., Hi. "	9	18	25	18	43	70	25	30	55	17	27	44										17	17	34	28	62	29	331	5416	F	
5417. 40.1j.2. Bal Raj S., M., Phy., Hi. "	16	15	24	18	42	73	37	42	79	44	35	79										22	23	45	27	72	34	337	5417	P	
5418. 40.1j.25. Jagdish Mitra S., M., Phy., Hi. "	16	25	22	16	38	79	45	36	81	75	75	150										32	28	60	29	89	28	427	5418	P	
5419. 40.1j.26. Harbans Lal Gugnani. S., M., Phy., Hi. "	20	22	26	19	45	87	64	70	134	75	75	150										33	32	65	35	100	33	504	5419	P	
5420. 40.1j.8. Sukh Dyal S., M., Phy., Hi. "	22	31	31	14	45	98	57	53	110	64	74	138										33	29	62	20	82	34	462	5420	P	
5421. 40.1j.5. **Abdus Salam** A., M., Phy., U. "	24	32	30	25	55	111	57	52	109	75	75	150										43	50	93	45	138	47	555	5421	P	
5422. 40.1j.7. Amir Chand P., M., H., Sk. "	22	27	30	15	45	94	67	52	119	74	75	149	30	44	74												40	476	5422	P	
5423. 40.1j.21. Partap Sain P., M., H., U. "	19	29	22	16	38	86	58	44	102	65	75	140	35	42	77												37	442	5423	P	
5424. 40.1j.59. Harbhagwan Das P., M., H., U. "	16	21	25	19	44	81	58	49	107	75	75	150	31	39	70												36	444	5424	P	
5425. 40.1j.16. Ahmad Khan Naim P., M., H., U. "	19	14	27	19	46	79	58	50	108	46	73	119	27	34	61												27	394	5425	P	

(15)

P. E. Press, Lahore—28-4-42—(83)—450

Totals checked by ____________
Sheets rechecked by ____________

Grand Total and Passing and Failing checked by ____________
Old Postings checked by ____________

Roll Nos. (Marks later cases) ____________
Roll Nos. (Result later cases) ____________

Total Number of Passes Seventeen
(To be filled in by the Scrutineers in ink and signed)

Roll No.	*Name of Candidate.*	*Marks obtained.*
	F. C. College, Lahore.	
3705	Pran Nath Khosla	293
3712	Hari Parshad Gupta	267
3713	Dyal Singh	223
3714	Mohan Parkash Khokhar	226
3715	Joginder Dass	254
3718	Om Parkash Sachdev	288
3722	Baupinder Singh Johar	232
3723	Aziz Ullah Khan	247
3725	Iqbal Krishan	292
3727	Kewal Nand Kashyap	201
3728	Saarnagat Singh Uberai	191
3738	Abdul Latif	181
3741	Hari Chand	387
3743	Shakumbri Diyal Malik	350
3744	Gurlal Singh Tandon	334
3745	Oakar Chand	233
3746	Sansar Chand Sood	237
3747	Saran Singh	311
3751	Rajinder Mohan Sood	242
3752	Ravindra Nath Ummat	276
3756	Gulshan Rai Luthra	265
3757	Hans Raj Mendiratta	278
3758	Jagdish Chander Khurana	301
3761	Manohar Lal Chopra	263
3762	Mohammad Tufail Butt	232
3765	Siri Ram Kumar	273
3769	Chandra Mohan Sapru	237
3770	Narendra Kumar	230
3772	Raj Kumar Kalra	347
3774	Tilak Raj Dhir	346
3776	Bal Mukand Ahuja	277
3778	Sayed Kazim Hussain	203
3783	Rabindra Nath Aggarwal	203
3784	Bharat Bir Vohra	255
3785	Hari Singh Gulia	265
3786	Parkash Chand Gupta	228
3787	Ashwani Chadha	191
3789	Jitendro Kumar Sircar	224
3791	Joginder Singh Chandok	195
3792	Mohd Din Dhillon	196
3793	Ram Kishan Dharmani	206
3796	Sukh Dev Bahl	261
3797	Tarjit Singh	206
3798	Chandar Prakash Ohri	183
3799	Russel Lazarus	254
3801	Surindar Pal Singh	220
3802	Abdul Hamid	196
3804	Yahya Bakhtiar	210
3806	Rashid Gauba	183
3810	Satya Pal Aggarwal	211
3811	Sita Ram	273
3812	Surendra Prakash	240
3813	Gurdial Singh	182
3814	Indar Pal Singh Kondal	220
3815	Sarupindar Singh Sidhu	222
3816	Devender Singh	214
3817	Kashoe Chandra Rai	260
3818	Mohan Singh Grewal	293
3819	Tilak Raj Vij	195
3820	Harcharan Singh	197
3821	Kulbir Singh	181
3822	Om Perkash Bansal	248
3823	Ranvir Singh Bhalla	235
	Government College, Lahore.	
3827	Raghbir Vohra	219
3828	Darshan Lal Malik	270
3829	M. Aslam Avais	312
3830	Mumtaz Ahmad	341
3831	Ghulam Murtaza Piracha	288
3832	Inayat Ullah	334
3833	Abdur Rehman Qureshi	259
3834	Raja Mohd Ikramullah Khan	288
3835	Nasir ul Mulk	291
3836	Ahmad Raza Bokhari	221
3838	Javid Iqbal	286
3839	Ghulam Mujaddid Mirza	240
3840	Masud ul Hassan	303
3841	Zulfiqar Ali Khan	221
3842	Agha Ahmad Raza	285
3843	Liaqat Hayat Khan	265
3845	Amin Ullah	265
3848	Ijaz Ahmad Naik	340
3849	Abdul Waheed Qureshi	256
3850	Nisar Ahmad Sethi	240
3852	Jagdish Chand Bhatia	278
3853	Samindra Nath Deogan	246
3855	Brijinderpal Singh Maan	219
3856	Joginder Singh Lamba	273
3857	Pritam Singh Gill	268
3860	Ijaz Razi Syed	254
3861	Manjit Singh	252
3869	Jaswant Singh	248
3870	Anand Kumar Malik	321
3871	Amir Chand Chawla	317
3872	Madan Mohan Talwar	410
3873	Sudarshan Singh	270
3875	Shahzad Hussain Sayed	238
3877	Abdus Salam	451
3880	Dharamvir Nagia	338
3881	Chaman Lal Malhotra	227
3882	Joginder Singh Narang	346
3883	Avtar Singh Jassal	281
3886	Joginder Mohan Byandri	M.L.
3889	Izzatuddin Ahmed Khan	M.L.
3890	Mohammad Asaf Khwaja	326
3891	Mohammad Sadiq Rajput	271
3892	Aslam Murad	234
3894	S. M. Latif	245
3895	Abdur Razzaq Qureshi	332
3896	Mohd Akhtarullah Khan	255
3898	Altaf Hussain	332
3901	Gurbir Singh Garewal	195
3902	Kirpal Singh Bawa	243
3903	Parduman Singh	254
3905	Krishan Lal Chhabra	322
3907	Satish Batra	256
3909	Amar Kumar Kapur	257
3911	Ramesh Chandra Khanna	222
3912	Dharam Vir Sawhney	309
3915	Lalit Mohan Pasricha	257
3916	Shiv Narain Mathur	333
3918	Naresh Chand Bhatnagar	218
3919	Bal Krishan Khanna	316
3920	Tej Singh	259
3921	Tilak Raj Lall	293
3922	Naresh	279
3923	Bashir Ahmad Ch.	302
3924	Mohd Salim Akhtar	222
3925	Mohd Safdar Khan Janjua	187
3926	Pratap Sain	261
3927	Janki Nath Monga	198
3928	Harbans Lal Gugnani	308
3929	Ranjit Singh Talwar	285
3930	Eric Alfred Isaac	213
3931	Muzaffar Hussain	263
3932	Bhagwan Sitlani	233
3933	Ashok Kumar Kashyap	261
3936	Aziz Mohammad Khan	256
3937	Pavanjit Singh	186
3938	Krishan Iqbal	184
3939	M. Hashim Khan	217
3940	Swarn Kumar Mehra	235
3941	Rajinder Nath Aggarwala	181
3942	Amarjit Singh Ahluwalia	285
3944	Suresh Kumar Sahgal	320
3945	Prithvi Raj	210
3946	Ravindra Mohan Chopra	203
3947	Tejindar Pal Singh Chawla	253
3949	Altaf Ahmad	260
3951	Vishwambhar Nath	326
3952	G. W. Duckworth	285
3953	Thomas Lobo	224
3954	Saadat Ali Syed	236
3955	Mohan Lal	195
3956	Amrit Lal Grover	268
3958	B. M. Singh	268
3959	Ajit Kumar Poplai	223
3960	Krishan Kumar Sethi	193
3961	Raj Kumar Lall	213
3962	Daljinder Singh	205
3963	Rajinder Singh Sehmi	212
3965	Madan Lal Saigal	320
	Islamia College, Lahore.	
3966	Maqsud Ahmad	225
3971	Mohd Iraj	236
3973	Syed Ijaz Hussain Bukhari	226
3975	Ghulam Rasul	321
3976	Mohammad Saeed Akhtar Chaudhary	231
3977	Mir Qamar ud Din	273
3978	Mohd Husain	261
3981	Mohd Aslam	260

1st Divn. 325 marks or more; 2nd Divn. 250 marks or more; 3rd Divn. below 250 marks.

Form No. E. 473.

Result of the Examination for the Degree of Bachelor of Arts of the University of the Panjab held in 194

First Division—325 Marks or more.
Second Division—Not less than 250 Marks.
Third Division—Less than 250 Marks.

FIXED AND ELECTIVE SUBJECTS.

NAME OF INSTITUTION AND CANDIDATES.

Government College, Lahore (Contd.) B-1944.

No.	Roll	Name	Subjects	Fictitious Roll No.	English (a) Prose 50	English (b) General 50	English (c) Poetry 50	English Total 150 (60)	Economics (a) 75	Economics (b) 75	Economics Total 150	A Course Maths (a) 75	A Course Maths (b) 75	A Course Maths Total 150		B Course Maths (a) 75	B Course Maths (b) 75	B Course Maths Total 150	Physics (a) 50	Physics (b) 50	Physics Total 100	Physics Oral and Practical 50	Physics Total of Subject 150	Astronomy (a) 50	Astronomy (b) 50	Astronomy Total	Astronomy Oral and Practical	Astronomy Total of Subject 150	Aggregate of Subjects 450 (180)	Additional Paper in Modern Indian Language 50 (20)	Military Science (a) 25	Military Science (b) 25	Military Science Total 50	Grand Total 500	Division	Roll No.
3876	42.g.179	Yusuf Jamil	E.M.A.B.U	3549	18	24	21	63				36	29	65	5	Cm a	Cm a													23						3876
3877	40.ij.5	Abdus Salam	E.M.A.B.U	3550	45	37	39	121				75	75	150	[illegible]	75	75	150											421	30				451	I	3877
3878	40.d.128	Iqbal Ahmad Chaudhary	E.M.A.B.U	3551	a	a	a					-	-			-	-													a						3878
3879	40.y.251	Abdul Rahim	E.M.A.B.U	3552	a	a	a					-				-	-													a						3879
3880	40.d.71	Dharamvir Nagia	E.M.A.Hi	3553	25	29	21	75				70	52	122	22	66	37	103											300	38				338	I	3880
3881	40.g.156	Chaman Lal Malhotra	E.M.A.Hi	3554	24	21	17	62				34	22	56	6	52	37	89											207	20				227	III	3881
3882	40.d.154	Joginder Singh Narang	E.M.A.Pb	3555	29	29	28	86				70	57	127	27	58	42	100											313	33				346	I	3882
3883	40.g.25	Avtar Singh Jassal	E.M.A.Pb	3767	22	27	22	71				60	25	85	35	52	39	91											247	34				281	II	3883
3884	40.f.10	Amir Chand Kumar	E.M(A) Ec.U	3768	17	22	16	55	28	35	63	46	27	73	3															0						3884
3885	39.g.144	Kewal Krishan Malhotra	E.M(A) Ec.U	3769	a	a	a																							a						3885
3886	39.g.260	Joginder Mohan Byandri	E.M(A) Ec.Hi	3770	26	33	32	91	47	58	105	75	57	132	32														328	23				351	I	3886
3887	40.g.67	Rattan Lal Wattal	E.m(A).M il.	3771	26	28	20	74	34	37	71	25	33	58	8														203		10	11	21	224	III	3887
3888	39.f.125	Khalid Mahmud Butt	M(A)Ast.U	3772	a	a	a					-																a		a						3888
3889	40.g.148	Izzatuddin Ahmed Khan	M(A)Mil.Sc.	3773	24	27	23	74				29	30	59	59									40	34	74	47	121	254	254	10	Abs		254		3889
3890	40.g.186	Mohammad Asaf Khwaja	M(A)Mil.Sc.	4223	26	35	31	92				53	43	96	16									41	48	89	49	138	326					326	I	3890
3891	40.g.7	Mohammad Sadiq Rajput	M.A.Phy.U	4224	25	30	30	85				51	13	64	4				35	30	65	30	95						244	27				271	II	3891
3892	40.g.90	Aslam Murad	M.A.Phy.U	4225	17	29	23	69				50	17	67	7				27	25	52	19	71						207	27				234	III	3892
3893	41.g.190	Abdul Rauf Hameed	M.A.Phy.U	4226	a	a	a					a	a	a					-			-								a						3893
3894	40.g.162	S.H. Latif	M.A.Phy.U	4227	15	27	24	66				48	34	82	2				31	21	52	20	72						220	25				245	III	3894
3895	40.g.31	Abdur Razzaq Qureshi	M.A.Phy.U	4751	35	27	27	89				75	49	124	24				37	30	67	26	93						306	26				332	I	3895
3896	40.g.169	Mohd Akhtarullah Khan	M.A.Phy.U	4752	34	20	23	77				48	29	77	17				27	20	47	25	72						226	29				255	II	3896
3897	40.g.19	Marouf	M.A.Phy.U	4753	a	a	a					a	a	a					-			-								a						3897
3898	40.g.53	Altaf Hussain	M.A.Phy.U	4754	33	18	26	77				75	65	140	40				38	28	66	25	91						308	24				332		3898
3899	40.r.87	Waheed ud Din Arshad	M.A.Phy.U	4755	25	20	26	71				34	38	72	72				15	9	24	31	[illegible]						[illegible]	22						3899
3900	38.y.67	Riazul Haque	M.A.Phy.U	4756	a	a	a					a	a						a	a		a								a						3900

To reappear in Eng. Economics + Urdu till April 1946.

appear in Physics till April 1946.

P. E. P.—350—12-5 44

Total checked by ________

Sheet Re-checked by ________

Grand Total and Passing and Failing checked by ________

Old Postings checked by ________

Roll Numbers of marks later cases 3884, 3885 2-5-44

Roll Numbers of result later cases ________

Total Number of Passes ________

(To be filled in by the Scrutineers in ink and signed)

UNIVERSITY OF THE PANJAB

NOTIFICATION

M.A. EXAMINATION (APRIL), 1946

THE following candidates have passed the Examination for the Degree of Master of Arts held in April 1946.

The names are given in order of merit :—

Merit No.	Roll No.	Registered No.	Name of candidate	Religion	Marks obtained.	Institution	REMARKS
			PERSIAN—concld.				
			(Second Class)—concld.				
13	23	35 z. 2426	Hari Kishan Rattan	Brahman	323	Jullundur District Private Student.	
14	28	34 z. 90	Mohammad Jahangir Sheikh	Mohammadan	311	Lahore District Private Student.	
15	269	37 i. 273	Khawaja Nazir Ahmad	Do.	309	Islamia College, Lahore.	
16	276	32 0-13/A	Abdur Rahman	Do.	303	Oriental College, Lahore.	
17	25	R i. 110	Mirza Mohammad Ishaq Beg	Do.	301	Jhang District Private Student.	
18	12	Y. z. 628	Sayeed Husain Khan	Do.	300	Dujana State Private Student.	
	32	28 b. 33	Amir Ahmad	Do.	300	Mianwali District Private Student.	
			Third Class				
19	268	41 z. 2002	Abdul Wahid	Muhammadan	296	Islamia College, Lahore.	
20	11	T i. 177	Chowdhri Mohammad Abdur Rashid Ahmad Shaida.	Do.	291	Peshawar District Private Student.	
21	17	33 z. 2006	Muti Ullah Mahmood Sandhew.	Do.	290	Amritsar District Private Student.	
22	266	39 f. 101	Zafar Ali Zaidi	Do.	273	Government College, Lahore.	
23	21	28 ig. 33	Fazl-ul-Hasan	Do.	270	Gujrat District Private Student.	
			MATHEMATICS				
			(First Class)				
1	410	40 ij. 5	Abdus Salam	Muhammadan	573	Government College, Lahore.	
2	385	40 y. 56	Ranbir Singh Chadha	Sikh	559	Dyal Singh College, Lahore.	
3	399	40 q. 7	Chaman Lall Gupta	N.-B. H.	525	F. C. College, Lahore.	
4	406	40 il. 66	Krishan Kapur	Kapur	514	Government College, Lahore.	
5	388	40 p. 2	Bal Mukand Gupta	Aggarwal	499	F. C. College, Lahore.	
6	386	36 kl. 22	Ranjit Singh	Sikh	486	Dyal Singh College, Lahore	
7	405	40 ij. 59	Har Bhagwan Das Gulati	Hindu	485	Government College, Lahore.	
8	398	40 il. 123	Sohan Singh Sodhi	Sikh	479	F. C. College, Lahore.	
9	390	40 f. 65	Hari Chand	Hindu	457	Ditto.	
10	425	4 · ip. 7	Rajendra Nath Jain	Jain	449	S. D. College, Lahore.	
11	377	40 dr. 143	Krishan Lal Anand	Anand	443	D. A.-V. College, Lahore.	
12	422	40 u. 80	Hans Raj Sharma	Hindu	430	S. D. College, Lahore.	
13	416	40 i. 308	Nasir Ahmad	Muhammadan	421	Islamia College, Lahore.	
14	396	37 p. 16	Ram Lal Aggarwal	Hindu	418	F. C. College, Lahore.	
15	119	39 f. 206	Pran Nath Suri	Do.	393	Lahore District Private Student.	
16	114	39 f. 282	Vinod Chander	Do.	383	Ditto.	
17	426	40 v. 2	Tirloki Nath Langer	Brahman	380	S. D. College, Lahore.	
18	383	40 dj. 16	Shiv Kumar Sharma	Do.	376	Dyal Singh, College, Lahore.	
19	105	39 gl. 89	Sarwan Singh	Sikh	371	Nabha State Private Student.	

E—176

S.P.P.—20-2-46—100.

Result Statement of the M. A. Examination of University of the Panjab, held in June 1946.

SUBJECT: Mathematics

NAME OF INSTITUTION AND CANDIDATES.					Fictitious Roll Number.	Paper I. Marks in figures.	Paper I. Marks in words.	Paper II. Marks in figures.	Paper II. Marks in words.	Paper III. Marks in figures.	Paper III. Marks in words.	Paper IV. Marks in figures. (A)	Paper IV. Marks in words. (B)	Paper V. Marks in figures. (C)	Paper V. Marks in words. (D)	Paper VI. Marks in figures. (E)	Paper VI. Marks in words. (4)	Aggregate of Marks.	Class.	Passed or Failed.	Merit.	I Class—360 Marks or more. II Class—300 Marks or more. III Class—Less than 300 marks.
Maximum Marks							100		100		100		100		100		100	600				
Minimum Pass Marks							40		40		40		40		40		40 or 45 (for English)	270				
393	38.gm.12	Parkash Chandra Malik	"	"	193	27	Twenty Seven	12	Twelve only	9	... only	28		26	25		8			Fail		
394	44.f.207	Radha Mohan Vyas	"	" H	195	45	Forty five	40	Forty only	41	... one			27		57	45			Fail		
395	39.dj.7	Raghbir Singh	} Rai 9/7/46	" S	159	52	Fifty Two	51	Fifty one	48	... Eight		53	86			41	331	II	Pass		Sur. [illegible]
396	37.p.10	Ram Lal Aggarwal		"	140	79	Seventy Nine	76	Seventy Six	56	... Six	56		84			67	418	I	Pass		Sur. [illegible]
397	38.gl.154	Sanjodh Singh Grewal	"	" S.	138	22	Twenty Two	21	Twenty one	26	... Six		26	20			12			Fail		
398	40.11.123	Sohan Singh Sodhi	} Rai 9/7/46	" S	128	11	Seventy one	80	Eighty only	63	... Three		87	93			85	479	I	Pass		Sur. [illegible]
399	40.q.7	Chaman Lal Gupta		" L	120	96	Ninety Six	94	Ninety four	76	... Six		89	100			70	525	I	Pass		Sur. [illegible]
Govt. College, Lahore.																						
400	37.z.1938	Miss Umaila Arora	"	" H	111	8	Eight only	5	Nine only	22	... Two		1	32			14			Fail		
(7) Govt. College, Lahore M.A. Exam. April, 46. (contd.)																						
401	40.lx.19	Nirmala Devi Malhotra	Mathematics	Lahore H	214	30	Thirty only	7	Seven only	A			A	A			A			Fail		
402	42.r.434	Miss Santosh Satija	"	" H	201	53	Fifty Three	50	Fifty only	46	... Six		67	A			A			Fail		
403	40.z.20	Sudarshan Singh	" Rai 9/7/46	" S	225	53	Fifty Three	43	Forty Three	46	... Six		50	52			46	290	III	Pass		Sur. [illegible]
404	40.gm.148	Jiwand Singh	"	"		Absent		Absent		Absent			Absent	Absent						Absent		
405	40.1j.59	Har Bhagwan Das Guleti	" Rai 9/7/46	" H	243	56	Fifty Eight	66	Sixty Six	78	... Eight		100	56			77	485	I	Pass		Sur. [illegible]
406	40.1...	Krishan Kapur	} Rai 9/7/46	" H	256	89	Eighty nine	89	Eighty nine	83	... Three		93	81			79	514	I	Pass		Sur. [illegible]
407	40.d.74	Dharam Vir Sagar		" H	266	45	Forty five	53	Fifty Three	40	... only		41	45			69	293	III	Pass		Sur. [illegible]
408	39.g.214	Noor Mohammad	"	" M	271	25	Twenty five	40	Forty only	43	... Three		48	30			57			Fail		
409	32.g.31	Zulf Hussain Shah Haidri	"	" M		Absent		Absent		Absent			Absent	Absent						Absent		
410	40.1j.5	Abdus Salam	" Rai 9/7/46	" M	215	100	One Hundred only	89	Eighty nine	88	... Eight		100	100				573	I	Pass		Sur. [illegible]
411	39.gl.144	Mohd Bashir	"	" M	202	27	Twenty Seven	40	Forty only	53	... Three		27	37			35			Fail		
Islamia College, Lahore.																						
412	39.mk.35	Mohd Kifayatullah	"	" L	226	22	Twenty Two	27	Twenty Seven	10	... only		28	A			A			Fail		
413	38.mc.68	Mahmud ul Hasan	"	" M		Absent		Absent					Absent							Absent		
414	40.dh.1	Sana Ullah	"	" M	244	33	Thirty Three	11	Eleven only	50	... only		42	A			A			Fail		
415	37.me.10	Mohd Ashraf Khan	"	" M	257	21	Twenty one	9	Nine only	17	... teen		A	A						Fail		

Checked [signature] 9/7/46

Result Statement, forwarded to the Registrar's Office, must be signed jointly by the Examiners in the subject.

Examiners are particularly requested :—

(a) to write out the number of marks both in figures and in words ;

(b) to initial all corrections without exception ;

(c) to avoid all fractional marks ;

(d) to sign the result sheet in the place indicated ;

(e) to fill in the name of the subject at the head of the sheet.

Dated 194

Please sign here.

Examiner. Examiner. Examiner. Examiner. Examiner.

Bibliography

[1] A. Ali, C. Isham, T. Kibble and Riazuddin (Editors): *Selected Papers by Abdus Salam (With Commentary)*; World Scientific Publishing Co 1994.

[2] A. Ali, J. Ellis and Randjbar-Daemi (Editors): *Salamfestschrift: A Collection of Talks From the Conference on Highlights of Particle and Condensed Matter Physics; 8-12 March 1993, ICTP, Trieste*; World Scientific Publishing Co 1994.

[3] K.K. Aziz: *The Coffee House of Lahore - A Memoir 1942-57*; Sang e Meel Publishers, 2008.

[4] Criag Baxter (Editor):*Diaries of Field Marshal Mohammad Ayub Khan 1966-1972*; Oxford University Press, 2007.

[5] Abdul Hameed Chaudhari: *Alami Shohrat Yafta Sciencedaan Abdus Salam* (World Renowned Scientist

Abdus Salam); published by Ahmad Salam, 8 Campion Road, SW 15, 6 NW, London; 1998; this book is written in Urdu.

[6] Robert P. Crease and Charles C. Mann: *The Second Creation - Makers of the Revolution in Twentieth Century Physics*; MacMillan Press 1986.

[7] Anwar Dil: *Science for Peace and Progress: Life and Work of Abdus Salam* compiled by Anwar Dil, publishers Intercultural Forum, San Diego and Islamabad (iforum@aol.com), 2008.

[8] Gordon Fraser:*Cosmic Anger: Abdus Salam The First Muslim Nobel Laureate*; Oxford University Press, 2008.

[9] Abdul Ghani: *Abdus Salam*; Ma'aref Printers Limited, Defence Housing Society, Karachi, 1982.

[10] Sheldon L. Glashow with Ben Bova: *Interactions: A Journey Through the Mind of A Particle Physicist and the Matter of This World*; Warner Books, 1988.

[11] F. Janouch: *Lev. D. Landau: His Life and Work*; CERN preprint 28 March 1979; also accessible at: http://image.sciencenet.cn/olddata/kexue.com.cn/upload/blog/file/2010/6/2010621214821385723.pdf

[12] Azim Kidwai: *The Greats in Science from the Third World: Abdus Salam*; Third World Academy of Sciences, Trieste, 1989.

[13] John W. Moffat: *Einstein Wrote Back*; Thomas Allen Publishers, Toronto.

[14] Abdus Salam: *Symmetry Concepts in Modern Physics*: Iqbal Memorial Lectures by Abdus Salam (Atomic Energy Center, Lahore) 1966.

[15] Abdus Salam and E.P. Wigner (ed): *Aspects of Quantum Mechanics*: Cambridge University Press, 1972.

[16] Abdus Salam: *Ideals and Realities: Selected Essays of Abdus Salam*: Second Edition edited by C.H. Lai 1987.

[17] Abdus Salam: *Science and Education in Pakistan*; Third World Academy of Sciences, Trieste 1987.

[18] Abdus Salam (ed): *From a Life of Physics*: World Scientific Publishing Co, Singapore; 1989.

[19] Abdus Salam: *Unification of Fundamental Forces*: The First of Dirac Memorial Lectures by ; Cambridge University Press, 1990.

[20] Abdus Salam: *Notes on Science, Technology and Science Education in the Developnment of the South*; (Red Book); Third World Academy of Sciences, Trieste, May 1991.

[21] Muhammad Abdus Salam: *Science and Technology: Challenge for the South*; Third World Academy of Sciences, Trieste, November 1992.

[22] Muhammad Abdus Salam: *Renaissance of Sciences in Islamic Countries*; Edited by H.R. Dalafi and M.H.A. Hassan; World Scientific Publishing Co, Singapore 1994.

[23] Jagjit Singh: *Abdus Salam: A Biography*; Penguin Books, India, 1992.

[24] C.N. Yang: *Selected Papers (1945-1980) With Commentary*; 2005 Edition, World Scientific.

Index